BLOOMING ENGLISH

English is a most creative, changeable and imaginative language. Some words are invented to meet temporary needs and are quickly discarded; others carry meanings hundreds of years old. Language fascinates us, and we spend a lot of time playing with it, creating everything from puns, riddles and secret languages to wonderful prose and poetry. We also worry about it a great deal, looking up and checking words in dictionaries and usage guides, and arguing about definitions. This book celebrates our capacity to play with language, as well as examining the ways we use it: in slang and jargon, swearing, speaking the unspeakable, or concealing unpleasant or inconvenient facts. It is a book for browsing, for finding intriguing snippets about language, history and social customs, and a formidable weapon in word games.

BLOOMING ENGLISH

Observations on the roots, cultivation and hybrids of the English language

Kate Burridge

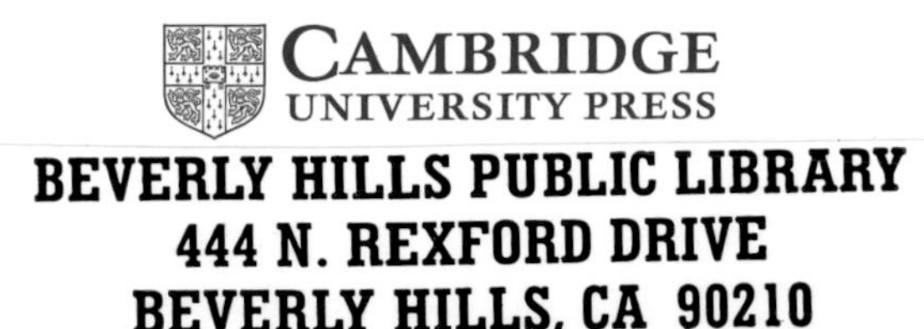

CAMBRIDGE
UNIVERSITY PRESS

PUBLISHED BY THE PRESS SYNDICATE OF THE UNIVERSITY OF CAMBRIDGE
The Pitt Building, Trumpington Street, Cambridge CB2 1RP, United Kingdom

CAMBRIDGE UNIVERSITY PRESS
The Edinburgh Building, Cambridge, CB2 2RU, UK
40 West 20th Street, New York, NY 10011–4211, USA
477 Williamstown Road, Port Melbourne, VIC 3207, Australia
Ruiz de Alarcón 13, 28014 Madrid, Spain
Dock House, The Waterfront, Cape Town 8001, South Africa

http://www.cambridge.org

First published 2002 by ABC Books for the Australian Broadcasting Corporation
GPO Box 9994, Sydney, NSW 2002, Australia. This edition published 2004 by
Cambridge University Press. Not for sale in Australia or New Zealand.

Printed in the United Kingdom at the University Press, Cambridge

Typeface Galliard 10.5/13 pt. and Formata *System* LaTeX 2_ε [TB]

A catalogue record for this book is available from the British Library

ISBN 0 521 83948 3 hardback
ISBN 0 521 54832 2 paperback

Contents

Why a Garden?

'Tis an unweeded garden, that grows to seed
William Shakespeare, *Hamlet*, Act 1, sc. ii

Most of the material in this book is provided by the 180 or so radio pieces that I've written for the Australian Broadcasting Corporation's (ABC's) *Soundbank*. These pieces are generated largely by 'talkback' calls during radio programmes I've been involved in – members of the public phone in to the radio station and put directly on air their observations on language and queries about usage. Very often these calls involve complaints about the language of others. We are all born with a keen ear for the ill-chosen word and the grammatical error of our fellow speakers!

What's obvious from these calls is the tremendous enjoyment people derive from their language. Most of us love messing about with English, it seems – looking up word origins, playing with language, manipulating it to create new and exciting expressions. Even something as everyday as slang illustrates over and over again just how inventive we can be. But our love of language is also reflected in the time we spend worrying about usage. Look at the hours we invest in checking things in dictionaries and style guides, thinking and arguing about the words and constructions we use – especially, of course, the words and constructions that others use. What is striking is the intensity of emotion that accompanies these worries. I could never have predicted the number of furious letters and emails that followed my suggestion that the possessive apostrophe was a useless addition to the English language and we would be better off without it. Such passionate support for a piece of punctuation we imported from the French nearly five hundred years ago!

When I was trying to think of an idea that would provide a framework to unite all of the short pieces on language that I'd written, I ended up choosing a gardening image. People's concerns about language bring to mind a picture of the English language as a garden that, if not carefully and constantly cultivated, would quickly become unruly and overgrown. As Shakespeare put it,''Tis an unweeded garden, that grows to seed'. Or, as one of the more passionate supporters of the possessive apostrophe put it to me – 'we shall have no formal structure of our language: it will become unteachable, unintelligible and, eventually, useless as an accurate means of communication'.

Language 'gardeners' can be found in all sorts of associations. They promote an array of causes from Plain English and simplified spelling through to Esperanto and Klingon. There are, for example, various apostrophe support groups out there – even one dedicated to the abolition of aberrant apostrophes like *Plea's Flush the Toilet* and *Canva's Hat's.* As a student I became good friends with the president of another group calling itself 'The Society for the Preservation of Old English Strong Verbs'. Strong verbs are those like *thrive*, *throve*, *thriven* – my friend is probably one of the few persons left for whom the past of *creep* is still *crope* and the past of *climb* is still *clomb.* But equally gardeners are those folk who simply enjoy looking things up in dictionaries and usage books, who spend time thinking and talking about language, and who like punning and playing Scrabble or Balderdash. We are probably all secret language gardeners of some sort.

And there is clearly a tremendous amount of pleasure to be had pottering about in the verbiage – edging, staking, cutting back, keeping bugs at bay. Why else would someone spend the time calculating that *foolish* could be spelt 613,975 different ways? Or that fifty million schoolchildren spend ten million hours daily on learning the English spelling system. (If that's not enough, this chap went on to calculate that this is roughly equivalent to the number of inches between London and Hull.) I mentioned Esperanto and Klingon. In fact there are hundreds of people out there all inventing languages simply for the pleasure of it – *conlangers* they're called, or 'constructed language creators'. And how many of you have lain awake at night trying to figure out just what it is that rhymes with *orange?* What is that third word in the English language that ends in *-gry*? There is even, as I write, a discussion on the Internet on this particular topic. In fact, there are hundreds and hundreds of different websites dedicated to language issues as diverse as word order, rhyming (where you can find out exactly how many words rhyme with *orange*), oxymorons, idioms, spoonerisms, phonetics, backformations, clichés and collectives. Most people create these websites for the sheer intellectual fun of it.

The garden is also an image that nicely caters for the arsenal of prescriptive texts (dictionaries, style guides, usage books, grammars) that give a standard language like English much of its muscle. These are the conservatories, the greenhouses and the hothouses that nurture our language, often artificially keeping alive features that have long perished in ordinary usage. It's in these linguistic nurseries that we protect and cherish endangered constructions, words, meanings and pronunciations. The neat lists and beautifully spun paradigms inside the dictionary and handbook provide the glasshouse counterpart to the outside 'wild garden' of language.

Why is it that people care so deeply about this garden? Is it simply because we now have these linguistic conservatories and hothouses that concerns with linguistic values and standards are so much greater? It appears not. People have been worrying about the garden for centuries. As Deborah Cameron's book *Verbal Hygiene* clearly shows, anxieties about language are underpinned by deep and complex social conflicts. We all refuse to leave language alone – it's part of our linguistic competence. Humankind would have to change beyond all recognition before these urges to cultivate and tidy up the language disappeared.

So where do linguists fit in? Are they the seasoned gardeners whose task it is to advise on what should be altered, removed or promoted in the garden? Should they be the ones controlling the pests, building the hothouses and performing the topiary? Linguists are in a tricky position here. They, of course, study language, in the same way that botanists study plants and zoologists research the physiology, anatomy and behaviour of animals. Should they therefore legislate language usage? Many people probably think so. For those people there's a very clear distinction between unwanted plants in the garden and those that should be encouraged. But let me put it this way. Should biologists denigrate certain species in the plant world that the wider community views as weeds? Should zoologists attribute evil to the cane toads which destroy indigenous species of amphibian? Should linguists disparage native speakers for dropping an *l* in *vulnerable* or condemn as 'linguistic atrocities' expressions like *youse*?

Linguists might argue that dropping an *l* in *vulnerable* is no different from losing the *l* in *walk* or *calm*. These sorts of reductions are a natural part of sound change. They will point out that *you* is historically plural, contrasting with singular *thou*. When social changes saw the disappearance of *thou*, *you* took over and dialects have been evolving new plural pronouns like *youse*, *you-all* and *you-uns* ever since. But while linguists might argue till they're blue in the face that all constructions are equally good and that change and variation are natural and inevitable features of any thriving language – it just so happens that most of the general community don't believe this is the case. Clearly, both parties approach language very differently. For linguists, it's a natural phenomenon, something that evolves and adapts. For many others, it's an art form, something to be cherished and preserved – understandably these people reject the neutral stance of the linguistics profession.

I recall a newspaper article that appeared in 1992 where linguists were described as 'categorically the dullest people on the face of the earth – rather than trying to present and explain information they try to shield people from knowing anything useful about the language'. I hope this book goes some small way to bridging the apparent gap between linguists and the wider community – and without getting up the noses of either camp! What I've always believed, in fact, is that the two have much in common – a love of language and a desire to know what it's all about. And let me reiterate. Most of the segments in this book have grown out of observations made by talkback callers. To all these people (especially Bob of Bermagui) I owe a special debt of gratitude. I've learned much and have derived a huge amount of pleasure following up their queries. This does not, however, include the hours spent trying to find rhymes for *orange* or words ending in *-gry*!

But let me continue with my thanks. In truth, this book has depended on the generous support of just so many people that I scarcely know where to begin.

Perhaps I should start with the obvious – the ABC. First, many thanks to those at *Soundbank* – Gary Bartholomew, Michael Taft and more recently Penny Johnston. I derive much enjoyment from writing these pieces and I am extremely grateful for their encouragement and their support. Many thanks also to both Terry Laidler and Peter Clarke for their regular linguistic programmes and for letting me take part. Their insights into language are remarkable and have been the inspiration of many examples in this book. To both Terry and Peter I owe a special debt. I believe those involved in the discipline of linguistics should also be grateful for the work being carried out by these presenters and producers at the ABC. We all need to pay more attention to the way language affects our lives, and their programmes have done much to bring language issues into the public arena as something we talk about with sport, health issues, economics and current events.

Many thanks to Ross Weber for putting up with those 4am starts, for patiently listening to and reading my endless attempts at rewording and for his fine ability to put me right. Thanks too to all those other dear and tolerant friends, colleagues and students who have also been so supportive during the time of writing this book. What would I have done without my colleague Margaret Florey who, after I'd been toying for days with such mundane titles as *Growing English* and *The Language Garden*, phoned and suggested *Blooming English* – it says it all! Jane Faulkner has given me constant encouragement and I am very grateful for her helpful comments. My special thanks to Eric Porter who bravely worked through the entire final draft and made extensive comments. Thanks also to Amy Williams who helped create the index and to that delightful pedant Kim Lockwood – I mightn't always agree with him, but I've certainly enjoyed and learned much from our discussions on language.

A special thank you to ABC Books who were a joy to work with throughout the production of the first version of *Blooming English.* Many thanks to Susan Morris-Yates and Matthew Kelly who made sense of my ramblings in the original proposal and to Jacquie Kent who was then so encouraging. I am also extremely grateful to Suzanne Falkiner for keeping me on my intellectual toes and for her wonderful editing. Now, here is someone with a keen nose (or should that be ear!) for ill-chosen words, grammatical errors, infelicities of style and punctuation. Her suggestions and insights – on virtually every page – were invaluable. More recently of course my thanks to Cambridge University Press, in particular to Kate Brett who was the driving force behind the release of *Blooming English* into the Northern Hemisphere. I am very grateful for all her hard work – and for her advice, especially when it came to pruning the Australianisms.

To conclude my thanks, let me point out I have numerous heroes in linguistics – fine writers like Jean Aitchison, David Crystal and Stephen Pinker who have shown that 'the pointy-headed abstruse strudel of academic linguistics' (to quote the same 1992 newspaper article) can make great bedtime reading. One real favourite of mine is Dwight Bolinger. Bolinger complained there was never enough debate about language, and using language to expose language was his life work – he was brilliant at it. The writing of these linguists has always been a great inspiration to me.

Finally, a note on the layout of the book. All of the sections are self-contained entities, as are the individual snippets presented within them. This is a book meant for grazing and browsing, not necessarily for reading from left to right, front to back, chapter by chapter – although readers can also do that if they wish.

Let me also emphasize that these pieces were originally written to be read aloud on radio. They are therefore chatty, informal and probably in style resemble something closer to speech than to writing. They contain no footnotes or endnotes. However, at the end of the book I have provided a list of references with the details of those authors I have cited. The list includes works of literature, linguistic books – and of course the gardening books that have also inspired me.

The Complexity of Language

The intricate and folded rose
Judith Wright, 'Woman to Man', 1949

Most of the time we simply speak without ever noticing the extraordinary complexity that underpins our language. Underlying every sentence we utter is a highly organized arrangement of layers. Like some intricate folded rose, around forty-four distinctive sounds are organized into the syllables that combine to form hundreds of meaningful segments of words. These in turn combine to construct thousands of different words that then combine and recombine into an infinite number of possible sentences and discourses.

Talking animals?

You've probably seen nature programmes on television that document dophinspeak, bird songs, bee dances – even talking horses. Perhaps you've read about the 'love songs' of the humpbacked whale. And some of those baby chimps do seem to communicate quite well with their trainers. I certainly had a parrot that said 'bless you' whenever anyone sneezed. But are any of these creatures actually communicating in a meaningful way? If not, what are the properties that distinguish our communication as unique?

It's a cluster of properties really, collectively known as the 'design features' of language. First, we humans initiate speech.

You don't have to dangle a cracker or a glass of red wine in front of my nose to get me to speak – though it might help. Not only that, I can talk about all sorts of things that are quite remote from the here and now. For instance, I can talk about my good friend Jill who now lives in Albany and who broke her leg climbing the Porongorups last year. Animals can't do this. Animals are 'stimulus bound'. Typically, they talk about nothing but the present moment and things they can see. Even bees, who do quite well reporting on the location of patches of nectar, can't report on that awesome patch of nectar they visited last week, or wonder about the plight of rural bees in drought-stricken New South Wales. Bees can't swap stories about great nectar sources they have known.

Another feature of human language is that it's conventional and arbitrary. Our words are symbols. For example, there's nothing about my physical or psychological make-up that causes me to use the word *book* to refer to the printed work you're reading at the moment. There's no natural, no necessary connection between *book* and its meaning. It's simply that we are all agreed on calling it 'a book'. In this regard, in *Alice in Wonderland*, Humpty Dumpty was undermining the very foundation of human language – when he used a word, you might remember, it meant whatever he chose it to mean.

By contrast, many animal signals are iconic; in other words there is a connection between the message that's being sent and the signal. For example, angry crustaceans will wave a leg, and those that are really cheesed off will wave a very large claw. The speed of beespeak directly relates to the distance of the nectar. However, not all animal signalling is so, and arbitrariness is not in fact unique to human language. More significant is that animal signals are based on the principle of 'one signal; one meaning', and this makes animals very limited in what they can say. Psycholinguist Jean Aitchison, for example, describes how one variety of male grasshopper has a choice of only six messages – 'I'm happy, life is good', 'I would like to make love', 'You are trespassing', 'She's mine', 'Let's make love' and 'Oh how nice to have made love'. Don't expect riveting conversation from a male grasshopper! By contrast we can talk about literally anything we like, when we want to and where we want to. We can if we choose say something completely ridiculous – 'the man in the moon bought himself a pink feather boa'. It's true some creatures, like monkeys, have quite impressive repertoires of signals, but they're fixed. The remarkable thing about human language is its ability to make infinite use out of a finite means. Sounds, syllables, parts of words, words, all combine and recombine into an infinite number of different structures. This organization of level upon level is what distinguishes human communication from that of other animals. No animal communication has this sort of infinite capacity. Even beespeak, it turns out, can't create a word for 'up'!

OK, you're probably thinking – what about chimp communication? Certainly it does seem chimps can cope with arbitrary symbols. They even show some creativity – but is there really linguistic processing going on? I'll let you decide. Here are some typical sentences from one of the success stories, Nim Chimpsky – 'Nim eat Nim eat', 'Tickle me Nim play', 'Me banana you banana me you give', 'Give orange me give eat orange me eat orange give me eat orange give me you'. So who would you choose to sit opposite at dinner – Nim or the male grasshopper? I think it's safe to say, for the moment at least, humans are unique in their ability to use language.

Blooming insertion

The parts that make up words are called 'morphemes'. These are the smallest units of meaning in the structure of a language. They include things like prefixes – the bits and pieces that come before the stems of words (such as *un-* in *unhappy*) and suffixes – the bits and pieces that come at the end (like *-able* in *readable*). Much rarer are things called infixes that are stuffed into the middle of a word stem. In English the only things that can be infixed are those expressive words which are used to intensify meaning. All of the seriously offensive intensifiers can be used this way, but there are plenty of sweeter-sounding remodellings too like *flippin(g)*, *friggin(g)*, *blinkin(g)* and *bloomin(g)*, as in *unbeflippinglievable* and *fanfriggintastic*. One of the most famous examples is, of course, Eliza Doolittle's 'absobloominlutely'.

'One Weetabick'

Even very young children are aware, at least unconsciously, that words have their own internal architecture. My colleague, Kersti Börjars, relates the following story about her son Nils. When, at the age of two-and-a-half, Nils was told off for having thrown his bowl of cereal on the floor, he declared it didn't matter because there was only one 'Weetabick' left in the bowl. In this case, Nils had analysed the final 's' sound of the brand name *Weetabix* as the English plural marker that you get in words like *trick**s***. Similarly, Katie, when her parents were waxing their boat, helpfully suggested they might give the boat another 'wack' – like Nils, Katie had analysed the final 's' sound (in this case of *wax*) as the plural marker. Nils' sister Ellen at the age of three fell over in the playground and tearfully informed nursery staff she had hurt her 'two-head'. When she'd calmed down a bit, she corrected herself and said 'I mean my forehead'. Ellen had already worked out that words can consist of more than one part and that these can exist as independent words. She thought of this word as 'four-head', but being so upset from her fall she got the number wrong. Paul, a neighbour to Nils and Ellen, was told by his father not to argue. He replied 'Well, don't arg-me then'. The final sounds of *argue* are identical to the pronoun *you* and Paul had therefore assigned the structure 'arg' + 'you' to the word. Finally, there's Nils' buddy Ben, who in the bathtub one evening pondered over the name *testicles*. 'So what do they test?' he asked his mother. As their wonderful misunderstandings of structure reveal, Nils, Katie, Ellen, Paul and Ben were all aware of the fact we can divide words into smaller units of meaning.

An internet discussion between linguists from around the world revealed that this sort of expressive infixing is widespread and appears in all the major English dialects. It's a complex process with an elaborate set of restrictions. For instance, infixing doesn't happen just anywhere in the word. Not all intensifiers can be infixed either. And not all words can take an infix. Let me run through a couple of the most important rules.

For a start, epithets like *bloody* must be infixed before a stressed syllable. So *absobloodylutely* is fine, but not *abbloodysolutely* or even worse *absolutebloodyly. Licketybloodysplit* works well but not *lickbloodyetysplit.* Hence we find *autofrigginmatic* but not *autofrigginmat*; he's *diplobloodymatic* but not he's a *diplobloodymat.* If a word has only an initial stress, it's impossible to infix anywhere. Try something like *criminal* – *crimbloodyinal* just doesn't work!

The syllable pattern of the word is important too. Infixing is much more likely in words of three or more syllables – *ecobloodynomics* and *imbloodypossible* sound perfectly fine. The infixes themselves need to have more than one syllable, at least in my variety of English. Examples like *absodamnlutely* which you find in the United States sound rather odd to Australians. Better would be something like *absogoddamnlutely. Goddamn* is rather rare outside of American English, but at least it has two syllables.

Meaning restrictions also apply to certain infixes. Apparently in some varieties of English you can infix the word *bastard*, but not to all words. While these speakers might use *telebastardvision* they would never say *fanbastardtastic* – *bastard* can only be infixed inside a word for an object which you could describe as 'bastard', like your television!

As a final rule, if the infix is followed by a vowel, most dialects of English will repeat the consonant from the first syllable. Hence, *fanbloodynatical* not *fanbloodyatical* and *hilbloominlarious* not *hilbloominarious.*

Now, all this might look like a really trivial aspect of English wordplay, but it does illustrate a serious point about language and its speakers. We mightn't be aware of the complex structure that underpins our language. We mightn't be able to articulate the rules of stressing and syllable structure. But at some level we are all sensitive to these things and we certainly know when something goes wrong – *abbloominsolutely* is a violation of the rule for 'blooming insertion' and no native speaker of English would produce it.

The longest word?

Many claim *antidisestablishmentarianism* is the longest word in the English language. In fact, *floccinaucinihilipilification* beats it by one letter. It's a useful word too – defined in the Oxford English Dictionary as 'the action of estimating something as worthless' as in 'I loved him for nothing so much as his floccinaucinihilipilification of money'. But there are names of chemical compounds and nasty lung diseases that are far longer – they seem limitless. This 'longest word' record is one that will repeatedly be broken. As linguist Stephen Pinker points out, we can go on to create *floccinaucinihilipilificational* 'pertaining to the estimation of something as worthless'. That's got two more letters. Then again *floccinaucinihilipilificationalize* 'to cause something to pertain to the estimation of something as worthless' has another three. Or how about *floccinaucinihilipilificationalization* 'the act of causing something to pertain to the estimation of something as worthless'? But wait; from that I can build *floccinaucinihilipilificationalizational* 'pertaining to the act of causing something to pertain to the estimation of something as worthless'. And so we go on – theoretically, there is no limit. There is, of course, a practical limit that has to do with the limited brain space available to keep track of all these *-als*, *-izes* and *-ations*. But in theory morphemes can combine and recombine in this way into an infinite number of different words. It's this structural complexity and creativity that distinguishes our communicative behaviour from that of animals. The infinite capacity to express and understand meaning is not found in the language of any other species.

Stuffedshirtdom – creating words

Some time back, Australian comedian Wendy Harmer wrote the following: 'And as I confront my unthinking lookism, I begin to ask myself is it possible I could also have been guilty of "hearism", "tasteism" and "smellism"?' Here Wendy is playing on the current success of the *-ism* and *-ist* endings. Few of her *isms* appear in even the most recent of dictionaries, although you will find them and many others in articles on political correctness. These *-ism* and *-ist* endings have become highly productive.

What exactly is meant by 'productive' here? Basically, the description covers any process that is frequently or actively used in forming new words. On the surface it's quite a straightforward notion: the more frequently an ending like *-ism* is used, the more productive we assume it is. But, as usual, things are more complex than they at first seem. First, we are dealing with a gradient, not a clear-cut division. Processes aren't simply productive or unproductive, it's a matter of degree. Moreover, even the most productive of processes are never one hundred per cent effective. For instance, the hugely successful *-er* ending is maximally productive. This is one lively little ending – *baker*, *singer*, *runner*, *player*. Yet there are still anomalies. 'Someone who types' is not a *typer* but a *typist*. This is not to say that productivity is a simple matter of numbers, either. A lot depends on the nature of what it is the suffix or prefix is attaching to. For example, the *-ade* ending hasn't given us many new words, but is very active when it comes to forming the names of flavoured (usually fizzy) soft drinks like *lemonade* or sports drinks like *Lucozade* and *Gatorade*. And there are practical forces at work here too. The survival of *-ade* in something like *lemonade* depends on a drinking audience. The shape of words can also affect the likelihood of a process taking place. The suffix *-ize* is extremely lively when it comes to forming verbs from nouns or adjectives, but they have to have more than one syllable, like *burglarize* and *prioritize*.

Secondly, productivity is affected over time. Some processes can be productive for a limited period but atrophy with the years. The now deceased negative prefix *wan-* was once highly productive, forming words with the same ease as the current prefix *un-*. In Old English it was responsible for a large number of expressions, now obsolete or dialectal, like *wanbelief* 'disbelief', *wanchance* 'ill luck', *wanfortune* 'misfortune' and *wanweird* 'ill fortune'. The only survivor is *wanton*, although the original sense 'undisciplined' has now shifted to 'sexually promiscuous'.

Then again, it's sometimes unwise to declare an ending no longer productive. For example, the suffix *-dom* is one that is currently coming back from the dead, especially in American English, with a burst of new creations like *parentdom*, *PCdom*, *fandom*, *moviedom*, *professordom*, *stuffedshirtdom*, *suckerdom*, *wifedom*, *womandom* (I might redress the balance and suggest *husbanddom* and *mandom*!) – even *lawnmowerdom*!

The fashion analogy is perhaps a useful one here. Whether it be Mohican haircuts, sun-dried tomatoes or cascading geraniums, suddenly for some reason these things capture people's imagination and they become fashionable. In the same way, affixes can suddenly take off (although obviously without the same deliberate manipulation that you find in the fashion industry). Some affixes come to achieve almost voguish popularity, like the *-ize* suffix. Nowadays we *burglarize* not *burgle*, *prioritize* not *rank*, *diarize* instead of entering things in a diary. Like modes of dress, furniture and hairdressing, affixes can come in and out of fashion. Apparently we even *condomize*!

Scrabble players will immediately recognize the ticklish nature of productivity. What do you do when your opponent defiantly puts down a word like *typer*, claiming quite reasonably that it means 'one who types'. Do you allow it or not? The *-er* ending can create agent nouns from most verbs. Now, the word *typer* doesn't happen to be in my dictionaries, but that doesn't necessarily mean the word doesn't exist. Dictionary makers are constantly having to redraw the admission/exclusion boundary for marginal vocabulary items. For example, the words *belongingness* and *apartness* have now been included in the Webster's and Oxford but were absent from previous editions (and are still missing from the Macquarie). Conversely, dictionaries are full of entries no longer in use (some were never frequent). My New Shorter Oxford has rarities like *comer*, *studier*, *presider*, *cycler*, *raper*, *supposer*, *stealer*, even *groaner* – a local Massachusetts term for 'whistling buoy' – although its entry is probably due to the fact that it appears in a celebrated work 'The Dry Salvages' by T. S. Eliot. So why not *typer*?

Favourites

Apparently the favourite word of the British in 2000 was *serendipity*. The London Festival of Literature ran a poll – fifteen thousand responded with their favourite words and *serendipity* won.

Why? Well, it seems there were two reasons. People liked the meaning – and there is something rather nice about the idea of making 'useful discoveries while looking for something else'. They also took pleasure in the sound of the word. It *is* a rather lovely assortment of vowels and consonants, and also echoes pleasant words like *serene* and *serenity*. It has an interesting etymology too. Serendip is an old name for Sri Lanka. The name came into English initially via a Persian story called 'The Three Princes of Serendip'. I don't know the story but apparently the heroes were always making accidental discoveries and this encouraged Horace Walpole, some time during the eighteenth century, to then coin the word *serendipity* for exactly the sort of discovery you make quite by accident.

What about the other favourites? Well, to my mind, there were some surprising ones on the list of finalists. A close second to *serendipity* was *quidditch*, a game played by witches and wizards in the Harry Potter books – but given the vogue status of these books at the time perhaps it's not a surprising choice. In fifth place was *onomatopoeia*, perhaps chosen for its sound, or maybe it's simply that once you've worked out how to spell the wretched word it takes a special place in your heart. Other high scorers were probably chosen for their positive meanings – *love*, *peace*, *hope*, *faith*, but also *family* and *football*. These last two tied with *muggle*. Would that be *muggle*, the obsolete Kentish word for 'tail'; or *muggle* the American slang term for 'marijuana'? I suspect once again it's the *muggle* from the Harry Potter books! In ninth place a truly curious assortment of words tied for the spot – *bollocks*, *compassion*, *home* and *fuck* (perhaps your least favourite?). I'm not sure whether those who voted for *bollocks* meant the bawdy body part or the derived meaning, 'balderdash' or 'blather'.

It's difficult to choose just one favourite word. I've got lots, and for different reasons. *Gobbledygook* for its sound, *glarpo* ('the juncture between ear and skull where pencils and pens are stored') for its usefulness and *alloloutrophilist* ('one who drinks another's bathwater') for its delightful pointlessness. I have plenty of dead favourites too – and here it's really hard to decide. But if I had to vote, it'd likely be *velleity*. The Oxford English Dictionary describes it as 'the fact or quality of merely wishing or desiring, without any effort of advance towards action or realization'. You must all have experienced *velleity* – that sense of desire that's, well, not quite strong enough to motivate you to do anything about it. How could we let that word slip away?

But maybe a more interesting survey would be one that asked what were people's least favourite words. For me it'd be the sort of language that turns 'doors' into *entry systems*, 'toothbrushes' into *home plaque removal implements* and 'fans' into *high velocity all purpose air circulators*. Of course, as a linguist, I'm supposed to find all words, accents and constructions equally endearing, even coagulated clumps of English like these. But it's hard to love this sort of jargon, especially when you suspect it's being intentionally murky; when you suspect it's deliberately disguising facts that are perfectly ordinary or simply inconvenient. So, what sort of words get under your skin, on your nerves or perhaps on your wick, up your nose, into your hair, or even under your feet; what sort of words set your teeth on edge, tread on your corns, turn your stomach, stick in your throat, make your hair curl, your flesh creep or your blood run cold? Disagreeable words, it seems, when they irritate and irk can touch most parts of the anatomy. They really are a lot more interesting than favourite words.

Leximania

How many words are there in the English language? At a conservative estimate, probably around one million. But then, who really knows – in fact, how could we ever know? To begin with, this figure excludes hundreds and thousands of scientific terms. And what about the New and Other Englishes now dotted around the globe? The figure of one million includes only very few items from their lexicons. Indeed, what about slang – those thousands of expressions that belong to our everyday colloquial language that, yes, may one day make it into recognized dictionaries like the Macquarie, Oxford and Webster's but equally well may simply drop by the wayside to be replaced by new and more colourful expressions?

What's more, the figure of a million overlooks another important group of English words, the so-called 'nonce' words. A nonce word is one that is created for temporary use. It's a one-off form;

Linguistic flummery

Present-day English has a remarkably rich vocabulary of wonderful-sounding expressions for loquacious nonsense. Many would appear high on the list of my favourite words. What a gorgeous assortment: *baloney, bumpf, bunk, codswallop, drivel, hooey, mumbo-jumbo, piffle, poppycock, tripe, waffle*. There's no end to them. Two of my real favourites are *discombobulation* and *gobbledygook*. How beautifully these words capture that bizarrely turgid and pedantic prose peculiar to official documents. *Gobbledeygook* was apparently the inspiration of a Texan. He is quoted as saying 'People ask me where I got gobbledygook. I do not know. It must have come in a vision. Perhaps I was thinking of the old bearded turkey gobbler back in Texas, who was always gobbledy-gobbling and strutting with ludicrous pomposity. At the end of this gobble there was a sort of gook.'

Since 1900 there has been a virtual explosion of these expressions, especially ones for official nonsense. It's hard not to conclude that ours is the era of incomprehensible, insincere blather. Or perhaps the eighteenth-century word *flummery* is a better description – the image of coagulated wheat germ seems particularly appropriate for this kind of language!

hence the name – for the nonce or 'for the once'. (If you'd prefer a more fancy description, nonce words are also *hapax legomena*, from the Greek meaning 'said once'.) Nonce words fill a gap felt at that particular moment. They're made up on the spot, usually with no lasting effect on the language. Speakers create nonce words all the time in their conversation, and nonce activity is a very important part of our playing with language.

Many of the made-up words on those electronic vocabulary lists currently winging their way around cyberspace and clogging up everyone's email are probably nonce. Creations like *onosecond* – that minuscule fraction of time when you realize that you've just done something inexplicably ghastly (you know, you've hit the wrong computer key and the fruit of your last two hours of hard labour has just disappeared); *kinstirpation* 'the painful inability to move visiting relatives'; *lullabuoy* 'that idea that keeps floating into your head, preventing you from drifting off into sleep'; *foreploy* 'any misrepresentation or outright lie about yourself that leads to sex'.

Strictly speaking, nonce words should be uttered only once and forgotten as soon as they're uttered. But once you start repeating and referring to nonce words, as I am doing now, or once they start to appear regularly in print, they gain currency and then cease to be nonce. Take *floccinaucinihilipilification* 'the act of estimating something as worthless'. This most certainly started life as a nonce word, but now makes regular appearances in different collections of lexical curiosities; in fact this impressive little brainchild is now nurtured by highly respectable dictionaries like the Oxford.

It can, of course, happen that nonce words are taken up to become legitimate words in the language. Perhaps they fill a genuine gap in the lexicon. The expression *bagonize* I feel is an excellent candidate – how well it captures the action of waiting anxiously at the baggage carousel for luggage to appear. Or *loobry* 'the collection of books for browsing in the toilet'. How about the *bozone layer* for 'the substance surrounding our workmates and colleagues that successfully prevents the penetration of any bright idea'? How have we managed without them?

Finally, there are nonce words that have been planted for a purpose, perhaps to trap people or simply just to frustrate. A couple of American newspapers once wanted to see whether people read their classified advertising section, and so they ran advertisements for *witzonsnickles* and *gitzensnorkers*. It's sometimes claimed that dictionary makers once deliberately planted such words to catch out any plagiarists.

There have been thousands of nonce words recorded but most, sadly, will remain lost. Many are truly lexical gems; imaginative brainchildren (brainchilds?) hatched by a kind of congenital *leximania*. Leximania, by the way, is the name now given to describe the compulsive coiner, driven by an in-built passion, so it seems, to invent new words – like *leximania*!

Gladly the cross-eyed bear

One of the many linguistic miracles we perform every day is the way we manage to recognize words in speech. For a start, words themselves are simply strings of merging noises. Take something as simple as the word *dog*. We all think of this as being made up of three distinct sounds, represented by the letters 'd', 'o' and 'g'. But this is an illusion. We don't make a 'd', then pause to make an 'o' and then a 'g'. Sounds will always change their shape depending on where they occur in a word and what they sit next to. For instance, if we reverse the order of these sounds on a tape recorder the word we get won't sound like *god*. How we differentiate words from each other is also based on an illusion. One word simply merges into the next. There are no convenient little gaps between spoken words, equivalent to the little white spaces between written words. It's astonishing how we manage to distinguish words in the unbroken streams of sound that we encounter daily. As the psycholinguist Stephen Pinker puts it – what we are actually doing is hallucinating the word boundaries whenever we reach the edge of a stretch of sound that matches up with some entry or other in the dictionary that we carry around in our heads.

Because of the seamlessness of speech, speakers occasionally end up hallucinating the boundaries in the wrong place. For example, some stretches of sounds can be carved up into words in a number of different ways. Many of you will remember famous childhood errors like *Gladly the cross-eyed bear* instead of *Gladly the cross I'd bear*. Pairs such as these are called 'oronyms'. You've probably also encountered examples like *ice-cream* versus *I scream*, *Iced ink* versus *I stink*, *The stuffy nose can lead to problems* versus *The stuff he knows can lead to problems*. Student bloopers are a good source for these kinds of slips of the ear. A simple shift in word boundaries can have hilarious consequences – 'In 1957 Eugene O'Neill won a Pullet Surprise' [= Pulitzer Prize]. This particular howler gave Amsel Greene the title for her collection of *Pullet Surprises*.

And as you might expect, people play with this feature of our language. Many Australians still remember those car bumper stickers that read 'Be alert – Australia needs more lerts'. Wrong boundary assignment can even lead to significant changes in the language. But that's a whole nother story.

Nidiots and uckleheads

Some of you might recall a very memorable Peanuts cartoon where Lucy called poor old Charlie Brown *a nidiot* and *an ucklehead*. This lovely example actually illustrates a quite serious force behind change in our language. It's something called 'reanalysis'. As the name implies, it refers to a process whereby a form comes to be analysed in a different way. Reanalysis can affect many different aspects of structure. One of these involves where we place the boundaries between words.

We can lose boundaries, for example. Strings of words often become compressed over time and turn into one word. We have spectacular examples of this such as *goodbye* from *God be with you* and *lord* and *lady* from *hlafweard* ('loaf warden') and *hlafdige* ('loaf kneader'). We create new boundaries, too. Speakers responsible for the word *chino* (as in 'a mug of chino') have done exactly this – they invented a word boundary in *cappuccino*. So did the speakers who created *mini* from *miniature* back in the mid 1800s. We also become inventive by simply shifting word boundaries about. This is precisely what Lucy in the *Peanuts* comic strip was doing when she produced *nidiot* from *an idiot* and *ucklehead* from *a knucklehead*. English has many examples like these. Word boundary shifts have given us modern-day *newt* from earlier *ewte*, *nickname* from *ekename* and personal names like *Ned* from *mine Ed* and *Nelly* from *mine Elly*. In Shakespeare you also encounter the occasional *nuncle* from *mine uncle*. The initial 'n' of all these forms comes from the end of the preceding word. An incorrect word division has been made and the 'n' has attached itself to the following noun. This can also result in words losing their 'n' as in *umpire* from *noumpere*, *adder* from *nadder* and *apron* from *napron*. In the last case, the related words *nappy* and *napkin* preserve the original initial 'n' now lost from *apron*.

If you think of the potential confusion between the words *an aim* and *a name* you can see how this sort of thing arises. You have to enunciate these very carefully in order to hear the difference, while in normal speech they sound the same. Speech is seamless – one word runs into the next. And it's because of this seamlessness that speakers (like Lucy) are able to shift the boundaries between words and move sounds from one word to another. What Lucy wouldn't have realized is that at one time it looked as if we'd all be saying *nidiot* (or possibly *nidget*). These forms came very close to being the accepted ones – they even retain an entry in the Oxford English Dictionary. This sort of boundary shifting was more usual in Early English, when fewer people were literate and there wasn't the same emphasis on writing. The changes occur more easily if we have no notion of the written word, but become less likely with a knowledge of spelling. It was a new spelling consciousness that returned *nidget* to *idiot* – but it came too late for *newt* and *nickname*.

Pluppayuping wuppith luppanguppuage

Secret languages, sometimes called 'pig Latins', appear all over the world. They're not peculiarly Anglo-Saxon. They're not even peculiarly European. There are Chinese pig Latins, Yakut pig Latins and Indonesian pig Latins, for example. They're not confined to the young either. Pig Latins occur in all age groups and wherever they occur they seem to serve a dual purpose – secrecy and solidarity. They prevent bystanders or eavesdroppers from easily understanding what's being said and so they're often associated with activities that conflict with the more mainstream aims of society. They form part of criminal jargon, for example. But of course they needn't always conceal the disreputable. Some Dutch fishermen disguise their speech simply so that other fishermen won't discover their secrets. But there is a more social function for secret languages too, and this I suspect is their primary function. They operate as a kind of in-group recognition device, to indicate membership within, and the integrity of, a particular group of people. Being able to manipulate language in this way means that you're automatically included in the group.

Most of these secret languages distort words in some way. It's a kind of remodelling. They might involve the addition of some sort of affix. Upp-Upp language, for example, inserts 'upp' before the rhyme of each syllable of a word. That's the vowel(s) and any consonant(s) that might follow: 'Hello, how are you' becomes *huppelluppo, huppow uppare yuppou.* To which you might reply: *Vupperuppy guppood thuppank yuppou.* Others can be even more complex. Try adding 'lf' after the vowel(s) of each first syllable, and then repeat the vowel(s) to finish the word. A doublebarrelled shotgun becomes a *dulfubble balfarrel sholfot gulfun.*

These two examples involve adding something, in both cases infixes that are shoved inside the syllables. Others involve distortion in different ways – speaking backwards, for instance. Backslang, as it's known, was once used extensively by barrow boys, hawkers, and traders such as greengrocers and butchers, so they could talk without their customers understanding. 'Give her some old bit of scrap' would come out *Evig reh emos delo tib fo parcs.* Backslang nowadays is usually a simplification of this – you only speak partially backwards. For example, it can involve moving the final sound to the front of the word. 'Shut your trap' becomes *Teshu eryou petray.* The original pig Latin is something similar. In this case you move the first consonant, or cluster of consonants, to the end of the word, but then you add an ending 'ay'. So 'fruit loops' becomes *uitfray oopslay.* 'Joe Bloggs is a pig' becomes *Oejay Oggsblay isay aay igpay.*

Some of these secret languages are mind-bogglingly complex. One Portuguese secret language, called 'Language of the Letter p', requires four different manoeuvres. They go something like this – add 'p' at the end of each syllable; after the 'p' you've just added copy the rhyme of that syllable; change all closed vowels in open syllables to open vowels (in other words, vowels made high in the mouth cavity are made lower but only in those syllables that end in a vowel); and finally disregard the original stress and instead stress the copy of each rhyme. And, of course, do all this at normal conversational speed!

Secret languages like this one show just how highly structured and organized the patterns of languages are. As speakers we're all sensitive to these patterns. We mightn't be able to say exactly what they are, but we have internalized them unconsciously and we can play with them and skilfully manipulate them as we do in the case of these secret languages. Small children can speak 'Upp-Upp' and similar languages fluently (and often do, much to the irritation of parents who can't understand what they're talking about). Yet these children don't have a clue what a syllable is, let alone where the onset, nucleus and coda of a syllable occur. It's an impressive performance they give, but we don't usually think of it this way because, as for so much of our language, we just take it for granted.

A conjugation of linguists

There is no doubt we love to play with our language. We always have. One particular game we've been playing for centuries involves the creation of new terms to describe groups of animals and people. There are manuscripts surviving from the 1400s containing long lists of these collective expressions, many of which made it into ordinary language and are still around today. For example, *a host of angels*, *a swarm of bees*, *a litter of pups*, *a colony of ants* and *a flock of sheep* date from this early time. But these are quite colourless really when you think what was available then in the way of collectives – *an unkindness of ravens*, *a skulk of foxes*, *an exaltation of larks*, *a murmuration of starlings*, *a parliament of owls*, *a murder of crows* and *a kindle of kittens*. These give a hint of the rich exuberance that once existed. It's a shame that so many have dropped by the wayside. We could certainly do with a few more collectives in my variety of English. That way Australians wouldn't have to rely so heavily on that – admittedly handy but rather overused – omnibus collective term *mob*.

There happens to be no handy single collective for these collective terms. They are known simply as 'collective nouns', 'terms of association', 'company terms', 'nouns of multitude', 'group terms' – and even 'terms of venery' or 'venereal terms'. These last two are not to be confused with *venery* meaning 'the practice of sexual pleasure'. The *venery* that has to do with collectives is indeed a related term but refers specifically to 'the practice or sport of hunting' – in other words, not the pursuit of sex but the pursuit of animals. Venereal terms are therefore terms belonging to the hunt, as in *a herd of deer* or *a pride of lions*. Many of the early examples developed in the context of hunting. Undoubtedly, there was originally a social need for these venereal terms, but there is also no doubt that people have always had a lot of fun with them. It's the challenge of coming up with appropriate terms that simultaneously refer to a gathering of entities and at the same time play on the characteristics of the group (for example, their appearance or personality). Even better is if you can involve sound play – alliteration, as in *a bevy of beauties*, or onomatopoeia as in *a gaggle of geese*. We think of these as collectives – and that's how I've been referring to them – but clearly many refer to animals that don't actually live in flocks or communities. Terms like a *sloth* or a *slowness of bears* and *a labour of moles* simply play on the most salient characteristics of these animals.

You'll find that some of these expressions are nicely revealing of the spirit of earlier times. Collectives like *a superfluity of nuns*, *a skulk of friars*, *a lying of pardoners*, *an untruth of summoners* and *an abominable sight of monks* give us quite an insight into medieval attitudes to certain members of the clergy. And we catch glimpses, too, of the attitude to women that was around at that time in collectives like *a gaggle of women*, *a nonpatience of wives*, *a herd of harlots*, *a rage of maidens* (*rage* here relates not to ill-temper, but to the presumed wantonness of these not-so-maidenly maidens).

Centuries later, speakers are still making colourful contributions. Who could forget the story of those four Oxford dons who, upon seeing a group of prostitutes, muttered in turn – 'a jam of tarts', 'a flourish of strumpets', 'an essay of Trollope's' and 'an anthology of pros'! More recently a doctor in California came up with a superbly inventive set of collectives for the medical profession – *a brace of orthodontists*, *a joint of osteopaths*, *a rash of dermatologists*, *a flutter of cardiologists*, *a pile of proctologists* and *a smear of gynaecologists*. The American poet James Lipton has contributed a number of his own – *a wince of dentists*, *a shower of meteorologists*, *an unction of undertakers*, *a flush of plumbers*, *a shrivel of critics*, *a wrangle of philosophers* and *a lot of used car dealers*.

Since I started to think about these terms, I have of course been trying to play the game myself. It's irresistible. *A deposit of bankers*, *a babble of broadcasters*, *a palaver of politicians*, *a scoop of journalists.* Then of course there's the problem of an appropriate term for a gathering of linguists. *A conjunction of linguists*? Perhaps *a conjugation* or *a declension of linguists* – *a paradigm of linguists* better still! Then again, I rather like an *eloquence of linguists* – or should that be *a loquaciousness of linguists*? Don't start this game or you'll never stop.

Language Change

The garden is far from static
Stefan Buczacki, *The Conran Beginner's Guide to Gardening*, 1988

As gardening wizard Stefan Buczacki puts it, 'no sooner do you turn over the spadeful of soil, put down the watering can or firm in the newly planted shrub than things begin to happen'. Most of the time we fail to see the stirrings going on around us. Changes in language are as gradual and imperceptible as the changes in the growth of a plant or tree. But the clues to where our language is heading are everywhere. The infinite variation in everyday language – this is what provides the basis for real change.

Sneaky diffusion

Currently in Australia we hear two pronunciations of the word *mandatory* – 'mandat**o**ry' and 'mandatry'. This is exactly the sort of variation that suggests a change is under way. Sound change is not a purely mechanical process that affects all eligible vocabulary at once. It's gradual, slowly sneaking through our vocabulary and affecting different groups of words at different times.

All words ending in *-ory*, *-ery*, *-ary* and *-ury* used once to be pronounced as if they ended in something like *-urry*. In other words, the vowel before the 'r' was pronounced in *factory*, *scenery*, *elementary*, *century* and so on. My dictionary still gives this as a possible pronunciation for these words, even though in practice the vowel is now omitted in many of them. Most of us say 'factry' and 'scenry' not 'factory' and 'scenery', but dictionaries have to provide a combination of older and newer pronunciations.

American linguist Joan Bybee is someone who has studied this particular change, and, as she observed, the first words to lose the vowel were the everyday words like 'evry' and 'factry'. This is typical of pronunciation shifts of this kind. As Bybee puts it 'repetition has a reductive effect on-line'; in other words, we make short-cuts when we chat and especially when we're in familiar territory. This is very obvious in the way we pronounce words for those places and objects we refer to often. For example, Australians pronounce *Australia* with a reduced, almost inaudible, first vowel; the final vowel is also reduced – some speakers drop the [l] as well, and perhaps even that first vowel. So 'ostralia' becomes 'straya'. The UK has many such examples – Gloucester, Barnoldswick, Chiswick, Leicester, Salisbury, Shrewsbury and Daventry are all placenames in England with spellings that in no way reflect their actual pronunciations. When I lived in London I used to live near Theobald's Road. I pronounced it according to its spelling, that is until one nice taxi driver put me right by politely pointing out that it was in fact pronounced 'Tibbalds' Road! I was extremely grateful. (Of course it's not simply frequency effects at work here. There are also mischievous social reasons for these absurd pronunciations – they identify you as an insider, one of the gang. If someone says 'ostralia' or 'awstralia', then you know they're an outsider.)

Sound change is generally reductive. So when sounds are on the move it's usually the everyday common-usage words that will be at the forefront of the change. In this case a less usual word like *mandatory* or *desultory* will hang on to the vowel for a bit. But once a change has its foot in the door, even uncommon words end up being affected. Hence, you now hear 'slavry' in place of 'slavery', 'cursry' in place of 'cursory' and, yes, 'mandatry' is becoming more common than 'mandatory'. But linguistic factors are also important. Even frequently used words won't change if the result is a more difficult pronunciation. For example, a word like *burglary* is much harder to say without the vowel because it makes for a nasty cluster of consonants – 'glr' as in 'burglry' (or we get 'burgelry').

This kind of word-by-word progress of a sound change through vocabulary is called 'diffusion'. A new pronunciation starts off slowly, first affecting a handful of common-usage words. It then experiences a sudden spurt of energy and many words are affected within a short period. The change subsequently often slows down, leaving a handful of words that one day may fall in line and change, but also may not. Other competing changes may have interfered by then. It all happens so very, very slowly.

Predicting change is a dicey business. We can observe what we imagine are changes while they are in progress, but we can never be sure they will be carried through to the bitter end. Some changes peter out over time. Some changes even end up reversing themselves. For instance, in England speakers cheerfully stopped pronouncing 'r' in words like *cart* at the same time as a spelling-enthused eighteenth century saw the restoration of 'h' in words like *helmet*. Suddenly, 'dropping aitches' was a bad thing. But why did 'h' suddenly come to the attention of speakers and not 'r'? There are just so many complex social and psychological factors that underlie language changes.

Yod-dropping

A fine example of sneaky diffusion is something linguists call 'yod-dropping' (and no, it's not some kind of nasty new linguistic disease or Olympic sport. 'Yod' is simply the name of the tenth smallest letter of the Hebrew alphabet and refers to the 'y' sound at the start of words like *yes*). As Laurie Bauer discusses, we've been dropping our yods before 'u(e)' and 'e(w)' since the seventeenth century, but the change is so gradual we're hardly aware it's happening. The first words to lose their yods were those where it appeared after 'r' – like *rule* and *true*. Nowadays, we all say 'rool' not 'ryule', but for a long time this was considered a 'vulgar' and 'indolent' pronunciation. Yods were also dropped after 'l', especially where a cluster of consonants was involved, as in *blue*. No one pronounces *blue* as 'blyue' any more.

Where yods are proving most difficult to shift is in words like *beautiful, cute, fume* and *mute*. These are all words beginning with consonants formed with the two lips, like 'p', or with the back of the tongue like 'k'. Pronunciations like 'bootiful' for *beautiful* tend to be jocular – except, that is, in some East Anglian dialects which drop yods even in these words. These speakers pronounce *beauty* as 'booty'.

Where most variation occurs is in words like *dew, new, tune, suit, enthusiasm*. These are all words where the yod follows sounds made around the teeth ridge – that's the little bump behind your teeth. Americans are the greatest yoddroppers with their 'toon', 'doo', 'noo' and 'enthoosiasm' for *tune, dew, new* and *enthusiasm*. British English speakers are reluctant yod-droppers here. Many still say things like 'syut', 'enthyusiasm', even 'lyud'. As usual, my downunder English lies somewhere in the middle. Many of us probably say 'tyune', 'dyew' and 'nyew' but 'soot', 'enthoosiasm' and 'lood'. Given the systematic way that change often works its way through the language, we'd expect these yods eventually to go as well – 'tyune' will give way to 'toon', just as 'enthyusiam' gave way to 'enthoosiasm'. But there's a competing change that may interrupt this sneaky diffusion. In these words, yods may get fused with the preceding consonants – as in 'chune' and 'djune' for *tune* and *dune*. Many speakers appear to be opting for the 'chune' pronunciation with an embalmed yod rather than 'toon' with a lost yod. But time will tell.

Linguistic chameleons and peacocks

A striking feature of ordinary speech is the tendency for sounds to become more like their neighbours. For example, say the word *pancake* in a sentence and you'll most probably say something that sounds like 'pangcake'. What happens is the 'n' sound of *pan* anticipates the following 'k' sound and changes to become more like it; hence, *pangcake*. Nasal consonants – the chameleons of the phonological world – are notorious for doing this sort of thing. Think of the negative prefix *in-*. The nasal is always changing its shape; for example, in *impossible* it becomes more like the following 'p' – both sounds are made with the lips. Sure, in careful speech you may say the words *handbag*, *seven* and *eleven* as they are written, but in ordinary conversation they're much more likely to come out as 'hambag', 'sebm' and 'elebm'. But the thing is, our everyday speech is so fast and furious that these kinds of short cuts usually go unnoticed.

Very occasionally consonants and vowels alter because of nearby sounds, but in such a way that they become **less** like these sounds. These changes are much more likely to attract attention. This sort of change is usually attributed to the fact that we find repetition of the same muscular activity hard. Nearly everyone has experienced at some time the difficulty of repeating the same action over and over again – whether it's on a computer keyboard, folding paper, stuffing envelopes or repeating sounds in a tongue twister. Suddenly you find yourself doing something weird, often substituting a totally different action. It seems it's hard for us to get our brains firing the same way in rapid succession. So, when we come to repeat something like *The sixth sheik's sixth sheep's sick*, our tongue slips and we start substituting other sounds.

The difficulty doesn't have to involve the same sounds, simply ones that are similar. Take that tricky word *diphthong*. In the middle of it is a particularly nasty cluster of consonants 'fth'. It takes considerable articulatory effort to enunciate them; so the solution for many speakers is to replace 'f' with a completely different type of sound; hence *diphthong* becomes 'dipthong'. *Chimney* has two nasal sounds close together. Kids often change the second one to an 'l'; hence 'chimbley' (there's an extra 'b' here too – more on that later).

Certain sounds such as 'r' and 'l' are particularly susceptible to this process. For example, the word *grammar* has two 'r's and for some dialect speakers during the late Middle Ages this proved just far too tricky. So they changed the first 'r' to an 'l' and *grammar* became *glamour*. Of course, in this case both pronunciations prevailed and eventually led to a spectacular meaning shift. Speakers also remodelled the Latin words *marmor*, *turtur* and *purpur* to *marble*, *turtle* and *purple*. (Compare the colour *purpure* in heraldry, which is conservative and retains the original 'r'.) This sort of change is typically sporadic. Unlike other sound changes that are more systematic, this is much more like a speech error – which also means we're more likely to notice it.

There is, however, a more extreme variety that is less obvious. In a word like *library*, for instance, we don't substitute one of the 'r's, we typically drop it. *Library* becomes 'libery'. An 'r' often disappears in pronunciations of *contrary* and *February* too – in fact entire syllables are often pruned. This sort of change is much more likely to slip by us unobserved. Even the language inspectors can occasionally be heard saying 'libry'.

Humble and humility

You've probably encountered pronunciations like 'umberella' for *umbrella* and 'fillum' for *film*. Here speakers have inserted a vowel where previously there wasn't one. It's a kind of simplification. There's plenty of evidence to suggest that speakers prefer a consonant-vowel syllable structure; hence, vowels get inserted between consonants to help the pronunciation of what are otherwise difficult clusters. 'Fillum' might be longer but it's easier to say than 'film'.

We also find consonants intruding in this way, but the motivation is quite different. It's more a case of 'mistiming'. Say the words *mince* and *mints*. Now, you probably think you pronounce them differently, but in fact you don't. It's just the spelling that suggests this. For both, you would insert a 't' between the 'n' and the 's' sound. Whenever we have a cluster of a nasal sound and a following consonant, as in the word *mince*, we typically insert a sound like 't'. It's hard not to. This has to do with our soft palate – that's the fleshy bit at the back of the roof of your mouth with the little teardrop uvula dangling from it. When we say nasal sounds like 'm' and 'n' our soft palate lowers so the air can escape through the nose. This gives the nasal resonance. For other sounds like 'b' and 'd' the soft palate is raised so that the nasal passage is blocked. Really, the sounds 'b' and 'd' are not very different from 'm' and 'n'. Nasal sounds are just like oral sounds except that the nasal passage is left open; in other words, it's the nasal resonance that turns 'b' into 'm' and 'd' into 'n'. (You've all experienced those times of a cold or hay fever when the passage of air through the nose is impeded. All your nasals turn into oral sounds. 'Good morning' sounds a lot like 'good bordig'.)

When we say the word *mince*, what happens is that our soft palate is lowered for the 'n' and air passes through the nose. Because the following 's' sound is oral not nasal, we need to raise the soft palate to stop the air escaping through the nose. But if the soft palate is raised too early, before the tongue position has changed, you produce an oral stop made in the same place of articulation as the nasal – that's why the 't' appears between the 'n' and the 's'. It's this same process that has inserted a 'b' in *thimble* and a 'd' in *thunder*. Even the 'p' in the name *Thompson* is an intrusive 'p'. Extra sounds are added as the vocal organs move from one sound to another. In cases like *thimble* and *Thompson* the intrusive sounds now show up in the spelling. The same mistiming has produced curious alternations like *tremble* versus *tremulous* and *humble* versus *humility*. The words *tremble* and *humble* show the 'b' intruder. It's also why children say *fambly* for *family* and *chimbley* for *chimney*.

Occasionally consonants get added to the ends of words. Again it's a kind of wrong timing but the motivation is different. When you finish saying something, your speech organs go back to rest position. But if you do this more abruptly, somewhere in the vocal tract there's a closure and this means an extra consonant. The informal (also more expressive) pronunciation of *no* as *nope* is usually attributed to this process. Usually though, it's an extra 't' that gets added. The tongue rests against the bump behind your teeth before articulation is complete. This explains the 't' at the end of words like *(a)midst* and *whilst*.

Changes like these are going on all the time in our speech. Usually they pass unnoticed. Sometimes they're noticed, then discarded. But sometimes they're noticed, appreciated, taken up by others – and are here to stay.

Pig's arse!

When people are asked to say what they regard as really bad grammar, many will give the example of double negation, as in ***I don't** understand **nothing**.* Like many features of English we object to, this particular construction has been in the language for many centuries. It wasn't condemned until the first grammars of the late 1700s.

Nothink/nothin'/nothing

There are four words of English whose pronunciation every now and again catches the critical ear of certain speakers. I am referring here to those little pronominal 'thing' words *something*, *nothing*, *everything* and *anything* – in particular, the pronunciation 'somethink', 'nothink', 'everythink' and 'anythink'. The story behind this pronunciation is complicated. Originally, all words ending in *-ing* were pronounced exactly as their spelling suggests – with a final 'g' sound. Then a sound change took place that deleted all final 'g', 'd' and 'b' sounds after nasals. Hence, the silent 'b' at the end of words like *climb* and *lamb*. So something like *sing* lost its 'g' and came to be pronounced as we do today. There are some conservative dialects in places like Birmingham, Stoke-on-Trent and Liverpool where the final 'g' didn't vanish – for these speakers *singer* still rhymes with *finger*.

In pronunciations like 'nothink', the final 'g' didn't drop off but lost voice and turned into a 'k'. This '-ink' pronunciation is recorded as early as a thousand years ago and today it's still scattered throughout the Midlands and also in some parts of south-eastern England. It features strongly in Cockney too. These are many of the dialects in the original melting pot that gave rise to Australian English and it's clear from early nineteenth-century descriptions that '-ink' was here downunder from the very beginning. It seems it was always restricted to the pronominal 'thing' words like *nothing* and *something*. There is no evidence of pronunciations like 'I'm goink runnink' or 'hello darlink' – unless, of course, a speaker is attempting a Zsa Zsa Gabor impersonation.

Of course, '-ink' also competes with 'in' as in 'somethin' and 'nothin''. This is also a very old pronunciation. Linguistic variation of this sort can indicate a change in progress, but it can also exist without ever leading to change. The 'nothink/nothin'/nothing' variation appears to be the latter type. The struggle between these forms has been going on for centuries and in many dialects too. Time will tell whether any one form does eventually win out. At the current state of play, it's difficult to predict. The 'nothink/nothin'/nothing' variation looks like hanging around for a good deal longer.

Because of its expressive nature, negation is, in fact, an aspect of language that is prone to extremely rapid change. The history of English negation is a spectacular illustration. One thousand years ago we were forming negative sentences with the little word *ne*. More usually, though, this *ne* was complemented with additional expressions. Two, or even more, negators in the one sentence became the norm. Here's some advice from the fourteenth century (literally, 'there not-is nothing that so quickly smites with grievance the head as wine') – *þere nys noþinge þat so sone smyteþ with grevaunce the hed as wyne*. One of these extra negative expressions was *ne-a-wiht* (literally 'not-ever-anything'). This eventually reduced to *noght*, the predecessor of Modern English *not* (and *nought*). Although it began life as a reinforcing element, in the course of Middle English it became so common that it lost its emphatic quality and in combination with *ne* emerged as the normal expression of negation. We then got something called 'embracing negation' – the two negators *ne* and *not* snugly wrapped themselves around the verb. For example, *Hit* ***ne*** *swelleth* ***not*** ('it not swells not'). Eventually *ne* dropped out altogether and *not* triumphed as the exclusive negator.

At this stage things start looking more familiar, but there were more changes to come. Here's a piece of sixteenth-century advice on how best to sleep – *Sleep* ***not*** *grouellynge upon the stomacke*. This is not bad Modern English, but it sounds better with the addition of the verb *do*. We are more likely to say – *Do not sleep grovelling upon the stomach.* This use of *do* spread slowly. For quite some time people continued to say things like *I know not* and *Fear not* – we have to wait until well into the eighteenth century before the system we now know stabilized.

So what's the current state of play? Well, in normal speech *not* is reduced to *-n't* and squishes onto the verb as in *won't* from *will not*. In fact, it often disappears entirely. In normal rapid speech, all that's left is a bit of nasality on the vowel – much like the Cheshire Cat's grin, the nasality lingers on. Sound change has now left *not* a fragment of the original expression *ne-a-wiht* from which it derives. Small wonder linguist Ron Langacker describes language as 'a gigantic expression compacting machine'! With *not* being now so tiny, Standard English negation is ripe for renewal.

Change is typically marked by rivalry between variant forms and there are several competitors here. One is the teenage negative construction involving a stranded *not* at the end of the sentence as in *I like you – not*. Certainly novel expressions can take off, but this one probably won't – it's just too weird to wait so long for the negative. Another candidate is the expression *a bit*. This derived originally from *bite* and was used to strengthen negative sentences involving eating (along the lines of *I didn't eat a crumb* and *I didn't drink a drop*). Nowadays of course we no longer even connect *bit* with *bite* and it appears in all sorts of places – *It didn't hurt a bit*. (If you think the development of *bit* into a negator is far-fetched, bear in mind French *pas* derives from Latin *passus* meaning 'step' – *pas* would have originally strengthened verbs of walking.) Other likely contenders for the job include *no way* as in 'No way I did it!' and *never* as in 'I never did it' (here the meaning is 'I didn't do it' not 'I didn't ever do it'). I was once asked if *pig's arse* was a potential negator in Australian English. Certainly it's used to reinforce negation, and could be expanding. However, its taboo quality probably means it's unlikely to ever gain the currency needed to start the grammatical ball rolling. But *pig's arse* as grammar in the making – an interesting idea!

Mongrel verbs

Language change can have curious effects. For example, it can happen that historically quite unrelated forms for some reason end up colliding. This then produces totally irregular and eccentric patterns in the language.

One spectacular example is the verb *be* as in *I am*, *you are*, *he is* and so on. This is one mongrel verb showing a combination of at least three, possibly four, originally distinct verbs. One source is *bēon* 'to become'. It provides the modern forms *be*, *being* and *been*. Another *wesan* 'to dwell' gives us the past tense forms *was* and *were*. There's also the ancient verbal root *es-* 'exist' that provides modern *is*, *am* and possibly also *are* (though there may be a fourth source here *er-* 'arise' – no one is quite sure).

Another outlandish verb, though not quite as impressive, is *go*. Most of its forms are built on *go*, but it derives its past form *went* from the verb *wend* 'to make one's way'. This verb *wend* has fallen out of general use, although it's preserved in the expression *wend one's way home* and, of course, it has generously donated *went* to the verb *go*. It now has a new past – *wended*. The verb *go* seems a word unable to keep its hands off the past tense forms of other verbs. Before it stole *went* from *wend* some time during the fifteenth century, *go* already had an irregular past – *ēode*. This wasn't its original past either, but stolen property from yet another verb that has since disappeared. It all becomes even more complex when you factor in other irregular dialect forms of *go* like the *gang* of Scottish English. This has a different past again. So, what's wrong with a verb that it has to filch past tense forms from other verbs?

The actual process that combines unrelated forms in this way is called 'suppletion'. Typically it involves frequently used items, but how it actually happens is complicated and not at all clear cut. Somehow the past tense form of a verb like *wend* gradually disassociates itself from the other forms of that verb and becomes synonymous with *go*. It's not peculiar to English – the verbs *go* and *be* are suppletive in many languages. The process affects common adjectives as well. Many adjectives for *good* and *bad* have aberrant forms akin to English *bad*, *worse*, *worst*, and *good*, *better*, *best*. Something went awry in the history of these words and somehow the forms of completely different adjectives converged to produce these 'bitser' forms.

Our disappearing endings

Typical adjectives are gradable. This means they refer to properties or states that can be possessed in varying degrees. Most adjectives you'll find take part in a three-term system. For example, something is *tasty*, *tastier* or *tastiest*. The endings adjectives take to reflect degree are *-er* and *-est*. These are known as the comparative and superlative forms.

Not all adjectives take these endings, however. In fact the group is becoming smaller. Phrases with *more* and *most* like *more tasty* and *most tasty* are pushing out forms like *tastier* and *tastiest*. Rather

Bought? Brought?

Two verbs in Antipodean English are currently on a collision course. The verbs *buy* and *bring* are confusing their past tense forms. More and more the form *bought* is appearing as the past of *bring*. This can take place because the older past *brought* is already highly irregular and very distant from *bring* in the way it sounds. And of course *buy* and *bring* also share an element of meaning, so they appear in similar contexts. Certainly these are early days, but the fact that *bought* now commonly appears in print as the past of *bring* suggests that the change is well and truly entrenched. Here's an example I came upon in a newspaper: 'Mr Eric Grant of Glen Iris **bought** in a couple of his 1975 Bin 389 for evaluation'. Once this sort of error would have provoked cries of outrage from media watchdogs. But those on the lookout for linguistic crimes have fallen curiously silent on this one.

than a clean takeover, however, we find the usual messiness associated with language change. Typically, it's adjectives of one syllable which are managing to hang on to the endings; for example, *bigger/biggest*. Adjectives of three or more syllables have lost the fight completely and require *more* and *most*. You can't, for example, say *beautifuller* or *beautifullest* – which is why Alice in Wonderland's response 'curiouser and curiouser' sounds so comical. Adjectives of two syllables have a kind of split personality, some do, some don't, some go both ways and not all speakers agree. For example, do you prefer *tastier* and *tastiest* or *more tasty* and *most tasty*? But how about *wickeder* and *wickedest* versus *more* and *most wicked*? Certainly, Shakespeare's *horrider* and *certainer* sound odd to us now. Of course, in Shakespeare's time double constructions were possible – forms like *more larger* and *most unkindest* where speakers had a bob each way. By the end of the seventeenth century, however, these double comparisons had become linguistic outlaws and remain so today.

A striking theme running through the story of English is the unrelenting erosion of grammatical endings. The *-er* and *-est* on adjectives belong to a tiny group of seven survivors. It's conceivable that all will disappear with time. More than likely, phrases such as *more tasty* and *more big* will eventually evict *tastier* and *bigger* just as *more beautiful* evicted *beautifuller*. Possessive *-s*, past *-ed* and plural *-s* are also endangered. But it's always a hazardous business trying to predict linguistic change. It's true we might go the whole way and totally lose these endings, but we also might end up hanging on to them. In fact, we might even reverse the trend and create some new endings, too. If you look at the languages of the world you can find examples of both outcomes. Chinese used to have lots of endings, but these have now gone. Hindi, on the other hand, lost a good many of its endings but then invented a whole heap of new ones.

We may take note of what we imagine to be changes under way in the language, but we can never be sure they will run their full course. Look at the fate of *ain't*, once a perfectly respectable contracted form – who could have foretold its fall from grace? Predicting the path these changes might take is one of the most tricky (trickiest?) tasks confronting historical linguists.

Whatever happened to 'thou'?

Over the years there have been massive changes affecting the pronouns of English, especially those pronouns that refer to the second person or the person spoken to – in other words, 'you'. In fact, that's all we've got left now in Modern English. The form 'you' refers to all persons addressed in every function and regardless of number; there can be one of you, two of you or even more.

Once upon a time we had a 'thou' series of pronouns – *thou*, *thee* and *thine*. These three different forms represented different cases. They changed their shape to mark their relationship to other nouns and to the verb of the clause. Originally they were all different forms of 'you (singular)', and a separate series of pronouns marked 'you (plural)'. In fact, way back there was another series to mark 'you (dual)' – in other words, 'two of you'. In late Middle English, and for some time after, these *thou*, *thee* and *thine* forms also came to mark intimacy. In contrast, the plural forms marked respect (or non-intimacy). This was an idea we borrowed from the French some time during the thirteenth century. It's a common linguistic strategy to use plural to show politeness – compare the so-called 'royal we'.

So when, why and how did the *thou* forms disappear from English? They were definitely on the way out in the 1500s and by 1650 had virtually disappeared, confined to some conservative rural dialects, for example in the north of England. Quakers continued to use *thee* for some time, though nowadays rarely. Undoubtedly it was the spread of feudal ideology that originally caused European languages like French and German (and eventually English speakers) to adapt the singular and plural pronouns in this way, and the social changes that ensued were also responsible for the breakdown of this system in English. The spread of egalitarian ideology eventually saw the pronoun *you* emerge as the all-purpose second person pronoun, regardless of status or familiarity.

But why did *thou* disappear and *you* triumph? There are probably a number of factors. First, the desire not to offend. If you weren't sure of the social standing of the person you were addressing then it was safer to err on the side of politeness (especially if you wanted something). To flatter someone you would use *you* rather than running the risk of offence with the intimate pronoun *thou*. (The Quakers of course avoided this sort of politeness and status issue and retained *thou* to mark humility.) The *thou* form was also a more demanding pronoun. It required an extra ending on the verb that followed it. The *you* form simply used the same ending that all the plural pronouns took. Now, English was in the business of getting rid of such endings; so it suited speakers to dump *thou* for this reason also. Even the plague probably had a role to play. A disaster that has the effect of bumping off huge numbers of speakers (in some areas three quarters of the speech community) will tear social networks apart and if a change is already lurking in the wings, it'll be precisely at times like this that it can take hold. Social upheaval often goes hand in hand with dramatic linguistic change.

Languages like French and German are now experiencing the same breakdown, but curiously the successful pronoun is not the polite 'you' pronoun but the intimate 'thou' pronoun. It would seem that egalitarianism and social democracy this time are seeing the solidarity function of these pronouns winning out over the status function. An interesting difference.

Finally, remember that *you* was originally plural. With the breakdown of the formal–informal distinction we also lost the singular-plural distinction. Many dialects have repaired the loss with new plural pronouns. Southern American English has *y'all* and *you-uns*; East Anglian has *you-together* and Australian English has *youse* which it shares with North America, Scotland, Ireland and New Zealand. Whatever you feel about such forms as *youse*, it does seem that this singular-plural distinction is a useful one, and Standard English will probably eventually adapt to it.

How changes take hold

None of us behaves linguistically the same way all the time. Our language varies constantly in response to a complex interaction of different factors in different situations. Change any one factor, and our language changes accordingly. Are we at a football match or in church? Are we debating who'll win the Melbourne Cup or the existence of God? Are we chatting to our friends or to our local priest?

But how much are we affected by those we speak to? Certainly, the better we know someone, the more relaxed our speech will be and the more vernacular forms we'll use. These are linguistic forms that tend not to have official sanction – they might be swearing or simply slang. But in situations where we don't know another person well, fewer of these vernacular forms will occur. People will naturally steer more towards standard language. Typically, we will also try to match our speech to those we're talking to. This could be to aid comprehension, of course, but also it's a way of gaining social approval. It's all part of polite behaviour. Most of the time we operate with the idea of conversational harmony in mind, with a preference for agreement and compromise. And so we accommodate to other people's vocabulary or accent as a way of getting along together.

This is all the more likely to occur where it's in a speaker's interests to accommodate. In a very famous study involving a Cardiff travel agent and her customers, it was shown quite clearly that this travel agent matched her accent to that of her customers – if they dropped their 'h's she would too. Of course, she had to relate well to them in order to attract business, and wanted them to like her. But we all do this sort of thing. Basically, people chatting together will partially imitate each other, incorporating certain features of the other person's language into their own, at least for the time they're chatting. But there may be long-term effects too, for this is the way language change is able to take off in a speech community and spread a feature from one group to another. Changes begin as the temporary shifts we make while chatting to those outside our immediate group, but can then be incorporated into the everyday speech we might use when chatting to our mates, for example.

We don't just accommodate to people we're chatting with face to face. Look at musical groups who adopt a pseudo American accent when they sing. There are others that take on British working-class features. These singers aren't adapting to their immediate audiences, but they are clearly identifying with the values of outside groups and are shifting their language accordingly.

I shouldn't give the impression that speakers always accommodate in their linguistic behaviour. Certainly, there might be times that you want to increase rather than reduce the distance between you and the person you're speaking to, and so you make your speech different from that person's. Perhaps you want to emphasize your allegiance to some other group, your ethnicity for instance; or you might even have negative feelings towards the person you're addressing. There are situations, too, where speaking differently has a prestige of its own. For some reason, certain accents or dialects come to be highly valued in a society. A divergent style can then be admired. We all love a French accent and there are undoubtedly speakers around who exploit their Frenchness to add to their appeal.

But to conclude, let me emphasize that linguistic accommodation can be a tricky business. I've just said that we accommodate our speech in the hopes that our interlocutor will like us better, but this strategy can backfire. On the one hand, matching your speech to the speech of someone else can flatter that person (you're saying that their speech is worth imitating). On the other, your behaviour might be taken as patronizing, perhaps even insulting. Your hearer might well think you're taking the mickey. Nothing in language is ever straightforward.

Word Creation

Just as woods change their leaves with the onward movement of the years, the first leaves falling: even so when words advance in age, they pass away, and others born but lately, like the young, flourish and thrive.
Horace (Quintus Horatius Flaccus), *Ars Poetica*, 19–18 BC

There are several reasons why words disappear. Most obviously, when objects, ideas or institutions are no longer important to us, the words for them will drop from our mental dictionary. In areas such as clothing, lexical obsolescence is probably a matter of course. Battle fashions have changed, not surpringly, and we no longer recognize medieval terms for armour like *vambrace*, *rere-brace*, *crinet* and *peytral.* Also on the danger list are fashion items like *codpiece*, the highly conspicuous decorative bagged appendage which once used to be attached to the front of men's close-fitting breeches. The word might well have dropped out long ago if *Blackadder* hadn't thrown it a lifejacket. Clearly it's the comic value that has kept this one alive. *Bustle* as a clothing item has also disappeared from the modern lexicon. Like *codpiece*, it had the dual function of highlighting the body part (in this case a woman's buttocks) at the same time as keeping them well and truly hidden under copious quantities of material. It seems we no longer go to the same lengths in this kind of 'doublespeak' dressing.

Disappearing words often indicate societal change. The traditional vocabulary of sin and virtue provides us with an interesting example. As lexicographer Geoffrey Hughes has discussed, terms such as *honour*, *virtue*, *temperance*, *modesty*, *chastity* and *virginity* no longer form part of our meaningful moral vocabulary and this is revealing of changing mores and attitudes. Gone too are all those *bounders*, *cads* and *rotters* – we've lost a whole category of morally based bastards!

Examples like these also illustrate another fact of lexical life – words wear out. There are certain areas of our vocabulary, like abuse, that are more prone to weakening than others. It's no longer effective to insult someone by calling them *a slubber-degullion druggel* or *a fondling fop*, *a blockish grutnol* or *a grout-head gnatsnapper. Mangy rascal*, *drowsy loiterer*, *flouting milksop*, *base loon*, *scoffing scoundrel* and *ruffian rogue* just don't pack much punch any more. Expressive words will soon become insipid and alternatives have to be found. We see this in many areas of vocabulary. Speakers are always on the lookout for new and exciting ways to express themselves, and inevitably many fine expressions will fall by the wayside.

Words can also disappear if they get too short. It seems that they have to retain a certain amount of phonetic saliency if they're to be a useful part of the vocabulary. Sound change is generally reductive and it can happen that the mutilation is so severe that words are reduced to virtual fragments. Examples like *ae* 'custom' or *ig* 'island' are no longer useful – except perhaps in Scrabble when you're stuck with those pesky last two or three letters!

Sometimes words disappear because they sound too much like other words. You'd be surprised how many single-syllable words beginning with 'f' and ending in 'k' have disappeared from the English language. During the Victorian era we lost *feck* meaning 'efficiency'; *feckless* must have sounded different enough to linger a little longer. Typically, we will drop words like hot cakes if they sound too much like expressions that are offensive or embarrassing. Such is the power of taboo.

But having said all this, I have to admit that huge numbers of English words seem to drop out of use for no obvious reason at all. We still have *gormless*, so why did we lose the noun *gorm* meaning 'understanding'? Once upon a time we could be *kempt*, *corrigible*, *ert* and *wieldy*, and full of *ruth* and *list*, but for some curious reason these words have left us. Why would such an apparently useful word like *gry* 'dirt under the fingernails' disappear? The same goes for *horrorfiliation* meaning 'goose bumps', *ugsome* 'horrid', and handy verbs like *apricate* 'to bask in the sun', *fibulate* 'to perform the action of buttoning and unbuttoning', and *groof* 'to lie face down on the floor' (here at least we've retained the related noun *grovelling*). Certainly the term *firkytoodling* would seem a more amusing substitute for modern English *foreplay*. But for some curious reason these words, like thousands of others, have just slipped quietly away.

Nostrils and froot loops

The simple process of compounding is responsible for many new words. Just look at recent additions to the world of *dance music* – *mosh pit*, *crowd surfing*, *crowd diving*, *heavy metal*, *thrash metal*, *speed metal*, *slamdancing*, *breakdancing* and *headbanging*. How to write these compounds is always tricky. For instance, I write *headbanging* and *slamdancing* as one word, but I've seen them written with a hyphen and as two separate words. Even dictionaries don't agree on the conventions they adopt, although on the whole American editors abandon hyphenation more quickly than others do. Often it boils down to the length of time a compound has been around. Well-aged compounds will typically lose their hyphens and appear as one word

Not only will familiarity remove hyphenation in well-established compounds, but it can bring about even further reduction. As the elements of the compound become more and more closely associated, the boundaries between them can become quite blurred. Look at what's happened to the pronunciation of *cupboard* and *forehead*. Here the spelling preserves the original compound, but this is not always the case. Consider *daisy* and *nostril*. Only the real word enthusiast will be aware that they began life as compounds: Old English *dægesēage* 'day's eye' and *nosþyrel* 'nose thirl [=hole]'. Occasionally spelling restores the full pronunciation. For example, *forehead* is now often pronounced as 'fore + head' (as in *forelock*). This is more likely if the word becomes unfamiliar. When we stopped wearing waistcoats, we stopped pronouncing them 'wescots'.

The 'one-wordedness' of compounds becomes obvious when we look at the way they behave in the grammar. For example, the noun *still-life* is very different from the noun *life* when it comes to forming the plural – *still-lifes*, not *still-lives*. Similarly, you would probably say *jack-in-the-boxes* and not *jacks-in-the-box*, thinking of *jack-in-the-box* as a fused word. You can also tell by the stress pattern. There's a heavy stress on the first syllable and the following parts are all squashed together: ***Jack**-in-the-box.* Of course, purists will insist that the plural of something like *attorney-general* should remain *attorneys-general*, but most of us have probably regularized it as *attorney-generals*, just as we've begun to do with *mother-in-law* and *runner-up*.

The fact that we are thinking of these expressions as single units is also obvious from their unified meanings. Take, for example, the wide range of relationships possible in noun-noun compounds. In *flu symptoms* flu causes the symptoms; in other words, A causes B. But in *flu virus* A is caused by B, and in *flu shot* A is prevented by B. In *orange juice* B is made of A. In *rubbish bin* B contains A. In *frogman* B resembles A. In *needlework* B is made with A. These are just a few examples. So how do we know that *health food* promotes health and not prevents it? And what about those compounds with highly idiosyncratic meanings like *sex appeal*, *bag lady*, *spaghetti western* and *black sheep*? The meaning relationship between the parts of a compound is often quite capricious. And this is used to great advantage in advertising, particularly food advertising. For example, what does it mean to say that something has a *fruit flavour*? It could be flavoured with fruit, or it could have a flavour resembling that of fruit. So something might have a fruit flavour without having any fruit in it. *Fruit juice* usually contains fruit, but not a *fruit drink*. *Froot loops* aren't loops of fruit; in fact they don't have any fruit in them at all – but they are 'naturally' flavoured, which a *fruit drink* needn't be. Exploiting the fact that word compounds can be interpreted different ways, advertisers can make all sort of claims that are difficult, indeed impossible, to verify.

In their search for vivid expression, advertisers use compounding to great effect. The novelty comes not from the actual words themselves, but from the strange collocations. We learn of *taste-tempting tomatoes* and *thirst-quenching cucumbers*; *oysters* with *mouth-filling freshness* and *in-your-face saltiness*. The expression has more impact because compound phrases are perceived as single concepts. For example, *once a year* is normally a phrase and is written as such. But if we describe turkey as *a once-a-year treat* (where *once-a-year* is a hyphenated word) it designates a single quality. This way we're less apt to question it, too, which makes the modifying compound a handy device indeed. When we read, for example, that Kitchen Collection bread mixes are available in *value-for-money 6 kg boxes*, the compound *value-for-money* attributes a special property to the product and is much more effective than saying something like *these 6 kg boxes are value for money*. Putting it as a statement, it can be questioned – are these boxes value for money? Verbs are to be avoided in advertising – they just invite questions.

Din-dins, dilly-dally and argy-bargy

The odd expression *argy-bargy*, as in 'argumentative talk, wrangling', illustrates another of the ways English creates new words – 'reduplication'. Essentially, it's a repetition process, where the whole or part of a word stem is doubled, and the resulting form is a kind of compound word. I've always found reduplication a rather under-appreciated word formation process in English. Most textbooks describe its contribution as a marginal one and the examples they cite are those of the nursery like *bow-wow* and *din-dins*. Really, reduplication is much more interesting than this. Around two thousand words have been coined this way and new ones are being created all the time.

They fall into three basic groups. One involves repeating the whole stem of the word. Nothing else changes. For example, *goody-goody*, *fifty-fifty*, *never-never* and *hush-hush*. A second group involves some sort of modification of the vowel. For example, *shillyshally*, *dilly-dally*, *mishmash*, *riffraff* and *flipflop*. The third group is much more plentiful than either of these two. It involves repeating the rhyme of the word. Sometimes this involves actually existing words like *fat cat*, *stun gun*, *brain drain*, *flower power* and *culture vulture*. But more usually, one or both of the elements are meaningless, as in *super duper*, *argy-bargy*, *ridgy-didge*, *teeny-weeny*, *lovey-dovey*, *helter-skelter*, *higgledy-piggledy*, *namby-pamby*, *hanky-panky*, *hokey-pokey* and *hoity-toity*.

Often expressions start life as meaningful, but over time speakers stop identifying the repeated elements with independently existing words. For example, I don't believe anyone associates a *nitwit* with *nit* 'louse' and *wit* 'intellect'. This would be true

The dishonest compound?

In some types of Modern English compounding is particularly popular. I am referring here to those superliterate varieties like Bureaucratese, Educationalese and Linguisticalese. The characteristic practice of many of these 'eses' is to take a phrase like 'the congruency between occupational choice and vocational interest' and replace it with the handy compound *occupational choice-vocational interest congruency*. Now why on earth would someone prefer a clotted clump of English like this? Compounds like *young driver risk-taking research* and *prototype crisis shelter development plans* might serve the interests of economy, but not intelligibility. Mind you, when 'doors' become *entry systems*, 'girdles' *anti-gravity panties*, 'teachers' *learning facilitators* and 'potholes' *pavement deficiencies*, there's little question of economy either. You can't help but suspect that the real function of these compounds is to puff up the speaker's self-image by making even the simplest of things sound complex. There may be an even more sinister motivation too: consider gems like *value minutes* (they're radio and television commercials), *monitored retrievable storage site* (well, that's a US Department of Energy nuclear fuel dump), and Canadian politicians who apparently engage in a little *reality augmentation* (of course they never, never lie). These were just some the nominees for the annual Doublespeak Awards – and these ones didn't even win a prize.

also of recent creations like *hi-fi* from *high-fidelity*. Links are often severed because of sound change, or else the words simply drop out of use. *Argy-bargy* probably comes from the longer expression *argle-bargle* with the same meaning. The verb *argle* was around in Shakespeare's time. Some claim it was a perversion of the Latin word *ergo* 'therefore', but more likely it was simply a corruption of either *argue* or *haggle* (perhaps a blend of the two). But *argle* is no longer with us, and *argy-bargy* is left behind as a kind of relic.

Hob-nob derives from the forms of two now obsolete verbs *habb(an)* and *nabb(an)*, literally 'have' and 'not have'; *willy-nilly* from the expression *will I nill I* based on the verbs *willen* 'want' and *nillen* 'not want'. *Hocus-pocus* comes from the first part of the string of mock Latin *hocus-pocus, toutous talontus* (supposedly parodying the first words of the consecration).

Many of these reduplicated compounds are undoubtedly expressive. Some are obvious imitations of actual sounds like *bow-wow* and *choo-choo*, and with a bit of imagination even *ho-ho* and *tsk-tsk* are a bit like noises we make. Dictionary makers, I think, must have more imagination than the rest of us. They see all sorts of sound–meaning links. Take the word *hurdy-gurdy* – a rhyming combination, says the Oxford English Dictionary, suggested by the sound of the instrument. Now, as a player of a hurdy-gurdy I fail to see how the word could possibly resemble what in sound is something like a cross between a bagpipe and harpsichord. In truth, *hurdy-gurdy* probably goes back to fifteenth-century *hiddy-giddy* (from *heady* and *giddy*) meaning 'confusion, disorder'. After all, *hurdy-gurdy* was a derogatory term given to the instrument after it fell from grace in the 1600s. Gentlemen of quality apparently didn't play the hurdy-gurdy. Beware of the label 'imitative' in dictionaries – it is used rather loosely.

You're the butler – butle!

It can happen that complex words exist in the language without their simple forms. Speakers will then often create new simple forms to fill the gap. This is something called 'backformation', and it's another way we have of creating new words. For example, Australian English speakers have 'backformed' a new verb *bludge* meaning 'to scrounge' from the noun *bludger*, interpreting the final *-er* as the agent suffix. Well, if a baker bakes and a singer sings, then a bludger must bludge. This of course has great comic potential: if a baker bakes and a singer sings, then a butler must butle, an usher must ush and a fishmonger must surely mong.

Backformation often gives rise to new singular words, derived from forms that people assume (wrongly) to be a plural. In the comic strip *The Wizard of Id* there was a time when the one-eyed monster Cyclops was found scrounging around on the floor, apparently looking for his lost contact 'len'. Cyclops had just back-formed a new singular noun *len* – one *len*, two *lens*. This was a joke, but in fact quite a lot of singular words have come about this way. Take the word *peas* as in 'a plate of peas'. The final *-s* of that word is now the plural *-s* ending, but it wasn't always – it wasn't even an ending. The word was originally the singular noun *pease*. Hence, the curious rhyme 'every pease has its vease [=fart] but every bean fifteen'. People mistook the final *-s* for a plural ending and some time during the seventeenth century backformed a new singular word *pea*. It would be the same if you took *cheese*, assumed it to be plural and then on this basis created a new singular word *chee* – one *chee*, two *chees*. During the eighteenth century this is exactly what some speakers did to *Chinese* – they back-formed the singular form *Chinee*.

Creating affixes

Probably the most common way we have of forming new words is via affixes. English has over sixty prefixes and more than eighty suffixes. Many of these have their origin in ordinary words. For example, the ending *-dom* goes back to an Old English word *doom* 'judgement' (related to the verb *deem*). At a time when words like *kingdom* and *Christendom* were created these were undoubtedly compounds, but twentieth-century creations like *Nazidom*, *newspaperdom* and the more jocular *slobdom, suckerdom* and *gardendom* (which I've just created) demonstrate that *-dom* is now a good example of a versatile and fully productive ending. Similarly, *-hood* in *gardenhood* 'garden-like character', goes back to a noun meaning 'condition'. The *-ship* ending of *gardenership* 'the art of gardening' also goes back to an ordinary noun – the same word in fact as our word *shape*. It meant 'creation, condition'. Over time, when these words shift to become endings, they lose stress and change pronunciation. We no longer connect *shape* and *-ship*.

The *-ly* in a word like *beastly* provides a truly spectacular example of the life cycle of an ending. This derives from an Old English word *līc* meaning 'body' (the same word as in *lychgate* 'gateway where the corpse is placed'). It originally appeared in compounds with the meaning 'having the appearance of'. You could compare something like *godlike*. Over time it evolved into an ending. We no longer connect the *-ly* in *godly* with *like* in *godlike*, although historically they are the same – a nice example of linguistic history repeating itself.

Twentieth-century slang gives us glimpses of how new affixes come about. The word *buster* has been around in compounds since the mid nineteenth century, but it was really the 1984 blockbuster movie *Ghostbusters* that catapulted it to affixhood. Recent times have seen a flurry of copycat creations, such as *alley busters*, or 'bowling balls', *ball-busters* or 'sexually emasculating women', *cold busters* or 'doctors', *line busters or* 'queue jumpers', *fare busters or* 'travel agents', *virus busters* or 'vaccines'. There are also *bank busters, crime busters, dam busters, chart-busters, stress busters* (a masseuse service) and *Gutbusters* (a diet clinic for men). It's too early to call *buster* a 'suffix'. Yet clearly it's on its way.

It's also possible for the opposite process to occur; in other words, an original plural ending is misconstrued as part of the singular stem. The other day, for example, I caught myself talking about having a pocket full of 'five-centses'. On the hop I'd reanalysed the plural *-s* ending of *cents* as part of the noun stem, and then put on another *-s* ending to make it plural; hence, *five-centses*. Now, you might well laugh at this invention, but exactly the same thing happened to the word *pence*. *Pence* was, after all, the collective plural of the word *penny*, but was reinterpreted as a singular noun. Hence, it became possible to say something like *one pence*. Back then, people would have had pocketfuls of *twopences* and *threepences*.

We did the same with *quince* (originally the plural of *quin*), *chintz* (originally the plural of *chint* 'a painted calico from India') and *bodice* (from the plural of *body*, as in *a pair of bodice*). Just like my *five-centses*, these words *quince*, *chintz* and *bodice* now have the new plurals *quinces*, *chintzes* and *bodices*. This same process is currently affecting the word *dice*. *Dice* was traditionally the plural of *die* 'small cube with six faces', but is now being reinterpreted as singular. In this case we've also got a split happening. In specialist contexts *die* is still being used as a singular noun for 'metal stamp for coining'. It preserves the original singular and has a regular plural *dies*. The *dice* used in gaming has a new reformulated plural, technically a double plural, *dices* (though some speakers still use *dice* as plural).

In all these cases, the original plurals were unusual. When speakers don't feel words to be plural enough, they add another plural marker for good measure. The original plural is then reanalysed as part of the singular stem and a new plural is reformulated. You might have noticed the arrival in colloquial speech of *incidentses* as the plural of *incident*. Confusion with the word *incidence* is undoubtedly a motivation – *incidents* doesn't sound plural enough and so it gets another *-s*.

Babelicious blending

Blends are new words created from the contraction of two (perhaps more) existing words. The new word then incorporates meaningful characteristics from the parts. Lewis Carroll's famous poem 'Jabberwocky' is full of them and some, like *chortle*, *galumph* and *slithy*, have made it into ordinary language. More recent successful blends include wonderful examples like *babelicious* 'gorgeous', *himbo* 'the male equivalent of *bimbo*', *cracker* 'credit card hacker', *fottle* 'collapsible bottle', *fanzine* 'magazine for fans', *Chunnel* 'Channel Tunnel', *slanguage* 'colloquial language', *humongous* and *ginormous*, both meaning 'shockingly big' (although I've never figured out exactly which words have blended to produce *humongous*). We've been doing this sort of blending thing for centuries now. *Flush* from *flash* and *gush*; *twirl* from *twist* and *whirl* date from the sixteenth century. There are examples going back as far as the twelfth century.

The blending process also enriches our language another way: that is, by giving rise to brand-new affixes that are then used to create more words. Take the ending *-holic/-aholic* meaning 'addict'; in other words, one who is addicted to or habitually does whatever the first part of the word denotes; for example, *chocoholic*, *sexaholic*, *golfaholic*, *newsaholic*, *junkaholic*, *icecreamaholic*, *worryaholic*, *beefaholic*, *bookaholic*, *sleepaholic*, *spendaholic*. The source

An elegant pant – a well-cut trew?

English has a group of so-called 'summation plurals' like *pants*. Typically, they are words for items that have two parts, like clothing or tools. Their singulars are formed with phrases such as *a pair of pants*. Occasionally, though, you hear backformed singulars like *a very nice pant* – especially from people who are into the business of selling these things.

A more colloquial version of *pants* is *trews*. Its final 's' was never plural, but came to be interpreted that way. Speakers analysed *trews* along the same lines as *pants, breeches* and *daks*. These words are always plural. And another thing – the word *trews* is not a shortened form of *trousers* as you might think. It's actually an older form. In this case the longer word *trousers* appeared later, probably formed along the line of other items of clothing with the same ending – *bloomers, knickers, drawers*.

for these new formations was eighteenth-century *alcoholic* 'pertaining to alcohol' (*alcohol* + *ic*). The sense shifted in the twentieth century to 'person addicted to alcohol' and in the 1970s this led to blend formations like *workaholic/workaholism*. This was all the encouragement speakers needed to then 'misinterpret' *-aholic* as a suffix.

Modern English has many examples of new affixes that have started life this way, like *-athon* in *danceathon* (from *marathon*), *-onomics* in *reagonomics* (from *economics*), *-ocracy* in *squattocracy* (from *aristocracy*), *-o/arama* in *cinerama* and *soundorama* (from *panorama*). All have been created via this same blending process. Sometimes such occurrences begin slowly and then all of a sudden proliferate. The *-(a/e)teria* suffix, for instance, first made its appearance in the 1920s in the word *cafeteria* (from American Spanish). It remained fairly dormant for many years, but suddenly became active in designating self-service retail or catering establishments. Newer arrivals include *bookateria*, *casketeria* (an undertaker's establishment), *chocolateria*, *hatateria*, *healthateria*, *pieteria* and *washeteria*. Recent newcomers on the scene like New

Zealand English *calfeteria* 'a bowl with multiple teats from which a number of calves may feed' suggest the suffix is still alive and well.

One of the most successful new endings of this kind must surely be *-gate*. Perhaps it's simply that there's been so much scandal and corruption about lately, but we've certainly seen a spate of *-gates* recently – *infogate*, *Dianagate*, *Irangate*, *oilgate*, *peanutgate*, *prisongate*, *winegate*, *papergate*, *Buckinghamgate* are a few of them. And who could forget *zippergate* or its variants *Monicagate* and *fornigate* that emerged from the Clinton–Starr conflict? The original *-gate* was of course *Watergate* – the mother of all *gates*. This was the name of the apartment and office complex where the events unfolded that led ultimately to US president Richard Nixon's downfall. It became a symbol for political scandal and produced enough blends that speakers were then able to reanalyse the words and derive the brand-new ending *-gate*. This kind of inventive restructuring is a significant part of our language play. But it also demonstrates an important way we have of expanding our vocabulary – and deserves to be taken seriously.

WYSIWYG, DINKS, WOOPIES and FUBAR – TIIC!

Acronyms are words formed from the initials of other words. For example, *Anzac* 'Australian and New Zealand Army Corps' (although today's bronzed Anzacs would never have been anywhere near Gallipoli), *okay* or OK from 'all correct' (or 'oll korrect') and *dwems* those 'dead white European males' currently on the top of the PC hit list. Examples pronounced as strings of letters like PC 'politically correct', PDQ 'pretty damn quick' and TIIC for 'the idiots in charge' are strictly speaking not acronyms but abbreviations (or alphabetisms).

Some acronyms become so fashionable they trigger copycat formations. The miliary acronym *snafu* 'situation normal, all fucked up' has spawned a number of similar acronyms including *commfu* 'complete monumental military fuck-up', *tarfu* 'things are really fucked up', *fubar* 'fucked up beyond all recognition'. Acronyms describing social types became very popular in the 1980s. Probably the first creation was *yuppie* 'young urban (or upwardly mobile) professional person'. It gave rise to a flurry of similar expressions: *dink* 'double income no kids', *pippie* 'people inheriting parents' property', *puppie* 'poncy yuppie', *scuppie* 'socially conscious urban professional', *woopie* 'well-off old people', *zuppie* 'zestful upscale people in their prime' and *nimby* 'not in my back yard'. Many of these die out as quickly as they appear, but they do illustrate the liveliness of the process.

Although we seem to be swimming in a sea of acronyms these days, you might be relieved to know the majority remain peripheral to the language. They serve either as proper names like *Qantas* (Queensland and Northern Territory Aerial Services) or are specific to certain occupations like *SOC* (Staff Observation Checks), part of the hamburgery lexicon of McSpeak. Words like these are never likely to become a part of our general lexicon.

The reasons for acronyms and abbreviations are probably obvious. Their primary function is precision and economy. How tedious it would be if every time we referred to the ABC or the BBC we had to use the full expansion of these letters. Small wonder *BSE* has come to replace *bovine spongiform encephalopathy*, the technical name for 'mad cow disease'. But there's a second function too and that is to promote in-group solidarity – to exclude those who don't understand. Acronyms and abbreviations act as a kind of masonic glue to stick members of the same profession together. If you can talk fluently of *ROM* and *RAM*, *DOS* and *WYSIWYG*, then to the computer literate you're immediately identifiable as a fellow member of the club. But if you don't know that *ROM* is 'read only memory', *RAM* 'random access memory', *DOS* 'disk-operating system' and *WYSIWYG* 'what you see is what you get', then you're obviously an outsider or just not worth talking to. So while these words facilitate communication on the one hand, they also erect pretty big communication barriers on the other. For those not in the know, acronyms are unintelligible gibberish. And if you find yourself in this position, you'll be relieved to know there is a club for you: the 'Association for the Abolition of Asinine Abbreviations and Absurd Acronyms', known of course as the AAAAAA or Triple A, Triple A.

Meaning Shifts

Out of the slimy mud of words, out of the sleet and hail of verbal imprecisions . . . There spring the perfect order of speech, and the beauty of incantation.

T. S. Eliot, choruses from *The Rock*, 1934, ix

At any one time words can hold a multitude of different meanings, along with a whole heap of associated baggage that arises from our experiences and personalities. Over time, these slip and slide as language evolves and adapts.

He was a daft and clever whore

Some time ago I encountered in a linguistics workbook by John Algeo an exercise for students where words were logically incoherent if we took them in their present meanings. I've often used this to illustrate the extraordinary nature of meaning shifts. Here's a rather embellished version of John Algeo's original paragraph.

We all liked Tom. He was a sad, daft whore – a happy clever cretin who we all agreed was above reproach in every respect. Tom had no neighbours and lived in a town with his unmarried sister, Mary, a wife of nearly thirty years. Now unlike Mary, Tom was a bit of a slut, but he was a good-looking girl – lean and stout, with shining hair, black as snow. A vegetarian teetotaller, Tom ate meat and drank liquor most days. He was a silly and a wise boor, and everyone really liked him. He was just so buxom. Now I often used to see Tom feeding nuts to the deer that lived in the branches of an old apple tree. But no more. Sadly Tom starved from overeating last year. So we buried him beneath that old apple tree. I remember well, it was full of pears at the time.

If you understand these earlier meanings, there are no inconsistencies here. Tom could be happy and sad because *sad* once meant 'satisfied'. He could be a daft clever cretin since *daft* meant 'humble' and *cretin* 'Christian'. He could be both a whore and a model of chastity, since *whore* originates from a term of endearment for both sexes. It was once possible to live in a town without having any neighbours, since *town* simply meant 'dwelling place'. Tom's unmarried sister Mary could be a wife of thirty years, if we take *wife* in its earlier sense of simply 'woman' (compare *fish-wife*). Unlike Mary, Tom was a bit of a slut. This means he was untidy. Tom's hair could be as black as snow because *black* derives from an original meaning 'shining white, bright' – it's historically related to words like *bleach*, *blanch* and even *bald* (originally, 'with white shining head'). Tom was also a lean and stout girl. This is possible because *girl* meant 'young person of either sex' and *stout* meant 'strong'. Tom could also be a meat-eating vegetarian and a liquor-drinking teetotaller because *meat* meant simply 'food' and *liquor* 'any type of fluid'. What's more our hero could be a popular *boor* because *boors* were 'farmers'. He could be wise and silly because *silly* meant something like 'happy, blessed'. Tom was also *buxom*. Now, here's a complex history. Originally meaning 'obedient', *buxom* then shifted to 'obliging, affable', then 'attractive, jolly' and later to 'plump'. Nowadays, of course, it's associated with a certain kind of plumpness – 'full-breasted' is how most of us understand it today. (Euphemism drove this shift, but of course the association with breasts is already contained in the sound of the word.) Feeding nuts to deer who live in the branches of an apple tree bearing pears contains a few little logical inconsistencies – but not when you take *deer* in its earlier sense of 'any animal' and *apple* in the sense of 'any fruit'. Finally, it was quite feasible for Tom to starve from overeating since *starve* simply meant 'to die'.

Clearly, words change in the weirdest of ways. It's that wild card human element – more than any other aspect of language, word meanings are linked to the life and culture of speakers. And this is responsible for some remarkable shifts.

Sluts and slags

They that wash on Monday have all the week to dry.
They that wash on Tuesday are not too much awry.
They that wash on Wednesday are not so much to blame.
They that wash on Thursday wash for shame.
They that wash on Friday wash in need.
They that wash on Saturday – oh, they're sluts indeed!
[Old rhyme]

As any cursory glance at the English lexicon will show you, there are many more derogatory terms used of women than of men. For a start there are the multitude of terms to describe women of loose morals – words like *slut*, *slag*, *slattern*, *hussy*, *whore*. I looked up 'woman' in my thesaurus. It's only a small one but it has well over a hundred expressions for sexually active or available woman, most of them quite negative. The comparable list for men is considerably shorter and noticeably less negative. There is nothing of the same pejorative sense of sexual promiscuity in words like *gay bachelor*, *not the marrying kind*, *philanderer*, *flirt*, *rake*, *lady-killer*, *gallant*, *gigolo*, *stud*, *womanizer*. Even the ostensibly pejorative terms refer at the same time to virility and sexual prowess. They connote a Don Juan or a Casanova and have associations of gallantry, much like the early English *squire of dames*, *roué* and *rake*.

One reason for this great imbalance in our vocabulary is the unfortunate fact that words denoting women are prone to deteriorate over time. The mildest form of deterioration occurs in words like *lady* or *dame*. These once referred to persons of high degree, but were then generalized to all people. *Lord* is still kept as a title for deities and certain Englishmen, but any woman can call herself a *lady* if she chooses. Most men wouldn't mind being called a *baronet*; not many women would want to be called a *dame*. Compare also *governor* versus *governess*, *master* versus *mistress*, *sir* versus *madam*. There are many such examples.

Even more striking is how quickly words meaning 'young woman' acquire moral overtones to do with sexuality and then decline. *Slut*, for example, referred simply to 'a woman of untidy habits'. Somehow even untidiness is linked to a woman's sexual mores – if she's messy, then she's obviously also loose. Compare

Rattle your dags

The word *dag* is a spectacular example of how a single word can undergo a number of transformations within its lifetime. Originally a British dialect word, *dags* specifically referred to the lumps of matted wool, dirt and dung hanging from the backside of a sheep (also known as *daglocks* or more colloquially as *dingleberries*). This is still current sheep industry parlance, but also occurs more generally in colourful slang expressions like *rattle one's dags* as in 'to hurry'. When used of a person in the early 1900s, a dag came to mean 'a tough but amusing character, an eccentric, a wag'. It's not clear how this sense arose but, as the lexicographer Gerald Wilkes suggests, it perhaps invokes a type of eccentric encountered in the wool industry. This is no longer current usage, however. During the 1960s, the adjective *daggy*, literally 'fouled with dags', came to apply generally to scruffy clothing and personal appearance – *dag* then became someone who was 'untidy, unkempt, unconventional in dress'. The word then shifted again to take on almost the opposite sense of someone who is conventional, square – someone who's definitely not 'with it'. No longer scruffy dressers, *dags* have been described for instance as 'the sort of boy every mother would like her daughter to bring home. His clothes are tidy, he wears shoes and is known to wear a tie' (Australian National Dictionary). More recently, it's become a more affectionate term for 'a chump, a silly sausage'. Clearly, in its lifetime an expression can go through a number of different changes and these can end up taking it far from its original sense. The modern Australian *dag* is a long way from the original locks of matted wool and dung hanging off the backside of a Derbyshire sheep.

this with *hussy*, originally short for *housewife*. Many of these terms started life being male or ambisexual in application. In Middle English, *wanton* meant 'undisciplined, unruly'. It could refer to both sexes, but it wasn't long before it narrowed to exclusively female reference and then came to mean 'sexually promiscuous'.

The term *wench* originally referred to both sexes. It goes back to an Old English word meaning 'child'. *Scold* 'a persistent nagging woman' comes from a word meaning 'poet'. From the mid 1400s it had exclusively female reference. Similarly, *shrew* (predecessor of the modern *bitch*) originally meant 'rascal, mischievous person'. As soon as these terms acquire female application, they take on associations to do with sexuality – and from there it's downhill. The oldest terms like *whore* are among the most offensive. They've had longer to deteriorate. *Whore*, by the way, is etymologically related to Latin *carus* 'dear'. It was at one time a polite term probably referring to 'a lover of either sex', but came to refer solely to women and later (no surprise) 'sexually promiscuous women'.

Lest you think this is a fact about vocabulary of the distant past, consider examples like *broad* and *floozie*. In the early 1900s they meant simply 'young woman' – there were no offensive connotations. *Tramp* 'male vagrant' shifted to *tramp* 'promiscuous woman' in the 1920s; *slag* 'piece of refuse' shifted to 'cheat, contemptible person' and since the 1950s 'promiscuous woman'. An even more recent example is *bimbo* – its shift from 'little child, baby' to 'sexually attractive but empty-headed woman' has been very rapid! In Australian English someone who's a *sport* is generally 'good humoured, generous', but when applied specifically to females it can mean 'woman who readily accords sexual favours'.

I've only ever encountered one term which apparently shows the opposite trend; in other words, a move from a female to a male domain and what's more an elevation in meaning. This word is *hunk*. According to some lexicographers it derives from a Scottish dialect word meaning 'sluttish indolent woman'. It now has exclusively male reference and has elevated to mean 'attractive, ruggedly handsome, well-built male' (with perhaps not a lot between the ears). This etymology is highly unlikely. Male *hunk* most certainly derives from the phrase 'hunk of meat' and not the Scottish dialect word for 'indolent woman'. The meat metaphor is a very persistent one for men. Think of *beefcake*, *meaty bites*, *piece of meat* and other such brawny terms referring to males. There is no doubt in my mind that *hunk* was inspired by the same meat metaphor – which means, as far as I know, there are no exceptions to the linguistic derogation of words referring to women. Our society clearly places very different values on male and female sexuality and this is reflected in the asymmetry in our vocabulary – in the sheer number of terms available and their different evaluative loadings. English has now amassed an extraordinary two thousand expressions to refer to women in a sexually derogatory way.

'The politickest sort of knaves'

Politics, *politicians*, *police* and *policy* – four Modern English words that derive from Greek *polis* 'city'. (Compare *metropolis* 'mother-city', *cosmopolis* 'world-city' and the *Multi-Function Polis.*) The meaning 'city' still glimmers through the basic neutral senses of these words. *Politics* is the art of governing the state. *Politicians* are those who are engaged in such a business. *Policies* are what they plan and pursue. The word *police* (or as it was once pronounced *police* with initial stress) originally referred to 'public policy'. It took on the meaning of discipline and control only during the 1700s, and then later, some time during the 1800s, shifted to its current sense of those entrusted with maintaining this discipline and control.

Politics and *politician*, in particular, have had tumultuous linguistic histories. *Politic* was the first to appear, some time during the 1400s. Its earliest senses were 'sagacious, shrewd, expedient', senses that still survive today. But the word deteriorated considerably and by the late 1500s the dominant meaning was 'scheming, cunning'. Dekker, for example, in 1609 describes Satan as 'a politick hunter'. The Oxford English Dictionary gives another quotation, somewhat later from 1667, describing certain persons as 'the craftiest and politickest sort of knaves' – clearly not complimentary.

It's around this time that *politician* first makes its appearance and with totally sinister connotations, too. A *politician* in the 1600s was someone who was 'a crafty, cunning intriguer', as is clear from one description of the Devil as 'so famous a politician'. Shakespeare has Hotspur say of Henry IV – 'this vile politician', where most certainly he means the King is 'a despicable schemer'. Heywood writing in 1632 states, 'I am a pollitician, oathes with me Are but the tooles I work with, I may breake An oath by my profession'. Sounds familiar? This sinister sense continues well into the 1700s. Adam Smith for example writes 'that insidious and crafty animal, vulgarly called a statesman or politician'. Samuel Johnson in his 1755 dictionary defines *politician* straightforwardly as 'a man of artifice; one of deep contrivance'. It isn't until much later, some time during the nineteenth century, that the word takes on a more neutral sense, the idea simply of 'one engaged in political life; in conducting the business of the state'.

But neither word has stood still. *Politics* has broadened enormously. Nowadays, all sorts of things have become politicized – the politics of food, of sport, even of language. And there are strong hints that the old sinister, suspicious and hostile senses are reattaching themselves. We have a new verb *to politic*, with its related noun *politicking*. Dictionaries define them something like 'engaging in political activity, especially with a view to striking political bargains, or gaining votes'. They are clearly tainted.

Words of this nature often show unstable histories because they are tied so closely to changes that go on in society. It was the shift from permanent monarchies to democratically elected representative governments that earlier helped these words climb out of the semantic abyss – so it's interesting to reflect on why these days they've taken such a turn for the worse. The old definition of *politician* as 'shrewd schemer, crafty plotter' seems highly appropriate and dictionaries that label these senses as 'obsolete' may well have to revise the entries.

Words of learning

Contrast the two simple words *learned* and *lewd*. The first clearly has a semantic halo, to use C. S. Lewis' description. There's certainly no sign of any halo on the second.

In medieval times the word *lewd* simply meant 'uneducated' (or 'unlettered', as it was then described). Its decline, however, was very rapid. Before long it had taken on the meanings 'foolish, stupid, worthless' with strong overtones of 'sloth'. The fact is, words that suggest a lack of education quickly become terms

All hail the pud!

Sometimes you encounter curious linguistic links between words, like that between pudding and botulism. Puddings were originally something like a sausage – the entrails or stomach of a sheep or pig stuffed with a mixture of minced meat, seasoning and oatmeal. The earliest cookery book in the English language describes the *puddyng of purpaysse* 'porpoise pudding' (porpoise was a considerable delicacy during the Middle Ages). 'Putte this in the Gutte of the purpays', the writer instructs us. This sense is of course preserved in *black pudding*, and don't forget the haggis. Now, the word *pudding* probably comes to us originally from the Latin *botellus* 'sausage', but via French, like so much of our gastronomic vocabulary. Then from the mid sixteenth century onwards pudding was used for a much wider range of dishes, both sweet and savoury, but cooked in a bag or a cloth. That was the connection – they resembled the sausage. As the foodie and splendid lexicographer John Ayto explains, it was puddings in which the cloth was lined with suet crust that led to modern savoury puddings (like steak and kidney pudding). On the other hand, puddings based on flour or some other cereal gave rise to modern sweet puddings: sponge puddings, treacle puddings, roly-poly puddings and Christmas puddings. The requirement that puddings be cooked in some sort of bag or cloth was later lifted and so we got modern rice puddings and bread and butter puddings. At this point, links with the original medieval pudding were totally severed. In current British English *pudding* has extended even further to become the general term for 'afters' – puddings can be any dessert.

So how did the unappetising link with botulism arise? The association is with the original Latin 'sausage'. It seems this food-poisoning germ was first found in cooked meats like sausages, or *botellus*. So you can put all thoughts of botulism out of your mind as you tuck into your next Christmas pud. The abbreviation *pud*, by the way, goes way back to the early seventeenth century – it's by no means a modern shortening.

of moral disapproval. Just look at examples like *simple*, *daft*, *silly*. These all started life imputing goodness and innocence, but are now quite contemptuous. There is a deep-seated prejudice about – if you don't know something, then you're incapable of learning. And *lewd* of course goes one step further. It eventually came to mean 'indecent, dirty-minded', or what the Oxford English Dictionary rather quaintly refers to as 'lascivious, unchaste'. Many words show this shift. Our current senses of *uncouth* developed from the earlier meaning 'unknowing, unlearned'. It's as if an inability to read, a lack of education, somehow reflects a lack of intelligence and also a lack of moral sensitivity. Meaning shifts (especially shifts in the values attached to words) are always revealing of what is valued in our society. Clearly we have always attached great importance to learning and education, even in those times when there wasn't much of it about.

These examples are well and truly in the past, but there are plenty of modern linguistic casualties too. The moralization of learning (to draw again on C. S. Lewis' insights) is still evident, in fact all the more intense now with widespread education and literacy. And the more education is made into a competitive activity, the more apparent this becomes. Geoffrey Hughes in his book *Words in Time* examines the status that now attaches to words like *learned*, *articulate*, *educated*. The semantic halo has also been extended to words like *intelligent*, *talented*, *gifted*, *capable*, *able*, *brilliant*, *genius*. Contrast these with the worthlessness and moral inadequacy implied by words like *uneducated*, *illiterate*, *ignorant*, *inarticulate*. What's more, English has seen a burgeoning of insults like *idiot*, *moron*, *cretin* and *imbecile*. Education has become one of those sensitive areas that we must now tiptoe around under cover of euphemism. Accentuate the positive – *backward*, *lazy*, *idle*, *stupid* become *less gifted*, *less academic*, *less talented*, *at the lower end of the ability scale*, *underachieving*. Both the clever child and the below-average child become the *exceptional child*.

Mind you, I'd be telling you only half the story if I didn't point out that words for the educated aren't immune to pejoration either. After all, *pedant* does derive from an earlier meaning 'schoolteacher' – but even *schoolteacher* hovers on the edge of disapproval (compare *schoolmarm*). It's certainly not all good news for academics either. Let's not forget that the Oxford English Dictionary defines *egghead* as 'an intellectual'. It joins that family of *head* words, mostly personal insults ascribing mental or physical inadequacy like *dunderhead*, *blockhead* and *pinhead*. There is now a linguistic cloud hovering around the words *academic* and *intellectual*. This decline undoubtedly stems from the contrast often drawn between the academic and the practical or pragmatic. The popular image of unworldly academics engaged in impractical contemplation is probably even stronger today with our overriding pursuit of 'relevance' and 'the real world'. But even back in the 1300s Geoffrey Chaucer expressed the view – to use his words – 'the greeteste clerkes ben noght the wisest men' by which he meant something like 'the most educated scholars aren't the most sensible of people'.

So far, *professor*, *lecturer* and *researcher* haven't suffered the same fate (although *professor* can be used as a sneer term; for example, in the schoolyard for 'a swot'). They seem to have remained pretty stable. But time will tell. Just look at what happened to the expression *a cunning clerk*. It might have meant 'a clever scholar' in Chaucer's writings, but few would be complimented by it today. *Clerk* has been thoroughly debased, shifting from the meaning 'scholar' to 'pen-pusher'. And *cunning*? Well, that reveals another disturbing but common shift, from 'knowledgeable, learned' to 'crafty, skilful in deceit'. It is extraordinary how quickly these words acquire dishonest senses. Why is it that we are suspicious of knowledge when it is attained at a high level?

Words will not sit still and meaning shifts like these are a fact of linguistic life. But they do make for a fascinating study of what is and what has been significant in our society. As Owen Barfield so neatly put it: 'in our language the past history of humanity is spread out in an imperishable map'.

'Like a gardener grafting a branch'

Metaphor isn't just the stuff of great literature. It pervades our whole language and without doubt is one of the most significant forces behind change in vocabulary. We are constantly adapting familiar structures from our experiences to new purposes in our language. Whether we're creating names for new concepts or simply adding to the names of old concepts, metaphor is very often behind it all.

Metaphor always involves the comparison of two items where there exists some sort of relationship. It's a kind of analogy. Let's say you call someone a *pig*. This sort of comparison takes salient characteristics from folk concepts about the appearance and the behaviour of the animal which are then attributed to that person. *A pig* is 'someone uncouth, slovenly'. We might want to convey a picture of someone totally disgusting in manner and character. Of course, taken literally, the statement is false. This person is not actually 'a pig'. But we are claiming there is a semantic connection between this person (the figurative meaning) and a pig (the literal meaning). All the colour and the expressive force here derive from this relationship. Back in the 1500s Baldesar Castiglione in his *Book of the Courtier* (1528) likened using words in a metaphorical sense to grafting a branch – a nice metaphor for metaphor!

One important type of metaphor is something called 'synaesthesia' (from two Greek words meaning 'together' and 'perception'). Basically, synaesthesia refers to an association of senses. Meanings of words are transferred from one sensory sphere to another. It has all the excitement, colour and emotion that we associate with poetic language but flourishes in ordinary everyday-speak. For example, when *hot* shifted from the meaning 'having a high degree of heat' to 'spicy' it shifted from the area of touch to taste. Other words that changed in this way are *cold*, *dry*, *smooth* and *coarse*. The word *faint* has shifted from colour to sound – out of the meaning 'pale, lacking clearness' grew the later meaning 'barely perceptible'. But synaesthesia can involve transfers of all kinds – from sight to sound, from touch to sound, from sight and touch to intellect, from taste to colour and so on. Dimension words like *big*, *deep*, *thin* and *high* transfer to both colour and sound. And they can transfer to taste too. Just look at current wine terminology that draws on images like *big*, *full*, *deep*, *even*, *thick*, *flat* and *small*. This is the bold metaphor of poetry and fiction.

Colours have particularly strong psychological effects for us and we often exploit this in figurative uses. Words for brightness shift to become terms to do with intellectual ability. We describe people as being *dull* and *bright*. Hue colour words shift to become words expressing moods and moral qualities. *Blue* has been associated with melancholia since the sixteenth century and we are still *singing the blues*. *Yellow* is typically associated with cowardice, *green* with envy (or inexperience), *red* with anger and so on. In this way, speakers can make sense of supposedly nonsensical utterances like Noam Chomsky's famous *colourless green ideas sleep furiously*. This was originally given as a sentence that's grammatically well structured but is unacceptable because it has no meaning. Yet *green* and *colourless* are perfectly compatible if we ignore their literal senses and assume the figurative senses – *green* as 'immature' and *colourless* as 'uninteresting, dull'.

In English (like many other languages) words for seeing, hearing and touching often develop to become terms of understanding. Think of expressions like *I see* and *I hear you* for 'I understand (you)' or *He finally grasped it* for 'He finally understood'. The verb *comprehend* also comes from something meaning 'to grasp, seize' in the original Latin. Of course, in all these cases we're no longer very conscious of the metaphorical links. This is the fate of metaphor – over time the imagery gets buried.

It's when metaphorical links are pushed below the level of consciousness that you encounter the dreaded mixed metaphor – 'As you go down the path of life, drink it to the full'. Many mixed metaphors go unnoticed, but when the metaphorical links come back to the level of consciousness the mixture of images can be irritating. Mind you, occasionally you do encounter a mixed metaphor that says it all. I'm very grateful to whoever it was who first used 'the carrot at the end of the long dark tunnel'. But 'cutting off your balls to spite your face' – well, it's a colourful image . . .

Sporting metaphors

I hardly need to point out the prominence of sport in our lives. We're up to our ears in it. But I'm not sure we are aware of the enormous contribution sporting terminology has made to our everyday language. People talk generally of course about *playing the game*, *lifting the game*, *giving the game away*, *levelling the playing field*, *moving the goal posts* and so on. But our language is also saturated with words, metaphors and idioms that have been borrowed directly from the specialist terminology of individual sports like cricket, baseball, football and boxing. Often it's no longer obvious that we're dealing with the extension of a sporting term. As with general expressions like *aim* and *goal*, even *tackling a problem*, the figurative sense has become the conventional meaning.

Cricket provides many of our current expressions. *It's not cricket* means 'it's not fair, not honourable' and *do something off your own bat* means 'to do something on your own initiative'. People *on a good wicket* could also be described as having *a fair innings* if they had a long life or a long and successful career. But others not so fortunate would be *on a sticky wicket* ('facing a difficult situation') – I'm no cricket buff but I've been told this alludes to the problems of a batsman faced with a rain-saturated wicket. People are *caught out* and *stumped*, if they are 'surprised' or 'defeated'. Here in Australia we describe things that are immoderate or unacceptable as being *over the fence*. We can also *hit someone for six* which means to overwhelm or surprise that person. The idea here is that the blow you deal that person is like the batsman hitting the bowler's ball way out past the boundary. The expression *go for six* or *go for a sixer* (in other words, 'to fall heavily, suffer a major setback') may well have been reinforced by cricket, the idea of hitting the ball out of the playing field without bouncing to score six runs, but this may not be the original source. The term *sixer* has been around a long time to refer to anything that counts as six, as in 'a six ounce loaf of bread' or 'six months of hard labour'. And it's been used in Australian Rules Football since the early 1900s as a synonym for a goal (a kick worth six points) and as a dicing term *throw a sixer*. It was then used as a euphemism for 'to die'. The expression *go for a sixer* has in all likelihood completely mongrel origins.

But what about forgotten or ancient sports that most of us no longer give a thought to? Medieval hawking or falconry, for example, has bequeathed us expressions like the verb *reclaim*, originally meaning 'to call the hawk back from flight'. This you did with a *lure*, a special pipe for the task. The verb *pounce* comes from this sport too, from the pounces or foreclaws of the hawk. The medieval tournament also provides the source for many current expressions like *break a lance*, *tilt at* and *at full tilt* meaning 'at full speed'. (The *tilt* was originally the barrier separating the combatants and later was applied to the sport itself.) *Jousting* was something similar. It was later extended to mean any sort of struggle or dispute between individuals. Knights would throw down a mailed glove or gauntlet and if their opponent picked it up the game was on. This gives us expressions like *throw down/take up the gauntlet* 'to challenge/accept a challenge'. Finally, if he was unlucky, a medieval knight fighting in a tournament might end up being *thrilled* (or what originally would have been pronounced 'thirled'). This verb *thrill* meant 'to pierce, penetrate'. Nowadays, of course, we're thrilled by emotions, not lances or spears.

Tennis is still alive and well, but modern-day lawn tennis didn't appear on the scene until the late 1800s. Original tennis (now 'real' or 'royal' tennis) dates from about the twelfth century and was played in castles or monastery quadrangles. It gives us our expression *bandy about*, originally a French verb referring to the action of hitting the tennis ball to and fro. It even gives us *bandy-legged*. In the seventeenth century *bandy* came to be used for an Irish game, much like modern hockey. The ball was also bandied about – but it was the shape of the curved stick the bandy players used that gave rise to the expression *bandy-legged*.

In all these examples, the expressions no longer convey any sense of the game that provided the original image. In this way, many forgotten sports like falconry have become buried in now dead metaphors. In fact, countless numbers of words in current English are entombed metaphors. So, as you're sitting back enjoying whatever sport you're watching or listening to, keep in mind the extraordinary way sports, both modern and forgotten, have been pervading and enriching our language.

'So fade expressions'

A powerful stimulus for meaning change is feeling. This refers quite generally to a speaker's desire to enhance expression and come up with innovative ways of saying things. As Leonard Palmer once wrote: 'It is wearisome to hear a spade always called a spade'.

One way emotional force can be achieved is, of course, through exaggeration. We know this well from the highly charged language of abuse. Hyperbole is often used to magnify the offensive intent, as in attested pieces of Australian colour like *You bloody great prick! You rotten bloody mongrel bastard!* It is also employed when diminishing and downgrading a person, as in *You peabrain! You slimy little toad!* But overuse of such language inevitably has the effect of bleaching terms of their offensive quality.

Emotional extravagance goes hand in hand with semantic weakening. Take words like *scamp*, originally 'highway robber'; *rascal* originally 'despicable, dishonest person'; *rogue* 'dishonest vagabond'; *scoundrel* 'base, vile character'; *scallywag* 'disreputable fellow, good for nothing'; *naughty* 'depraved', and *mischievous* 'disastrous'. Our language is full of such examples. All were strongly contemptuous at one time, but have now become mild terms of reproof. In fact some are really quite playful. Even a term like *ratbag*, once highly offensive, now pales in comparison with its modern relatives *scumbag*, *slimebag* and *dirtbag*. It'll be interesting to see how these newer expressions fare over time. Presumably we'll see their pejorative senses fade too. This sort of weakening often occurs through exaggerated playful use, like calling a small child *a little monster*. Terms of opprobrium can always be used in a jocular, even affectionate, fashion and Australian English is well known for this.

Intensifying expressions are particularly prone to weakening, which is why they are constantly being renewed. Intensifiers such as *terribly*, *awfully*, *frightfully*, *horribly* and *immensely* all rapidly lost their original strength and now mean little more than 'very'. Hence, 'contradictory' usages like *awfully good* and *enormously small* and the more colloquial versions like *helluva/heck of a good party*. A striking example is *bloody*. Once upon a time it was considered such an appalling word that it was necessary to render it in print as *b****y*. Nowadays, *bloody* has been totally emptied of its colour and force and certainly in Australia is little more than a variant of *very*. Even *very* has weakened from its original meaning 'truly, truthfully' (still preserved in adjectival uses like *my very word*).

Some have claimed that such intensifying expressions are characteristic of women's speech. Jane Austen makes a lot of them in novels such as *Northanger Abbey*. Her female characters are always saying things like 'excessively' this and 'amazingly' that. Lord Chesterfield, writing in the *World* (5 December 1754), also clearly associated this kind of language with women. He writes: 'A fine woman is vastly obliged, or vastly offended, vastly glad or vastly sorry. Large objects are vastly great, small ones are vastly little; and I had lately the pleasure to hear a fine woman pronounce, by a happy metonymy, a very small gold snuff box that was produced in company to be vastly pretty, because it was vastly little'. Otto Jespersen, writing in the early 1900s, described how 'the fondness of women for hyperbole will very often lead the fashion with regard to adverbs of intensity and these are very often used with disregard of their proper meaning'. This is not the case. Fondness for hyperbole is most certainly not a uniquely female thing – and both sexes use these words without regard for "proper meaning". Men and women might prefer different intensifiers, but that's hardly surprisingly – any social group will show differences of vocabulary.

What all intensifiers have in common is instability. Chesterfield's quote nicely illustrates just how quickly they come in and out of fashion. *Vastly* is not a word many would use today. Probably *excessively* and *frightfully* also sound a tad fusty. But there's no shortage of replacements. It's a familiar story in language change – the constant tug of war between creativity and expressiveness, on the one hand, and the tendency for things to become routine and mundane on the other. As Lord Byron appropriately put it – 'as forests shed their foliage by degrees, So fade expressions which in season please'. 'Terrible emphasis', as it's been dubbed, is a widespread, probably universal, phenomenon.

Two-faced intensifiers

Not only do intensifiers weaken and become insipid, sometimes they go down very curious semantic paths – more than just wear out, they actually come to mean the opposite.

Take, for example, a word like *just*, an odd word in Modern English because it holds the contradictory meanings 'very' and 'not very', as in *He's just brilliant* versus *It's just a little dirty.* This word has gone through some remarkable shifts. As borrowed from French, its original meaning was 'equitable, rightful' (still preserved in *a just person*). The word was then recruited as an intensifying expression and came to mean 'exactly, precisely', as in *Just how do you propose to do this?* This shift is understandable. After all, we can infer that whatever is *just* is done in exactly the right sort of way. More problematic is to account for the more recent shift to 'only, merely, barely', as in *She's just a linguist.*

Before I suggest how this might have come about, compare the word *quite*, which shows a similar development. This word *quite* evolved from the earlier meaning 'clear, free' also into an intensifier meaning 'exactly, precisely, absolutely'. For example, *I think he's quite superb.* But, like *just*, it's also done an about-face and can also mean 'somewhat, fairly', as in *It's quite good.*

Both *just* and *quite* show the same shift from concrete meanings to intensifiers that have then subsequently weakened. The initial change is driven by our constant need for new forceful expressions and our incurable tendency to overstate. However, this process can't explain the later shift from 'positive' to 'negative'. There's another type of social force at work here – and that is politeness. Most social discourse operates with the idea of harmony in mind, with a preference for agreement or at least non-hostile interaction. In other words, we're usually polite, whatever we might be feeling inside. Criticism is a threatening act; so we might try to minimize the threat by making a positive evaluation first, then following it with a negative one. You could imagine someone saying: *it's quite good, but . . .* Now, words occurring side by side can influence each other semantically. So by associating with the following negative, these little intensifiers invert their original sense and we see a shift from 'very, no less than, absolutely' to 'not very, no more than, merely'.

Clearly, in its lifetime an expression can go through a number of different changes which can end up taking it far from its original sense. As a final example, consider what's happened to the word *fair*. From an original meaning 'suitable, fit' the word *fair* elevated and came to mean 'beautiful, pleasant, agreeable'. In the context of appearance it shifted further from 'beautiful' to 'blond, light in colour' and in context of character and conduct to 'equitable, unbiased, just', as in *fair-minded*. We can see a number of cultural forces at work here. *Fair* was able to shift from 'beautiful' to 'light coloured' precisely because blonds were preferred in medieval England. In other contexts, *fair* shifted to mean 'just', probably because agreeable and pleasant situations were those that were free from injustice. I also mention *fair* because – as with *just* and *quite* – the word has done an about-face and has recently shifted to become more negative. In an example like *He's got a fair chance of succeeding* the word *fair* has lost its sheen and means something like 'moderately good'.

Change in this area of language is always a complicated business and likely to involve the interaction of a number of different factors, both linguistic and non-linguistic. Clearly, at any one time words will hold several different meanings, so that even the semantics of ordinary little words like *just*, *quite* and *fair* becomes as elusive and slippery as a bar of wet soap in a bathtub. Of course, over the years many people have tried to establish academies to ensure that the soap stays dry and well and truly in its original container. All have failed.

Words that are their own opposites

Other words, not just intensifiers, can also simultaneously hold two completely opposite meanings. A *blunt* instrument is dull, not sharp – but a *blunt* comment may be quite pointed, and can be very sharp. The verb *ravel* means simultaneously 'to entangle' and 'to disentangle'. Now, do *seeded* oranges have seeds, or have they had their seeds removed?

Words that are their own opposites are known as 'contranyms', 'autoantonyms', or if you want an even grander term 'enantiosemes'. But more often than not they're known simply as Janus words – two-faced words. Contranyms are appearing all the time. Take the word *literally*. In its core sense it means 'actually, not figuratively'. But now when people say something like 'I was literally climbing the wall', what they often mean is that they were figuratively or metaphorically climbing the wall – in other words, not actually at all. Human beings are natural exaggerators. We are constantly striving to enhance our expression and come up with new and exciting ways of saying things. It's this sort of emotional extravagance that has led to *literally* finding itself on the list of contranyms.

These words often draw from the same semantic field. For example, we now have the verb *cleave* which means simultaneously 'to stick together' and 'to split apart'. The verb *splice* suffers precisely the same confusion. Similarly, if you *clip* on something it means you put a little bit on – or *clip* can mean you take a little bit off. *Trim* typically means 'to cut things off' – unless it's a Christmas tree! *Cleave*, *splice* and *trim* form a natural set. We might even include *dust*. It can mean 'to free something from dust' – or the opposite 'to sprinkle something with dust'. Verbs that mean 'to examine carefully' sometimes simultaneously have the meaning 'to glance over'. *Look over* means to give something careful scrutiny – then again it might mean just a fleeting glance. We've got the verb *oversee*. But then, what's an *oversight*? To *table* something in British and Australian English means 'to put something forward for discussion' – but in American English 'to set it aside'. Words of transaction often turn into Janus words, too. They end up meaning both 'give' and 'take'. Think of *rent* and *lease* that involve both the granting and the taking out of a lease.

So, how does this sort of thing happen? One way is through sound change – two originally distinct words collide phonologically. In this way two words with contradictory meanings can end up with the same pronunciation. This is how we came to have *raise* 'to erect' and *raze* 'to tear down'. Originally these were distinct. Another example is the verb *let*. In Old English there were two verbs *lǣttan* 'to permit' and *lettan* 'to stop, hinder'. After sound changes these two verbs ended up being pronounced the same; hence, one verb *let* 'to permit' and another verb *let* 'to prevent'. Generally speaking, our language doesn't tolerate this sort of thing; so we end up discarding one of the words. In this case, the second *let* with the meaning 'stop' has now disappeared, except for relics like *without let or hindrance* and *let ball* in tennis. Precisely the same thing happened with the verb *cleave*. Old English had two verbs – *cleofian* 'to stick together' (compare related forms *glue* and *clay*) and *clēofan* 'split apart' (compare modern *cleaver* and *cleft*). After sound change we were left the one word *cleave*, with either the meaning 'to stick together' or 'to split apart'. Probably it's the latter sense that's now winning and *cleave*, meaning 'to stick together', is on the way out.

Another way these contranyms arise is through meaning change. It can happen that different senses of a word simply drift apart. *Spendthrift* 'extravagant person' and *thrifty* 'frugal' are different aspects of the condition of thriving, in other words *thrift*.

The original meaning of *fast* 'not moving at all, fixed firmly' (as in *it stuck fast*) sprouted the newer meaning 'moving quickly' (as in *she runs fast*). Perhaps it was the idea of sticking fast to something you're in hot pursuit of. This newer sense is now dominant. Something similar is happening to *sanction*. To apply *sanctions* involves measures forbidding something, but the verb *sanction* means the opposite 'to give permission to do something'. Both these senses have arisen out of the original meaning 'law, decree'. The words just went down different tracks. Perhaps the different grammatical contexts will ensure that both these senses continue, although the outcome is generally that speakers eventually jettison one of the forms.

The most famous contranym of all doesn't come from English but French. It involves the Latin words *gallus* 'rooster' and *cattus* 'cat'. In some rural French dialects sound change meant that these two words ended up merging. Imagine the potential problems in a country context – picture the poor farmer unable to distinguish whether a cat or a rooster had got into the henhouse! Or think of English *inflammable*. It means 'easily set on fire' (compare *inflame*). But you can't blame speakers for thinking the opposite, 'not easily set on fire' – after all, *in-* is our typically negative prefix. When they involve the same contexts, the effects of these contranyms are potentially disastrous!

Old expressions in a brand-new world

It's not always the words that shift – sometimes they stay still, and it's the world that shifts instead. This is 'subreption'. The dictionary defines it as a 'deceptive or fallacious representation', but in the context of language change it simply refers to the kind of meaning shift that involves the process of external change; in other words, change that occurs outside the language. Objects, ideas and institutions alter over time, but the names for them remain. It's almost as if the expressions somehow outgrow their original meanings.

Sometimes the changing world brings with it a widening of the original meaning of words. *Pictures* once used to be painted representations, but now include paintings, drawings and photographs. Indeed, they refer quite generally to any image, however

A 'couple' of drinks

Some meaning shifts are triggered by psychological factors; in other words, factors arising from our mental make-up. Take words to do with punctuality. These words always seem to shift from meaning 'immediately' to 'after a short time'. The word *anon* for example used to mean 'at once, instantly', but by late Middle English it had shifted to 'soon, in a little while', as in *I'll see you anon*. *By and by* used to mean 'at this moment' but has also shifted to 'soon, in a little while'. So too has *presently*, at least in Antipodean English. Even the word *soon* derives from something meaning 'immediately'. So why does this happen? Because humans are natural procrastinators, of course – 'why do today, what you can put off till tomorrow?'

Probably another incurable tendency is to underestimate the truth in certain situations and this is also responsible for changes. Take the typical shift we see in numerical words. Words for dual number (that is, words meaning 'two') frequently shift to mean 'a few'. Current changes to *a couple* give us a clue as to how this happens. For many of us now *a couple* means 'a few' in most contexts. Certainly someone announcing they'd had *a couple of drinks* would generally mean more than two!

it is produced. The word *napkin* comes from the original meaning 'linen cloth', but now napkins can be made of cotton or paper. We drink from *glasses* made of plastic and through *straws* made of paper. *Light* was once by definition that which made things visible. The idea of invisible light was absurd, a bit like a triangle with four sides or a round square. These days we have ultraviolet and infrared light and the meaning of *light* has shifted accordingly.

Often the changing world brings with it a complete meaning shift. In New Zealand and Australia, for example, the flora and fauna indicated by terms like *birch*, *magpie*, *robin* and *bream* are completely different from their British counterparts. The original colonists retained the familiar names, perhaps out of a sense of nostalgia, and applied them to things they saw as similar.

Raspberry tarts and cobbler's awls

Generally, speakers won't work any harder than they have to in making themselves understood; they'll use the minimum amount of energy needed to convey their message. Phrases like *how are you going* or *goodbye* (from *God be with you*) are shortened to fragments, even a mumble or perhaps a simple gesture. This sort of reduction can trigger shifts in the meanings of words, particularly when phrases become single words that then stand for the whole expression. *Fall* meaning 'autumn' derives from the phrase *fall of leaves*. This is a very old expression now surviving in American English. *Rifle* is short for *rifled gun*, in other words a gun with a special groove inside the barrel, *alarm* derives from *alarm clock* and *life* from *life sentence*. Shortenings of this kind can turn adjectives into nouns. Through economy of effort speakers drop the noun and the full meaning then transfers to the adjective that's left behind. In this way a *daily paper* becomes a *daily* and a *private soldier* becomes a *private*.

Sometimes these syncopations can result in meaning changes that are startling, as is the case of rhyming slang that loses its end rhyme. The curious verb *rabbit (on)* meaning 'to talk incessantly' comes from the phrase *rabbit and pork* [=talk]. A *raspberry* (as in *blowing a raspberry*) is short for *raspberry tart* [=fart]. Rhyming slang is a kind of verbal disguise (which explains why it once featured in the insider slang of the criminal underworld and now features prominently in the language of euphemism). The meaning derives from the unstated word that rhymes with the last part of the phrase; for example, *cobbler's awls* = *balls*. By reducing *cobbler's awls* to *cobblers*, however, the original significance is lost because the rhyme is clipped. The sense then transfers to the first part of the phrase and we have a meaning shift – although in the case of *cobblers*, most of us have forgotten what the original significance was.

Technological change sees many words adapt in this way. The advent of motorization, for example, has brought with it remarkable changes for words like *car*, *tyre*, *lorry* or *truck*. Think of the modern-day *dashboard* – no longer the board on coaches to stop the driver getting covered in mud and dung, it now refers to the control panel beneath the windscreen of a vehicle. The *visor* on a knight's helmet has transformed into the shield of the modern-day crash helmet (or in North America the peak of a cap). Despite the arrival of mechanical refrigeration, many continued to use the term *icebox* even though the appliance no longer involved a box for ice. The verb *write* derives from a Germanic word meaning 'to scratch, carve' and goes back to the time we wrote by scratching runes into wood or rock. With the arrival of Christianity came a different kind of writing. But even when we stopped carving letters and started to write on parchment with a feather quill we retained the old term for writing. What's more, we continued writing with *a pen* – originally 'a feather'.

Because changes in the world can be so sudden, the responses made by the language can also be sudden. Developments in telephonics have been considerable. Yet, we continue to *dial* numbers on our push-button and touch-tone phones. And we still listen for the *dial tone* – and why not? We're just putting the word to a new use.

Relics of Linguistic Change

As creeping ivy . . . hides the ruin that it feeds upon
William Cowper, *The Progress of Error*, 1782

Language change rarely occurs without leaving behind some trace or 'relic' of the original structure. The language garden is full of moss-grown remnants of linguistic building stones.

All those little linguistic eccentricities, the elements that are out of whack with the rest of the language – these irregularities are typically relics of past regularity. Language change, whether it involves alteration to words, meanings, sounds or grammatical structures, leaves behind in its debris a partial history of the language. For example, linguistic curiosities like *foot-feet* and *tooth-teeth* date back to a pronunciation feature of early English. This involved a kind of vowel harmony known as 'umlauting'. Specifically, the vowel in the stem of the word changed to be like the vowel that followed it.

Take *foot–feet.* Originally, the word *foot* would have been pronounced as it's written – with a long 'o' sound. Its plural was formed by adding an *-iz* ending. The vowel of this ending is something like an 'ee' sound. When you say it, the front of your tongue is bunched up high against the roof of your mouth. In eager anticipation of this vowel, speakers changed the pronunciation of the 'o' in the stem of the word to be more like it. Sounds often change to be more like their neighbours – in this case the vowels are harmonizing. But ends of words are awfully unstable and prone to erosion. The plural ending *-iz* eventually dropped off. With the

Cunnies in gravy

The following simple recipe for rabbit stew comes from the earliest surviving cookery book in the English language. It's around six hundred years old – and it's full of linguistic rubble.

Conynggys in grauey schul be sodyn & hakkyd in gobettys; and grynd gyngyer, galingale & canel, & temper it vp wyþ god almand mylk & boyle it. & nym macys and clowys and kest þeryn, & þe conynggis also, & salt hym & serue it forþe.

Roughly, here's what the recipe is telling you to do. Rabbits (in gravy) should be boiled and cut into pieces; grind ginger, galingale and cinnamon and mix with good almond milk and boil. Take mace and cloves and add these and also the rabbits; salt and serve.

Some of the words are totally unfamiliar. The word for 'rabbit', for instance, *connynge* or *coney* (pronounced like *honey*), no longer exists. We dropped *coney* when, as someone once quaintly put it, it took on 'inappropriate anatomical significance'. In other words, it sounded too much like the female bawdy body part. It's left a relic though in the placename 'Coney Island' – but note the cunning change in pronunciation!

Much of what is curious in this recipe comes from meaning shifts that have occurred. Take the strange reference to the 'sodden cunnies'. Now, these rabbits are not soaked to the skin! At this time *sodden* was the past participle of the verb *seethe* meaning 'to boil'. But no one connects *sodden* and *seethe* any more (just as no one connects *straight* and *stretch*, *wrought* and *work*). But an instruction to 'seethe rabbits' is no less curious. Nowadays, we only *seethe* figuratively, as in *I was seething with rage*. The verb has now been relegated to quite specific contexts of use.

We are also advised here to 'hack' the rabbits (into 'gobbets'). Other recipes from this collection suggest 'smiting' or 'hewing' them! All this hacking, hewing and smiting for a bunch of small rabbits seems a bit excessive. Of course, culinary activities are different today. Most of us no longer draw, gut, clean and bone, hack or even mince – death has been pretty well banished from the modern-day kitchen. But more importantly, these verbs would now only be used in quite restricted contexts to mean 'sever into pieces with violent cutting blows'; indeed, both *hew* and *smite* are archaic and would probably only be used for special effect; as in *hewing asunder*.

ending gone, the vowel change is no longer motivated. All we're left with is *foot-feet*.

This kind of vowel harmony is responsible for many of the irregular vowel alternations you find in Modern English; for example, adjective forms like *old-elder-eldest*. Once again, the endings triggered the vowel change so that forms like *strong-strenger-strengest* and *long-lenger-lengest* were widespread. Most have now disappeared. Even *elder-eldest* is giving way to *older-oldest*, although the vowel mutation lives on in fixed expressions like *elder statesman* and pairs like *strong-strength* and *long-length*.

There are other couplets connected in this way. For example, *fall-fell*, *food-feed*, *full-fill*, *drink-drench* and the dreaded *lie-lay*. These are also the result of vowel harmony with a now lost ending *-jan*. This suffix had a causative meaning; in other words, if you wanted to indicate that someone caused someone else to do something, you simply plonked on this handy form. In Modern English we have to resort to far more wordy constructions using verbs like *cause*. Think of the relationship between *fall* and *fell*. Originally the verb *fall* was *fallan* and the verb *fell* (in other words 'to cause to fall') was *falljan*. The 'y' sound of the *-jan* ending then triggered the vowel change that we now see preserved in *fall-fell*. But, of course, the ending has now gone and with it the original trigger for the change.

This kind of vowel harmony was a feature of early Germanic languages, and in Modern German is still very much alive and well. In English all that remains are these relic forms – eccentricities of Modern English that delight the historical linguist but drive foreign English-language learners to drink.

More relics

Compounds often contain remnants of words long since ousted from ordinary usage. The old word *hriff* for 'belly' would have totally disappeared if it wasn't for the *midriff*. We have many relics of this kind: *wer* 'man' + *wolf*, *garlic* from *gar* 'spear' + *leac* 'leak', *cobweb* from *coppe* 'spider', *hatred* from *hate* + *red* 'condition'. Some modern expressions retain earlier colloquial shortenings that speakers have since abandoned. *Bate* from *abate* now exists only in the fixed phrase *bated breath*; in other words, 'with breath held back'. We don't tend to bate our breath any more! *Scape* now survives only in *scapegoat*, *bash* lingers on in *bashful* and *noy* from *annoy* in *noisome*, or 'troublesome'.

Often we end up reinterpreting these relics to make more sense of them. For example, many speakers now understand *noisome* to mean 'noisy'. The *kith* in *kith and kin* has changed too. It used to refer to something that was known; in this phrase it meant 'one's friends'. But the word has disappeared, except for this phrase, and in order to make sense of it, we've reinterpreted it to mean 'kinfolk'. In other words, we treat the phrase *kith and kin* as a doublet, much like *will and testament* or *cease and desist*. Sometimes we end up remodelling the word altogether, getting rid of the problem that way. Take the expression *to be on tenterhooks* – it doesn't make a lot of sense nowadays, because *tenter* either as the instrument of torture or else the wooden frame used to stretch woven cloth doesn't exist any more. So some speakers have altered the word to *tenderhooks*.

When meanings shift over time, the older meanings can also get stuck inside fixed expressions which then renders the expressions nonsensical. Ones that always puzzled me as a child were *more haste less speed* and *the quick and the dead*. These make more sense if we take *speed* with an earlier meaning of 'success' (in other words, more haste less success) and *the quick* with the earlier meaning of 'living persons'.

Sometimes fragments of older meanings lurk for a long time inside words and phrases and often account for their peculiar behaviour. Take the verb *will*. Originally, this was an ordinary verb meaning 'to desire'. This older meaning is preserved in fossil expressions like *do what you will*. Today, of course, *will* marks

The legacy of 'she'

One great linguistic mystery is the origin of the pronoun *she*. Around one thousand years ago, the masculine pronoun was *hē* and the feminine pronoun was *hēo*. The form *she* didn't make its appearance until some time during the twelfth century. It became the dominant form in the Midlands dialect that eventually gave us modern Standard English, although relics of *hēo* survive in *her* and *hers* – they have developed directly from the original pronouns.

Via ordinary sound change, Old English *hē* 'he' and *hēo* 'she' would have collapsed into one form. We would therefore have had one pronoun meaning both 'he' and 'she'. The arrival of *she* overcame this ambiguity. But where did it come from? There have been many extraordinary and imaginative explanations for the appearance of *she*, but all fall short in some way. Of course, if *she* had never appeared, we would have been left with the result of the two collapsed Old English pronouns, pronounced something like Modern English *he* is today. This surviving pronoun would have provided a truly bisexual pronoun for both males and females. This was the state of affairs for many speakers during the Middle English period before *she* arrived. Indeed, there are still some conservative remote dialects in the United Kingdom that (in their spoken versions at least) have never felt the effects of *she* and preserve one pronoun form pronounced something like 'uh' and written sometimes as *a*. This is a truly gender-neutral pronoun and these dialects don't have the problem of coming up with clumsy alternatives like *s/he, his/her* or *her/him* when the sex of the speaker is unknown or irrelevant.

Of course, there is always the 'singular' *they*. This form also has the advantage of being gender-free. I know many people have a strong aversion to it, but it does have a long and distinguished history. Shakespeare certainly used it. So did many early writers before grammarians declared it ungrammatical and put a price on its head. *They* is a natural solution to the problem of no bisexual pronoun in the standard language – the legacy of the mysterious emergence of *she*.

future time. However, it still contains enough of its older meaning to make it difficult to say something like 'Will I help'. While it's fine to say 'Shall I help', even 'Will you help', *will* still sounds odd with 'I' when used in a question. Why? Well, there's enough meaning of desire still lingering in the word *will* that it sounds somehow inappropriate to ask a question of yourself. If someone said to me 'Will I come too', I'd feel like replying, 'Well, I don't know; do you want to?' The verb *will* has been evolving into a future marker for the last thousand years. Yet, the ancient meaning of 'desire' is still hanging in there.

Even earlier pronunciations leave behind relics. English speakers used to pronounce 'f' as 'v' and 's' as 'z' when they occurred between vowels. This is preserved in alternations like *wife-wives*. Or think of the curious plural form *women*. The 'i' vowel (spelt 'o') is left over from its Old English predecessor *wīfman*, literally 'female person'. Similarly, *hussy* from *housewife* better preserves the early pronunciation of Old English *hūswīf* – as does its spelling. Indeed, our spelling system is chock-a-block with ruins. It's not an ideal system, to be sure, but it does provide nice clues as to how English once sounded.

The Nature of Exotics

A remarkable hybrid
Lisle Carr, *Jud. Gwynne*, Act I, sc. ii

The English language is probably the most successful language of all time, and a mongrel tongue if ever there was one. Seventy-five per cent of English words are exotic – filched from somewhere else. Its current-day 'bitser' grammar also shows the effects of contact with many different languages. It is indeed a remarkable hybrid.

Stealing

An important force behind language change is incorporation from other languages. Often this contact is called borrowing, although strictly speaking it's theft. There's always some sort of gain involved: when English appropriates some linguistic element from another language it somehow benefits. Perhaps the transferred material replaces an expression that's become obsolete or has lost its expressive force. Perhaps the motivation is sheer necessity. It may simply be that a borrowed word fills a gap. The gain might even be social. Speakers often borrow words and pronunciations from more prestigious groups.

Different types of contact between languages will trigger different types of borrowing. Take a situation where the original inhabitants of a place adopt the language of a bunch of newcomers. Usually you'll find there's a period of bilingualism where the new language is spoken but with some interference from the first language. If elements from the primary language are transmitted to later generations of speakers of the prevailing language, it's typically pronunciation that's affected. This exactly describes the nature of Celtic–English contact. English didn't originate in Britain and when it arrived in the fifth century it came into contact with various Celtic tribes. The majority of Celts seem to have learned the language of their Germanic conquerors thoroughly. The Celtic underlay that lingered then gave rise to the very distinctive pronunciations you still hear in various parts of Britain. Otherwise the impact of Celtic is pretty slight – confined to place names like *Devon* and *London* and some cultural borrowings like the *bannock cake*. This is very similar to the impact of Australian Aboriginal languages on Standard Australian English; it's largely names of places and cultural items that have been borrowed.

But what if a bunch of newcomers end up being linguistically absorbed into the indigenous population? In this case the influence is most obvious in vocabulary. This is what happened after the French invasion. For several centuries after the Norman Conquest in 1066, English was well and truly under the Norman French thumb. The prestige, or educated, languages were French and Latin and these were what people typically wrote in. Of course, English eventually prevailed and French was ousted, but the effect of French on the English lexicon was remarkable. Some ten thousand French words were adopted – the majority between 1250 and 1400. It was the Normans who controlled the state, the military, and cultural and intellectual interests. French words flooded into these areas, sometimes as brand-new additions, sometimes supplanting English expressions, and sometimes existing side by side, but usually later diverging in meaning and style. Words of French origin often retain a highfalutin or posh ring to them.

Contact with Scandinavian languages was similar – just a different bunch of invaders. At various stages during the ninth and eleventh centuries there were Scandinavian raids on England. These culminated in twenty-five years of Danish rule, with large settlements of Scandinavians, particularly in the northern and eastern parts of the country, and considerable influence on native English. But this time the borrowings were very different. The expressions we pinched from Scandinavian are striking for their everyday nature. They include basic verbs like *die*, *get*, *give*, basic nouns like *husband*, *fellow*, *egg*, even grammatical words like *they*, *them* and *their*. These are just a handful of the hundreds of words that entered the language at this time. Borrowings of this sort suggest two things. First, unlike the French situation, Scandinavian and English existed side by side with more or less equal prestige. Second, the languages must have been very close – so close in fact, that it's actually difficult to assess the true extent of the Scandinavian contribution. There could have been many more borrowings. It's hard to tell.

All parts of the language can end up being borrowed, even grammatical patterns, though usually this requires more long-term and widespread bilingualism between donors and borrowers. But words are the most borrowable of all. The contact in this case doesn't even have to be that extensive. A bewildered foreigner just has to point at something and look puzzled, and the native speaker will usually supply the missing lexical item – sometimes having a bit of fun at the foreigner's expense. There are placenames in Australia that don't have anything near the picturesque meanings that appear in tourist books. Neither does the name of the famous street festival that happens in Melbourne every year on Labour Day – 'Moomba' almost certainly means 'buttocks'. Whether this was the result of a genuine misunderstanding or a bit of linguistic leg-pulling we'll probably never ever know.

The nature of our linguistic exotics

English shows a very interesting hierarchical patterning in its vocabulary that reflects nicely the historical development of the language with respect to borrowings. A carpet analogy is useful here (but like most analogies, only up to a point). Our native English vocabulary, of Germanic origin, provides the basic underlay, or our fundamental everyday stock of words. Typically these are short, concrete and stylistically neutral. They include grammatical words like *a* and *the* and, of course, the most basic offensive language – the so-called four-letter words. This Germanic underlay or foundation supports a quality carpet on top – a kind of lexical superstructure comprising those items of refinement and nuance that come to us from French. Dotted on top of this quality carpet are the classy scatter rugs. These are words with connotations of

Romance pairs

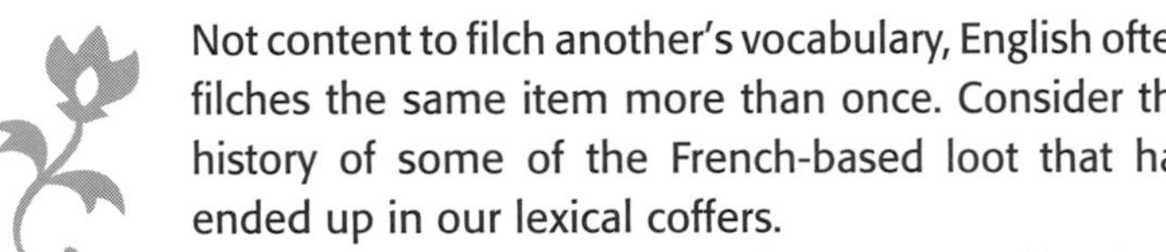

Not content to filch another's vocabulary, English often filches the same item more than once. Consider the history of some of the French-based loot that has ended up in our lexical coffers.

Occasionally, we knocked off the same word but from different French dialects. This had interesting consequences. Take the pair of words *warranty* and *guarantee. Warranty* shows the original 'w' of Norman French; *guarantee* shows the change from 'w' to 'gw' which occurred elsewhere. These are therefore historically the same word. So are *chattel* and *cattle*. *Chattel* reflects the Central French pronunciation 'ch' which evolved out of Latin 'k' and *cattle* reflects the Latin 'k' preserved in Norman French. The original Latin word was *capitale* meaning 'possession, stock' – we borrowed that too! So *cattle*, *chattel* and *capital* share a common origin.

If we abduct the same word at different times in our history, this too can result in doublets. Take *chief* and *chef*. *Chief* was borrowed in the fourteenth century and shows the 'ch' sound of Old French. Like *chamber* and *chant*, it's an early appropriation. *Chef* reflects the 'sh' pronunciation of Modern French and, like *chic* and *chiffon*, is a later borrowing.

Sometimes these doublets arise because of changes in English. The longer an exotic has been in the language, the more likely it is to have been beaten into shape and made to conform to the pronunciation rules of English. For example, the word *garage* is an early twentieth-century borrowing. It's now gradually naturalizing and adapting to the English sound system. Some say 'gar**a**zhe' (closest to French), some 'g**a**razhe' (with English stress), some say 'g**a**ridge' (more English still). However, no one would be tempted to say 'cab**a**zhe' – *cabbage* has been in the language for six hundred years! Doublets like *v**a**lour* and *vel**our*** show the effects of this. Like most older borrowings, *valour* fits the native English stress pattern. *Velour* is historically the same word, but was purloined two centuries later. It's pronounced closer to the French with the stress on the final syllable. Other doublets include *artist/artiste, critic/critique* and *gallant/gallant*. The first words in the pairs with initial stress are older. The others show the more typical end-stress of Romance and are recent loans. They've been adopted, but not adapted.

Finally, we can borrow a word just once, but we then get two for the price of one because it splits. Different pronunciations end up parting company and go off and develop their own meaning. This is precisely what happened with the pair *divers* and *diverse* (from Latin *diversus*). *Diverse* took on the meaning 'different in character or quality'. *Divers* broke free of this sense (around 1700) and retained only the vague numerical sense as in 'various, several'. Other words that have undergone such splits are *antic* and *antique*, *human* and *humane*, *urban* and *urbane*. To see how this happens, consider the word *garage*. You could imagine how in two hundred years time a 'garidge' might be the carport next to the house, and posher-sounding 'garazhe' the commercial building where you get repairs done and buy petrol.

learning, science and abstraction and come to us from the Classical languages Latin and Greek.

Take a simple example – the words for medical practitioners. We have native English expressions like *quack* and *leech* – neither terribly flattering! (By the way, *leech* comes from an Old English verb meaning 'to heal'; the meaning 'aquatic blood-sucking worm' was a later development.) The French language gives us *doctor* and Latin gives us *physician*. Or take the verb *ask*, which is Germanic. Compare it to the verb *question* of French origin or *interrogate* of Latin origin. The verb *rise* is Germanic, *mount* is French and *ascend* is Latin. Our language is full of examples like these. Each of the forms in these triplets has strikingly different social and stylistic connotations. Compare *a black eye* with *a circumorbital haematoma*, everyday *knee jerk* with *patellar tendon reflex* and you quickly get the picture. The contrast is also reflected in noun and adjective pairs. Germanic gives us the nouns and the Romance and Classical superstructure provides the adjectives. Compare the noun *mouth* with the adjective *oral*, *finger* with *digital*, *water* with *aquatic* and *town* with *urban*. Sometimes Germanic also provides

Panties versus undies

The effect of French on our vocabulary has been remarkable. Look at clothing. First, the sheer number of borrowings – words like *attire, boots, buckle, button, cape, cloak, collar, costume, dress, embroidery, fashion, frock, garment, gown, lace, satin, veil, wardrobe*, and there are hundreds of others. Colours like *brown* and *blue* – even the word *colour*. Second, much of the vocabulary has prestigious connotations. They may well be pronounced *à la française* to sound that bit more classy. Sometimes we make a token effort to give them a sort of quasi-French pronunciation – and we have a special nasal vowel for this. Look at French borrowings like *lingerie* and *ensemble*. It doesn't matter what French vowel we start with, they all get pronounced the same with the all-purpose nasal French vowel.

There's a fair bit of linguistic snobbery involved here – as in the area of food, French fashion connotes fine and classy, luxurious and chic. Even in casual dress, *déshabillé* is a pretty swish way of saying you're undressed. *Au naturel* versus *naked* – no comparison. As usual, English provides the basic vocabulary, French the garnish. You could use the English word *clothes*, but if you want to sound more highfalutin then use the French word *attire*.

Of course, French words are also used for unmentionable bits of clothing such as *lingerie, camisole, chemise, petticoat, negligée* and *bra*. Compare these French words to English *bloomers, drawers* and *girdle* – not a lot of lexical titillation there! Even French *briefs* sound sexier than English *smalls. Panties* versus *undies* says it all.

an adjective, but there's a world of difference between the two. Compare for example, *doggy* and *canine*.

Typically, what you find is that certain areas of speech are bottom-heavy and draw overwhelmingly from the stock of native English words. Think of as many terms as you can for drunkenness. You'll probably come up with a few elevated terms like *inebriated* and *intoxicated* but most that spring to mind are low-level slang expressions like *sloshed*, *smashed*, *stewed*, *sozzled* and *soaked*, to mention the ones more mentionable. (It's interesting how many of these begin with 's'.) Other fields are top-heavy and draw from the Romance and Classical languages. The language of poverty, for example, is full of impressive terms like *indigent*, *impecunious*, *destitute* and *impoverished*. Of course, one reason for this is that it's an area of social taboo. This makes it an inevitable target for euphemism – in other words, a never-ending chain of obscure vocabulary to avoid saying the dirty word *poor*. Recent times have seen a rise in dainty circumlocutions like *economically marginalized*, *negatively privileged*, *economically non-affluent*, *culturally deprived* or even *differently advantaged* – all largely Romance or classically inspired.

During the nineteenth century a number of writers became obsessed with the 'purity' of Anglo-Saxon. Some sought to abolish this Romance and Classical dimension to our vocabulary, even going as far as coining words like *speechcraft* to replace *grammar*. It's hard to imagine what our language would sound like without the lexical aliens. British humorist Paul Jennings has tried. He has rendered the opening lines of Hamlet's famous soliloquy into almost pure Anglo-Saxon.'To be or not to be; that is the ask-thing' – it doesn't quite make it, does it?

Bad Language

A weed is a plant you hate.
Patricia Thorpe, *The American Weekend Gardener*, 1988

Just as there is nothing intrinsically bad about those plants we call weeds, and just as pests are simply creatures that live in our gardens in ways that run counter to our objectives, there is nothing intrinsically bad about bad language either. Indeed, some of the greatest weeds in the garden are those we planted in the first place!

'Bad' bad language

So-called bad language comes in many forms – sloppy pronunciation, poor grammar, slang, meaningless little fillers like *you know* – and of course swearing. But there is something puzzling about all this bad language. If it really is so very bad, why does it persist?

Take those studies that evaluate standard and non-standard accented voices. They consistently show accents like Cockney as being rated negatively, even by Cockney speakers themselves. New Yorkers too, it seems, hold their own speech in low esteem. In fact the world is full of linguistic groups who think they speak badly. So, why don't all these people speak the way they think they should? Is this just another example of the sort of doublethink that underpins so much of our linguistic behaviour – or is it more complex than that?

The primary, or orthodox, function of language is, of course, to facilitate communication. But we also use language to locate ourselves within a social space. Accent, vocabulary, grammar and ways of speaking are potent symbols of a bewildering array of different affiliations: ethnicity, sex, race, sexual preference, religion, generation, abilities, appearance, profession. An accent isn't just something someone else has. We all have one and we all wear it like a badge. It defines the gang.

Changing your accent isn't like changing to another brand of toothpaste. It means giving up your allegiances to your own social group. It means turning your back on the values, aspirations and accomplishments of those people you most closely identify with. And it means adopting symbols of another group. What's more, it isn't a simple matter of one group having more prestige than another. Certainly, there are accents associated with power, education and wealth and these things are, of course, highly valued by many people. Such accents are said to have overt prestige. But so-called bad language can have a prestige all of its own, a covert or hidden prestige. Swearing and strong, broad accents, for example, are associated with toughness and strength and these can be highly valued qualities. Attitude studies also show that the low or powerless speech styles win big on the more human qualities like solidarity, integrity, social attractiveness and friendliness. In other words, what we have is a constant tug-o'-love between the overt prestige of the high status groups, symbolically the wider community, versus the covert prestige of the local, non-prestige groups.

Clearly, there is more to language than what is good and what is bad. As Andersson and Trudgill conclude in their marvellous book *Bad Language*, there is always something good in bad language or quite simply it wouldn't endure. This even goes for swearing. Whether it's via full-blown expletives or those many remodelled disguises like *Gosh!* and *Crumbs!* swearing is a means of emotional release and we all do it.

Language overkill

Those concerned about the wellbeing of our language worry greatly about redundancy, in particular the use of combinations of words that somehow overlap or copy each other in meaning. This is tautology – saying what you've already said.

I have an acquaintance who has a keen nose for this sort of thing and he has drawn my attention to a number of recurring examples. The football ground was *packed to capacity*. Even worse *a capacity crowd completely packed the stadium*. If a football ground is packed, why mention *to capacity* and why add a modifier like *completely*? Apparently, this particular game was so well attended that only those with *pre-booked tickets* had a chance of getting a seat. My friend is right, of course, *pre-booked* is about as silly as tickets *booked in advance* as 'beforehand' is contained in the meaning of *book*. More tautology. And what about *the invited guests arrived for dinner around 8.00*. In the context of a dinner party, what are these guests if they're not invited? Presumably they didn't crash the dinner, and they weren't dragged there against their will either. The flight attendant asks you to check your *personal belongings*. What are belongings if they are not personal?

Our language is full of linguistic overkill. My friend, like many people, has strong feelings about English and this sort of language makes his blood boil. One that really gets up his nose is the phrase *safe haven*. We read and hear a lot about safe havens these days. Strictly speaking the phrase is also tautologous since the word *haven* already contains the meaning 'safe'. The problem with this particular example is that it's one of those time-honoured expressions. The adjective mightn't add anything but the phrasing is now fixed. Similar to the tautologies of religious-speak like *joined together*, there's not a lot you can do about them. They're here to stay.

Politicians are particularly prone to tautology. So are radio presenters. Well, so is anyone who is required to talk for a long period and maintain a continuous output, especially if it's all done on the hop. It's a survival technique. Phrases like *new innovations*, *revert back* and *paid professional* trip easily off the tongue and provide breathing space. We've all been guilty of this sort of silliness. I've certainly caught myself saying, even writing, things like *8.00am in the morning*, *green in colour*, *past experience*, *definite decision*, *free gifts*, *grateful thanks*, *gainfully employed*, *may possibly*. My own list of crimes is quite long.

Lawyers are very good at this sort of thing. They've turned it into an art form with their elegant-sounding doublets like *will and testament*, *null and void*, *act and deed*, *goods and chattels*, *in my stead and place*, *cease and desist*. Some will tell you that these have to do with the need for greater clarity in the law. Not so, I suggest. Examples like these are not confined to legal prose and derive from a very early literary practice of conjoining usually one noun of Germanic origin with a synonym of Romance origin. It's always been largely a matter of stylistic ornamentation, even in legal language.

I'm certainly not wanting to suggest redundancy is necessarily a bad thing. It's not all linguistic flummery. Even tautologies like these can provide synonyms for words that may be less well known. There is also a lot of useful redundancy in language that we exploit for stylistic effects. We repeat things: *I'm ok*, *I'm ok*. We do this for dramatic emphasis. Who would want to condemn Shakespeare for his famous tautology in Julius Caesar: 'This was the most unkindest cut of all'? All right, so Shakespeare has expressed the superlative idea twice, but it has rhetorical force. The double superlative is effective – the linguistic equivalent of a trumpet blast. It signals this information is worth paying attention to. Of course, we should never overdo linguistic fanfares. The danger is that such extravagance ends up sapping expressions of their strength. Do you take perfection more seriously if it is *absolute perfection*? Certainly, overuse of intensifiers often has the effect of emptying words of their force. Unique is unique and it becomes less unusual when speakers intensify it with *very*, as in *very unique*. In this case it's actually stronger to leave out the modifier.

One function of redundancy we tend to overlook is that it does increase the likelihood of our message being conveyed safely. Double negatives like *I didn't do nothing* abound in different varieties of English around the world. That's non-standard English, you might be thinking. But what about the construction *neither–nor* as in *neither this nor that* – now, there's a perfectly standard piece of grammatical overkill. So is something like *She's the sweetest*, *dearest*, *loveliest person*. I've just expressed the superlative idea three times here, each time with the *-est* ending. Even something like *Those two linguists are mistaken* has grammatical extravagance in the form of a quadruple-marked plural – *those*, *two*, *linguists* and *are* all express the plural concept. Grammar is chock-a-block with inbuilt redundancies we never notice.

But let's face it, given the nature of the average speaker and hearer there's a real need for this sort of redundancy. Speakers sometimes mumble, they sometimes speak softly. Hearers typically listen with half an ear. And what if the channel isn't clear – a bad telephone connection, or the background din of a dishwasher? As unappealing as this may sound, linguistic overkill does mean we have a greater chance of getting our meaning across. Redundancy is fall-back. Look at addresses on letters. We don't need the suburb, city or state (county, province) if we have the postcode. But what if a digit is illegible? In language it's the same. If a bit of information were only expressed once, it would be intelligible only if all channels were functioning and free of interfering noises. Redundancy makes communication easier in situations which aren't ideal. If something is indicated more than once – say, a plural or a negative marker (just to be controversial) – then it may not matter if something gets lost in transmission.

I think it's safe to say that redundancy is generally useful. But is it still as useful as it has been? The linguist Dwight Bolinger suggests that we probably need redundancy less than we did in the past. We transmit information more easily now. It's physically easier to communicate. We also rely much more on writing, where we don't need redundancy in the same way. There is no background noise. Readers can go back and re-read a point they might have misunderstood. Recordings can be replayed, too. We don't need the reminders. Time will tell what impact this has on our language.

I mean, like sort of meaningless, you know

Every now and again people suddenly become very aware of small words. Like I mean the sort of meaningless words you know that people kind of throw into a conversation. Some time back I had a rather grumpy letter from someone about my own use of the phrase *sort of* – so I feel compelled to spring to the defence of these small words in the English language.

First, you need to distinguish two sorts of small words. One group includes the 'non-fluency features' – fillers like *umm* and *err*. Consider for a moment just what's going on when we chat. The spontaneity and speed of conversation mean instant feedback

Redundant negatives

Take the almost clichéd sentence opener: 'I wouldn't be surprised if . . .' Let's assume you want to say you think it'll rain, and if it doesn't, you'll be surprised. Should that then be 'I wouldn't be surprised if it rained' or 'I wouldn't be surprised if it didn't rain'? You hear both in conversation, but if you think it will rain, the logical expression is the first. The second version 'I wouldn't be surprised if it **didn't** rain' has an extra negative.

Redundant negatives often occur where no actual negation is present but there is some sort of negative sense lurking somewhere in the sentence. For example, you often hear in conversation sentences like 'That'll teach you to arrive early' **and** 'That'll teach you not to arrive early'. Both can mean the same thing; namely, you arrived early, this had some sort of unfortunate consequence, and you should learn from this and not come early in future. The illogical negative comes about because there is some sort of underlying negative idea present. This negative idea then comes to be expressed overtly with a negator like *not*, as in 'That'll teach you **not** to arrive early'.

The redundancy here arises from a processing problem. Multiple negatives, also negative ideas in combination with negative expressions, are particularly befuddling. It's not surprising negation is a target of the cleaning-up activities of the Plain English movement – official language is notorious for its confusion of negatives. Look at the stacked negatives in the following gem: *A term of a sale shall **not** be taken to **exclude, restrict** or modify the application of this Part **unless** the term does so expressly or is **inconsistent** with that provision*. Plenty of things make this particular sentence difficult, but much of the difficulty comes from the multiple negatives – the combination of the negative marker *not* with semantically negative words like *exclude, restrict* and the negative linking word *unless*. Of course, another earmark of officialspeak are phrases like *a not insignificant amount* or *not unnaturally*. Here an affirmative is expressed in terms of the negative of the contrary – and if you think this needlessly complicates things, then you're dead right!

and little or no time for planning. Speakers have to monitor what they're saying to make sure it's coming out as they intended and that their audience has understood it this way, too. Speech events are produced for immediate processing by the listener, who is also expected to respond in some sort of way (perhaps by gaze, nodding or some sort of listening noise like *hmm*). At the same time as speakers are doing this monitoring, they are having to plan what to say next. And all this is happening at breakneck speed. When you think about it, spontaneous speech is an extraordinary performance, especially when it involves conversation with another person. Our daily interaction with others is quite an achievement. So is it any wonder we occasionally hesitate?

Recently I had the experience of an audience member counting the number of times I said *umm* during a lecture. At question time this person reported on his findings. While doing so, he seemed remarkably unaware of his own hesitation phenomena. People who draw attention to fillers in the speech of others typically don't notice them in their own speech. Of course, these can be annoying. But let me draw an analogy with a piece of music on a scratched record. Sure, if those scratches get under your skin, they are all you'll hear. But focus on the music, and you probably won't notice them. When it comes to speech, cooperative listeners should be so hell-bent on the message that they simply edit out the fillers. Stop focusing on the message, and you might suddenly notice your conversational partner says *umm* a fair bit of the time. Sooner or later that's all you're going to hear. So it is with any feature of language. As soon as you notice something, perhaps a new word, you'll start to hear it all the time. It suddenly becomes the most common (and the most irritating) word in the English language. Yet it occurs probably no more frequently than before your attention was drawn to it.

Conversation is also dotted with many expressions like *you know*, *I mean* and *I think*. These 'discourse particles' are highly idiosyncratic features of our language. To find exact equivalents in other languages is difficult, if not impossible. People often sneer at them, lumping them with hesitation fillers, and imagining them as the sorts of things we plonk down when we have nothing else to say. But they play crucial roles in conversational interaction and politeness; roles to do with focus and change of topic or the expression of social relationships, personal attitudes and opinions. Some take on functions to do with turn-taking. When speakers start their turn they often do this by acknowledging the turn of the previous speaker. A current favourite with this function is *yeah-no*. 'Yeah-no I was quite sure he was mistaken'.

Spoken interaction is much more personal than writing and speakers constantly make reference to themselves and to their audience by using expressions such as these. They can convey subtle nuances of meaning and often have complex effects on our utterances – which brings me back to my own use of *sort of*. Certainly, this can express approximation or imprecision, as in *sort of pinkish*. But in its non-literal use, it's a typical hedging expression used in informal contexts to reduce the force of utterances. It can minimize distance between speakers and their audience by modulating the authoritative tone and creating friendliness.

Now, I realise these words can also become irritating. But again, people who grow irritated by other people's discourse particles typically don't notice their own – and you can be sure they are there! Like the seasonings and flavourings essential to good food, these expressive fillers spice up a conversation and without them our speech would be very lifeless indeed. Of course, you can argue that when they are too conspicuous, they become distracting. And this is true – don't overdo them. As food writers remind us, 'Nothing is more deadening to the tastebuds than a flavour repeated too often'.

Slips of the tongue

The world is full of self-appointed arbiters of linguistic virtue, always on the lookout for language crimes: a mispronunciation, a misplaced apostrophe, an incorrect word, a split infinitive. Some time ago one of these crime watchers compiled a list of errors committed by ABC radio announcers. These atrocities comprised mainly slips of the tongue and included examples like *spectra* for *spectre*, *reticent* for *reluctant*, *fluent drive* for *fluid drive*, *incredulous* for *incredible*, *presupposing* for *prepossessing*, *unfettled* for *unfettered* and *mercurical* for *mercurial*.

There are two things that need to be said in response to such a list. One, everyone's tongue slips – even, I dare say, those of linguistic crime watchers. Slips of the tongue are a normal feature of spontaneous speech. Two, these kinds of slips follow predictable patterns and provide us with valuable clues as to how our brain works – how we go about searching for words and how our mental dictionary is organized.

Some of the radio announcers' slips were errors of assemblage. Speakers chose the right item but simply the wrong order of sounds. For example, one announcer produced *spectra* for *spectre*. The segments got moved around. These sorts of mistakes are usually caught, but occasionally they slip through the net. We now say *third* not *thrid*, *bird* not *brid* and *wasp* not *waps*. These are standard pronunciations now, of course, but they would have started life as this kind of mistake. Modern-day *ask* was another that snuck through – *aks* was regular well into the seventeenth century! Spoonerisms are spectacular examples of assemblage slips. Here the transpositions occur across a whole sentence, as in the Reverend Spooner's celebrated 'Is the bean dizzy' for 'Is the dean busy'. With spoonerisms the switches tend to result in already existing words and the consequence can be hilarious, especially when speakers get stuck in a groove. I recall a moment of great embarrassment when this happened to me during a presentation on word order change in Dutch. Instead of 'the period of Middle Dutch' what kept coming out was 'the myriad of Piddle Dutch'. Needless to say, these sorts of transpositions don't have a long-term effect on the language!

Most of the radio slips listed involved an incorrect item. Something went wrong with the selection process – *reticent* came out in place of *reluctant*, *fluent* in place of *fluid*. In fact, as psycholinguists have shown, to say something like *reticent* for *reluctant* is really more a slip of the brain than a slip of the tongue. None of these mistakes, you might have noticed, was far off target. All were closely related in some way to the intended word. There is a chance, of course, they were Freudian slips; in other words, slips revealing the secret thoughts of the speakers. It's impossible to know whether these were the fallout of secret thoughts, but more likely the announcers simply slipped up while accessing their mental dictionaries on air.

Slips can be based on similarity of sound or meaning. Malapropisms like *conversationalists* in place of *conservationists* are the first kind. A similar-sounding word has been picked for another. Of course, not all malapropisms are genuine slips of the brain. They can occur through ignorance. I recall once receiving a memo concerning the Faculty Teaching Committee. It began 'Due to a lack of decorum'. I was sure we were pretty well behaved during that meeting – presumably the memo writer meant *quorum*!

As it happens, most of the radio slips in my examples involved both sound and meaning. For example, *fluent* in place of *fluid* – both begin with *fl* and both share the property of flowing. *Reluctant* and *reticent* involve some property of unwillingness and sound alike too. These slips suggest we activate more words than we need as we plan our speech, and from time to time other words inappropriately pop up. Sometimes speakers might fail to make up their minds between competing possibilities and what emerges is a blend. *Unfettled* was probably a blend of *unfettered* and *shackled*. Finding words involves two operations: selecting the meaning and, as psycholinguist Jean Aitchison neatly expresses it, finding the sounds to clothe this meaning. People are probably thinking about the meaning when they select the sound, since slips typically involve both meaning and sound.

Most of us care deeply about language, but we should try not to be too critical of the occasional slip or hesitation on air. Spontaneous speech is a biological miracle, and small wonder if now and then we slip up and accidentally let the wrong word through. We should guard against viewing speech through the spectacles of writing. Grammars of English are based largely on the fairly formal, careful usage associated with writing. Speech is definitely not 'spoken writing' and to judge it that way is a mistake. Recall what it's like when someone reads a talk instead of speaking it. The emotional contact isn't there, and it can be hard to follow, too. Occasional slips, repairs, repetitions and hesitations are natural features of speech, and of effective speech as well. After all, speech processing is slow, and as listeners we don't have the luxury of pausing and going back to a point we didn't follow.

It's true, we tend to favour the fluent speaker, but bear in mind that speech lacking errors and hesitation isn't likely to be spontaneous – it's probably well rehearsed, certainly pre-planned, or is simply a matter of stringing together some pretty well-worn and formulaic expressions. In short, be a little wary of the smooth talker!

Ain't ain't grand any more

In normal speech the word *not* typically occurs in the contracted form. Unless it's stressed, we're not likely to say *cannot, will not* or *do not* but *can't, won't* and *don't*. Once these latter forms used to be considered too colloquial for writing. Some editors still uphold this; but most now accept contracted forms, even in quite formal writing. When you think about them, they're curious little words. *Won't* is supposedly a contraction of *will not* but sounds nothing like it. This is typical of the fate of words that occur in combination, especially if they're frequently used. With time they compress. As with words like *marshal* (originally a compound of *mearh* 'horse' + *scealc* 'servant'), forms like *won't* and *can't* now no longer resemble their originals and behave no differently from single words.

These contracted forms have been in the language since at least the seventeenth century. All of the helping verbs like *can* and *will* have them, with one exception. There is no shortened form for *am not*. Well, not in our dialect at least. Some varieties have *amn't*, but the awkward cluster of sounds probably stopped it from catching on like the others.

What about *ain't*? This form first appeared around the same time as the other contractions. It was then perfectly respectable. Examples like *it ain't certain* were found in the speech of even the most highly educated speakers. Those from the best of society used it. Jonathan Swift, author of *Gulliver's Travels*, said (even wrote) things like 'I a'n't well' – though he described all these contracted forms as examples of 'the continual corruption of our English tongue'. Frederick James Furnival, a former editor of the Oxford English Dictionary, is said to have habitually used *ain't*.

Then for some reason *ain't* fell from grace. My feeling is that it became such an all-purpose contraction that it drew too much attention to itself and fell victim to the verbal hygienists (to use Deborah Cameron's wonderful description) of the time. Consider its history. When it first appeared it was pronounced 'ant'. Later this shifted to something like 'ahnt'. (This same change is responsible for the different pronunciations of *castle* you hear in Australia and Britain today.) This brought it in line with the pronunciation of other words like *can't* and also *aren't* (or *an't*), the contracted form of *are not.* Complications arose when this contraction of *are not* then acquired another pronunciation,'ain't', which came to serve as the contraction of *am not* and also *is not.* (Here you need to imagine a series of changes something like *is not* > *isn't* > *int* > *ain't.*) This leaves us with the perfect paradigm *I ain't, you ain't, he ain't, we ain't, they ain't.* And it doesn't stop here – *ain't* was also adopted by *haven't* and *hasn't.* Around this time, dropping an 'h' was quite acceptable and it was regularly dropped from *have* and *has.* If you then drop the 's' and the 'v' from the middle (the usual fate of consonants in contracted forms – think of *will not* to *won't*), you then arrive at *ain't* for both *hasn't* and *haven't. Ain't* really did become a kind of omnibus contraction – *am not, are not, is not, has not* and *have not* all at some time contracted to *ain't.*

It was because *ain't* fell into such disgrace that the confusion of *am not* and *are not* came about. People felt so uneasy about *ain't* that they overcorrected and started saying *are not* in place of *am not.* This confusion remains in the standard language today. Even those who wouldn't be caught dead saying *I are not* or *I aren't* say *Aren't I* in the question form. It's a curious little inconsistency in English that produces something like *I'm not coming,* ***am I*** but *I'm coming,* ***aren't I.*** It's little *ain't* getting its own back on the standard language that condemned it.

The 'r' intruder

Why is it, somebody asked the other day, that Australian speakers put an 'r' in the middle of the phrase *law and order*, so that it sounds more like 'law-r-and-order'? This man was a speaker of Scottish English and like many he found the idea of inserting an 'r' in the middle of this phrase quite peculiar. This is something called the 'intrusive r'. In fact, we insert these little 'r' sounds all over the place, but most of the time they go unnoticed. There is only a handful of examples that attract attention in this way. Most Australian speakers, and that includes me, will insert an 'r' between *idea* and *of* in a phrase like *the idea of it.* Yet, people don't seem to notice – at least, it doesn't attract the widespread condemnation that something like 'law-r-and-order' or 'I saw-r-it' does. To understand why Australians insert 'r' sounds we need to go back a few years and look at the history of the sound we represent with the letter 'r'.

Originally we assume that 'r' was pronounced as a trill, similar to the sound you hear in Scottish English today. A trill resembles a sequence of very rapid stopped sounds, with the tip of the tongue vibrating against the roof of the mouth. The quality of this sound then changed, so that it came to be pronounced further back in the mouth, and had the vowel-like quality that we give 'r' at the beginning of a word like *rabbit*. We know from spelling, and from other sources like some of the modern dialects, that at one time speakers of English also pronounced 'r' wherever it appeared in a word. So a word like *father* would have had a final 'r', as it does in American English. Some time during the 1700s speakers stopped pronouncing 'r' before consonants or at the end of words. As one disapproving writer at the time put it, 'r' is 'sometimes entirely sunk'. So this was the pronunciation that came out to Australia. The colonization of America took place earlier during the seventeenth century; in other words, before this pronunciation change took place. At this time the colonial settlers would have pronounced the 'r' wherever it appeared. Hence, American dialects and others like them are now known as 'r-ful' dialects – 'r's are pronounced everywhere.

As far as the 'r-less' dialects of English go, nothing terribly significant has happened – simply a slight change in the manner of pronunciation. We pronounce the word *father* without 'r', but when the word is followed by a vowel as in *father and mother* the sound surfaces again. It's 'father-r-and-mother'. This is called a 'linking r', and not to be confused with the dreaded 'intrusive r' in *law and order*. This '**intrusive** r' would have come about through people simply extending the '**linking** r'. It's a kind of analogy. Compare the word *father* with the word *idea* or *soda*. These words sound very similar, or at least they end in the same vowel sound. So if you say 'father-r-and-mother' with 'r', why not 'soda-r-and-ice'? And so the 'r' sneaks in this way. Like most changes of this nature, it continues to worm its way through the system. Many speakers have now extended the 'linking r' to cover any situation where two vowels come together. Quite simply the rule for many speakers is now to insert an 'r' sound between words ending in vowels and words beginning with vowels. Hence the pronunciations 'law-r-and-order' and 'I saw-r-it'.

But the story doesn't end here, as watchers of the 'intrusive r' well know. This rule is also extending to the interiors of some words. The word *drawing* often gets pronounced 'draw-r-ing'. Now, there's an 'intrusive r' that does attract ferocious criticism! But is this justified? Take words like *going* or *seeing*. Both these have vowels in the middle. But even those people who say 'draw-r-ing' would never dream of inserting an 'r' in these two words. Why? Well, quite simply because we already insert consonants there. They don't appear in the spelling, of course, and we may not be aware we're doing it, but they are there. The 'w' and 'y' sounds in 'go-w-ing' and 'see-y-ing' are what help the smooth transition from one vowel to another. It does seem unfair that poor little 'intrusive r' should get such bad press, when our language is full of these extra sounds that help words and syllables to run together more smoothly. In other words, they ensure fluent-sounding speech – and all of us, even the linguistic crime watchers, produce them.

One laid-back little vowel

I've had several irate calls from people insisting that most speakers don't pronounce correctly the vowels at the beginning of words like *official* and *event*. This got me thinking about one of the most important vowels in the English language – a seemingly insignificant little vowel that goes by the name of 'schwa'. Its curious name is actually the English version of the German name for a Hebrew vowel of roughly the same quality. It sounds something like 'ugh' and its phonetic symbol is [ə]. Schwa is actually the most common vowel in our language and is represented by a great variety of different spellings – it appears with all the vowel letters, in fact. When we make this vowel sound, the centre of our tongue is slightly raised, the lips are in a neutral position (not spread, not rounded), and there's no firm contact between the edges of the tongue and the upper molars either – it's an extremely relaxed little vowel.

In normal connected speech, all single syllable grammatical forms like *the*, *of*, *a*, *was* and *have* appear in their weak forms where the vowel is reduced to schwa. They receive a full vowel only if for some reason they're stressed. For instance, I might say 'He's **the** man for the job!' rather than the less emphatic 'He's the man for the job'. If you listen for it, you can hear schwa in all sorts of places where syllables aren't stressed – for example, at the beginnings of words like *official*, *occasion*, *event* and *fatigue*. Many people, like these callers, feel these 'schwa-ful' pronunciations are lazy, but really you would sound pretty odd if you did pronounce the full vowel in place of schwa in these words. Pronunciations like '**oh**fficial' and '**oh**ccasion' sound unnatural and rather theatrical. Schwa also occurs in the middle of words like *coronation* and *afterwards*. Again, it would be peculiar not to sound schwa in this position – for instance, 'cor**oh**nation' for *coronation*. Schwa also appears at the end of words as in *mother* and *beckon*. Say the word *Australia* and you'll probably hear it at the beginning and at the end. *Formidableness* has all schwa vowels except for one.

English is what's called a 'stress-timed' language. People might sneer at little schwa, but it is in fact an extremely important feature of our language's accentual pattern. It's been this way for at least as long as English has been recorded. You can tell by the confused spelling of unstressed vowels in Old English that this little vowel would have been around then. Schwa has been crucial to the heartbeat of English for a long time, and produces a rhythm very different from the rhythm of languages like French or Italian, where the syllables are spaced out at a fairly even beat. As some have described it, theirs is a kind of rat-a-tat-a-tat rhythm. But in English you typically find intervening reduced vowels. These vowels borrow time from the preceding full vowels, and this produces the more uneven beat that is characteristic of English. If I say 'Dad's firm flat feet', all you hear is full vowels. This is the rat-a-tat-a-tat effect. Compare this example to something like 'father's feet are firm and flat'. In this example, every other vowel is reduced to schwa. It's the tum-tee-tum-tee-tum rhythm of typical English.

Schwa usage varies greatly between dialects. Australian English speakers often put schwas in places where British and American speakers won't. Striking differences are also now appearing as a consequence of the worldwide spread of English. In India and

Africa, for instance, English is coming into close contact with languages that have the syllabic rhythm characteristic of French. In many of these varieties, now called New Englishes, schwas are replaced by stronger vowel qualities. The syllables have a more even force. This produces a very different rhythm and these Englishes can sometimes be difficult for us to follow. But bear in mind there will soon be more speakers of Englishes with the rat-a-tat rhythm than the tum-tee-tum rhythm. One wonders what impact this will have on World English.

Spellings that irritate

Spelling reform is a recurring preoccupation of people in the English-speaking world. Of course, complicating the whole business is the tug of war between the two giants – British English and American English.

First, there's the thorny issue of *-or* versus *-our* in words like *honour* and *colour*. As it happens, this is a variation dating from the seventeenth and eighteenth centuries. Spelling enthusiasts keen to show off their scholarship decided that *-or* should be used for words borrowed from Latin, and *-our* for words from French. However, in many cases it simply wasn't clear which was the donor language and so the choice between *-or* or *-our* was hit and miss. On top of this was the problem of what to do with the English words – something like *harbour* got an *-our* spelling even though it's a native. Really, matters of etymology don't belong in questions of spelling, especially when they introduce these sorts of irregularities.

On both sides of the Atlantic there was agreement that this *or–our* variation wasn't desirable and it should be got rid of. But, of course, getting both sides to agree on which spelling was another matter. Samuel Johnson's dictionary of 1755 became the arbiter of English orthography in Britain. Johnson prescribed the *-our* spelling. Noah Webster then published his American dictionary in 1828. Webster loved tinkering with questions of spelling reform and he opted for *-or*. This he did in the interests of consistency but, it has to be said, there was also a bit of linguistic chauvinism involved. As he put it, 'a difference between the English orthography and the American is an object of vast political consequence'. To be honest though, Webster's *-or* spelling was the more sensible choice. There is no doubt that Samuel Johnson's dictionary was an extraordinary accomplishment, but he did make a few dippy recommendations with respect to spelling. The *-our* spelling brought with it many inconsistencies – even one as obvious as his choice of spelling for *interiour* and *exterior*. Problems also arose with related words like *humour* versus *humorous*, *labour* versus *laborious*, *vigour* versus *vigorous*. In fact, the British themselves had already got rid of 'u' in a great many words like *error*, *author*, *doctor*, *horror*, *mirror*, *senator*, *emperor*, *governor*. So Webster was really following on from British spelling practices already in place.

In Australia, official usage has followed the British tradition, although both spellings are found. Many newspapers and magazines have been using *-or* spellings for quite some time. The Australian Labor Party has, of course, spelt its name without a *u* since early last century. In contrast, the Labor Party's counterparts in both Britain and New Zealand spell theirs as Labour.

The other great tussle exists between *-ise* which most British writers use and *-ize* which is prescribed in America. This is yet another instance where American practice is following British spelling habits. *The Times* newspaper, the various editions of Daniel Jones' famous English Pronouncing Dictionary, even the great Oxford English Dictionary itself – indeed many other prestigious British publications prefer the *-ize* spelling. To quote the Oxford on this matter: *-ize* is 'at once etymological and phonetic'. The suffix comes to us from the Greek ending *-izein*. So *-ize* is historically more accurate, but more importantly, it better reflects the pronunciation.

Another of Webster's recommendations concerns whether or not to double 'l' in words like *travelling* and *excelling*. The British double 'l' across the board but Webster's suggestion (he wasn't the only one to recommend this) was to double the consonant only if it occurred in stressed syllables. So *excel* and *propel* would double 'l' in *excelling* and *propelling*, but *travel* and *grovel* wouldn't. This remains American spelling practice. In fact, Webster made a number of recommendations that we all follow today. But he also proposed some very radical spelling changes – dropping the 'a' in words like *bread* and *feather*, spelling *soup* and *group* with ‘oo’ and *tongue* ‘tung’. Not surprisingly, they didn’t catch on.

Gobbledygook

If I were pressed to say what I felt qualified as truly bad language, then I’d probably say some examples of gobbledygook or jargon. Originally the term applied specifically to official language. In truth, we encounter gobbledygook in many different domains – Educationalese, Sociologese, Medicalese – even, I’m afraid, Linguisticalese. These occupational dialects, or ‘eses’ if you like, are the apex of a one thousand year old writing tradition, but they also represent probably the worst kinds of super-literate writing in our society. There have, of course, been backlashes – social and political movements pushing for clear and simple language. In fact, cries for understandable plain language have been heard throughout the history of English, and the current move against incomprehensibility reminds me strongly of the general opposition to Latin in fifteenth- and sixteenth-century Europe. During this time new, emerging literate groups from the middle classes were fighting to understand documents in which their legal and professional rights were set out. The breakthrough today of Plain English into arcane professional registers nicely mirrors the breakthrough of the various vernacular languages like English into the Classical stronghold of writing at this time.

The parallel is even more striking when you consider that many of the linguistic horrors of the ‘eses’ have their beginnings in original Classical models of prose composition, particularly Latin. It took many centuries for English to be accepted. Ours was deemed the language of the street, not of scholarship, and scribes writing in English attempted to emulate what they considered to be good Latin style. This then served as a prestige model for the new literate groups emerging at that time. In their pursuit of knowledge, especially of the law, the new urban bourgeoisie attached considerable importance to these documents and accordingly the style of language in which they were written. Regulating, polishing and refining English essentially meant making it look more like Latin!

As so often happens, this different sort of language then became the badge of the group. Jargon is no different from any other social language variety, whether it be the slang of ecstasy-users, the Latinisms of medicos and lawyers, the special vocabulary of interior decorators. Solidarity is conveyed through the jargon, which becomes a social password. We will never eradicate it. We can't abolish specialized ways of speaking or writing that establish our identity.

But I shouldn't give the impression that all jargon is bad. As much as we like to whinge about it, jargon can be efficient, economical and even crucial in that it can capture distinctions not made in ordinary language. For that reason, ordinary language is constantly borrowing from it. For example, the verb *to contact* was once jargon and early last century there was ferocious resistance. An outraged public used descriptions like 'lubricious barbarism' for this new arrival on scene. The Oxford English Dictionary has a small entry for the verb *to contact* with quotations like this one from 1927: 'Dreiser should not be allowed to corrupt his language by writing "anything that Clyde has personally contacted here"'. Of course it's hard for us today to understand what possible objections people could have had about the verb *to contact*. Seventy-odd years have gone by and we've lost any feeling for the objectionable connotations this verb obviously had for speakers at that time. It seems when it first appeared as a verb, *to contact* smacked of pretentious jargon – probably something along the lines of the verb to *impact on* today. But let's face it, it's more elegant than *get in touch with* and it fills a gap in our everyday language. The new verb *to stretcher* someone off a football field might be irritating, but it's also handy. As Dwight Bolinger once put it so beautifully: 'the familiar jargon is the alcohol of our verbal drug culture, the unfamiliar is its marijuana'. In language it's always been so.

The important thing is not to be taken in by jargon. Profound thought doesn't require difficult language – and difficult language shouldn't pass for profound thought.

Colloquial Today, Standard English Tomorrow

What is a weed? A plant whose virtues have not yet been discovered
Ralph Waldo Emerson, *Fortune of the Republic*, 1878

Variety holds the key to language change. The colloquial forms in everyday speech – probably the very ones that get up your nose – provide the basis for change. These slipshod pronunciations, mistakes in grammar, coinages, new meanings – the majority will drop by the wayside, it's true. But some will catch on, be used more and more, and will eventually form part of the repertoire of Standard English. Today's weeds may become tomorrow's beautiful and rewarding species.

'In forme of speche is chaunge'

The following snippet, a tenth-century cure for warts, comes from some of the earliest written English we have:

Genim hundes micgean & muse blod meng to somne smire mid þa weartan hi gewitaþ sona aweg

'Take dog's urine, and a mouse's blood, mingle together, smear the warts therewith, they will soon depart away'

There can be no doubt that English has changed, along with wart remedies. The further we go back in time, the stranger our language appears to us. This example doesn't even seem remotely English. Massive changes have occurred, and at all levels of the language.

Most people appear fascinated by word origins and the stories that lurk behind the structures in our language. Paradoxically, they may consider that change is fine as long as it's part of history – anything occurring now is calamitous. We've always been this way. In 1653 John Wallis railed against the use of the word *chicken* as a singular noun. In 1755 Samuel Johnson wanted to rid the language of 'licentious idioms' and 'colloquial barbarisms'. The sort of barbarisms he had in mind were words like *novel*, *capture* and *nowadays.* Others were fretting about shortened forms like *pants* for *pantaloons* and *mob* for *mobile vulgus.* More than five hundred years ago the printer Caxton also worried about the 'dyuersite & chaunge of langage'. Even two thousand years ago Roman verbal hygienists were complaining about changes they saw happening in spoken Latin. Of course, this 'bad' Latin continued to deteriorate until it turned into French, Italian and Spanish.

Take a straightforward example. English shows a handy flexibility in being able to convert words to other parts of speech without the addition of any sort of prefix or suffix. Such elasticity is an offshoot of the loss of inflection (endings added for grammatical purposes). Curiously, this is a feature of English that's not appreciated by all, and many speakers are quick to condemn usages such as *to impact (on)* and *a big ask.* New conversions often provoke hostility in this way. In the 1600s *to invoice* (created from the noun) was a horrid colloquialism. With time, such newcomers may come to sound as everyday as any venerable oldie, and the next generation of English speakers will be puzzling over what possible objections there could have been to them. By then, there'll be new weeds to eradicate. One such was reported to me by someone who overheard it in a Chinese restaurant. The waiter was praising a customer for having *chopsticked* so well. Will this verb catch on? Time will tell.

So what's really going on when people object to words and word usage in this way? Essentially, it's not a language matter we're dealing with here, but more a social issue. Words carry with them a lot of social baggage, and typically it's that which people are reacting to. Many rules of language usage like 'don't use "impact" as a verb' take their force from their cultural and social setting. People aren't objecting to *impact* as a verb as such. It's just that it sounds a bit like gobbledygook, either pretentious or uneducated, and maybe they don't want to be identified with the kind of people who use it. In the same way, fifty years ago people complained that the verb *to contact* was inflated jargon and they hated it.

Language often becomes the arena where social conflicts are played out. When Jonathan Swift complained about shortenings like *pozz* from *positive*, he blamed changes like these on the 'loose morals' of the day. But of course the social significance of many of these usages is lost to us today, and the objections to them now seem puzzling and trivial. American lexicographer Noah Webster wanted to rid his dictionary of English *-our* spellings like *honour* and also *-re* spellings like *theatre*. Why? Because they smacked of a smarmy deference to Britain. Compare the reactions of many Australians towards the current Americanis/zation of their 'beloved Aussie lingo'. In truth, hostility towards 'American' *-or* spellings in place of English *-our*, or *-ize* in place of *-ise*, is not based on genuine linguistic concerns, but reflects deeper social judgements. It's a linguistic insecurity born of the inescapable dominance of America as a cultural, political and economic superpower. These spellings are symbols of this American hegemony and become easy targets for anti-American sentiment.

If Alfred the Great had had the chance to read the language of Chaucer, over five hundred years after Alfred's own time, he would have been shocked at the changes to English – changes that we now see, another six hundred years on, as part of the richness and versatility of the language. The only languages that don't change are ones that are well and truly dead. English, with 350 million first-language speakers and about the same number of second-language speakers, is alive and well. The future for English has never looked so good.

Slanguage

'Slang' is a perfect example of a variety of language whose virtues are unrecognized. For many, it has all the features of bad language. For a start, it belongs to a highly informal milieu, perhaps even anti-formal. Slang is colloquial. It springs from speech, not writing. And for many it has a close connection with swearing and offensive language. Some speakers also view slang as some kind of adolescent disease that everyone eventually grows out of. This is not the case. Sure, teenagers use slang, but so do adults. It's not a modern disease either. We have evidence of very old slang. Admittedly it is hard to make stylistic judgements on slang from the past, but when we read a seventeenth-century description of someone as a 'shite-a-bed scoundrel, a turdy gut, a blockish grutnol and a grouthead gnat-snapper' it's unlikely the writer was using the neutral or 'proper' language of the time – I think we can safely assume he was using slang.

Another aspect to slang that causes irritation is its solidarity function – what is my slang may well not be yours. In this respect, slang has something in common with jargon. It defines the gang. The fact that I might use a piece of slang, and you might use the same term shows we're both jolly good fellows and part of the same club. Slang works much like masonic mortar to stick members of a group together – and of course at the same time to erect barriers between them and the outside. Try to identify examples of slang in your own speech and that of your friends. How would you feel about other speakers, outsiders, using these terms? Some teachers and parents might use expressions like *wicked* or *vicious* to describe something good, maybe to show empathy with their students and children, but it will always sound phoney.

Sometimes there's the added motivation of secrecy – in fact 'slang' originated as a term in the 1700s to describe the secret vocabulary and idiom of the British underworld. In today's criminal slang, it still serves to maintain in-group recognition devices and in this context, of course, it's even more ephemeral. The need to maintain secrecy will always ensure a constant turnover of vocabulary. As soon as a term's cover is blown, it has to be replaced. This must be the case in all so-called 'anti-languages' (in other words, languages that need to be unintelligible to outsiders). The language of those involved in unofficial or illegal activities, for example, changes constantly and rapidly, and this makes it extremely difficult for police to train informers to infiltrate these groups. As Andersson and Trudgill report, the rapid turnover of slang makes it easy for the group members to identify anyone from outside.

But the feature that almost guarantees slang a permanent place in some people's bad books is that it is language in a constant state of flux. Slang is creative. Slang has to stand out. It has to be novel. What is slang for one generation is certainly not necessarily slang for another. *Cool* might have made a comeback, but the language of the 'hip culture' of the late sixties is now pretty well passé – *far out* has been replaced by *awesome* and who knows what new 'awesome' words lurk in the wings. Current teenager slang might have a strong American dimension with words like *wicked*, *sick*, *mad*, *filthy*, *zesty* and *groovy* for 'good' and *seedy*, *krusty*, *festy* and *sad* for 'bad', but it probably won't endure. For slang to be slangy it has to startle, amuse, shock – but above all it has to be new.

The slang of today provides tomorrow's formal language. Just look in some early dictionaries, particularly at the entries labelled unfit for general use. In Samuel Johnson's dictionary of 1755, for example, we find *abominably* described as a word of low language, *nowadays* as barbarous usage, *clever* as a low word used in burlesque or conversation, *noways* as a word used by ignorant barbarians, *bamboozle* as a cant (or jargon) word not used in pure or grave writings. A lot of his entries were clearly slang of the time. It's just that the term *slang* for Johnson was the special language of tramps and thieves. It didn't get its modern meaning until the early 1800s. Clearly, slang expressions either intrude into neutral style and become standard usage (and therefore stop being slangy) or they drop by the wayside. Slang is simply a linguistic flower out of place.

Up the duff/dough?

Those who enjoy pointing out the inconsistencies of English spelling always give the example of 'gh'. Sometimes it's silent as in *night*. Sometimes it's an 'f' as in *rough*. And then there's *hiccough* where it's a 'p'. So is it the 'sluff' of despondency or perhaps the 'slou' of despond – or perhaps the 'slup' of despond? Do you 'sluff' something off or 'slou' it off?

The problems of 'gh' have come about because of the disappearance of the sound we represent in phonetics as [x]. It's a kind of guttural 'ch' sound made at the back of the mouth (as in German *ach*), not quite as far back as if you were gargling, but about where you make 'k'. Around a thousand years ago this sound was spelt with the letter 'h' and when it appeared at the beginning of words it was pronounced much like aitch is today. In other positions it was more like guttural 'ch'. In the Middle English period this spelling changed to either the yogh symbol (a 'z' with a fancy tail) or the letters 'gh' that have come down to us today.

But the days were numbered for this little sound. We know this from spellings of words like *night* as 'nite' and also words like *delite* that suddenly acquired a 'gh' spelling even though they had never had this sound. It was probably on the way out as early as 1400, but there was a lot of variation and for a long time. It always takes a while for sound change to work its way through the vocabulary and the speech community. We know, for example, that it disappeared earlier in the south of England and in other regions hung around a little longer. A chap called Coote writing in the 1590s described how 'some say *plough*, *slough*, *bough*; others *plou*, *slou*, *bou*'. There was considerable resistance too, as you might expect. (Just look at the concern today at the dropped 'l' in *vulnerable*!) Coote described the pronunciation 'dauter' for *daughter* as 'barbarous speech'. In fact, Coote had a little list of 'corrupt pronunciations' – they all make for fine English today.

The process was actually more complex than this. In certain positions guttural 'ch' also became 'f', as in *cough*. Again there was a lot of variation, both regional and social. Someone called Hart wrote a pronunciation treatise in 1569 – he pronounced *laugh* with a final guttural. Yet, it's clear that Shakespeare pronounced it as we do today, with 'f'. As late as 1700 some speakers were even pronouncing an 'f' in words like *daughter*, *taught*, *bought* and *naught*, where it has totally disappeared today. So in the 1600s the word *daughter* was pronounced three ways: 'dauter', 'dauchter' and 'daufter' (the vowels in these words would also have been different, but I'll ignore this fact here). This state of affairs sometimes led to a split, where the pronunciations parted company and became separate words. For example, today we have *dough* and *duff* 'a pudding' as in *plum duff* – British and Australian speakers probably know this better in *up the duff* (= *bun in the oven*; in other words 'pregnant'). Both words *dough* and *duff* derive from Old English *dah*.

So back to *slough*. This is tricky because there are actually two different words here. There's the *slough* pronounced 'slou' meaning 'muddy ground' and *slough* pronounced 'sluff' meaning 'skin'. Both words have distinct etymologies, but they show different pronunciation outcomes for the original 'ch' sound. As for *hiccough*. Some time during the sixteenth century, spelling enthusiasts, being under the impression that it had something to do with *cough*, had the bright idea to respell the word. Not a terribly helpful amendment.

Stressing about stress

Stress is one of those fiendishly difficult areas in English. It used not to be. If only we'd stuck with good old Germanic words, the stress probably would have stayed on the first syllable and that would be that. But we borrow, and when it comes to borrowing English is something of a linguistic omnivore. Huge numbers of loan words like *apparatchik*, *tureen* and *taboo* have entered English, all with their different stress patterns. The result – rules of stress placement that make your head spin.

There are four groups of words in particular that have especially provocative stress patterns. First, words like *ceremony*, *temporary* and *secretary*. These aren't new linguistic vices, as many imagine, but are conservative usages. Originally, these words were all pronounced this way, with a secondary stress on the second last syllable. This stress is now disappearing and the word ending is weakening. American English better preserves this older stress pattern. Indeed, many of the linguistic features British and Australian speakers think of as being quintessentially American are directly traceable to seventeenth-century British English.

Second, the dreaded *kilometre*. This was the first of this group of terms to enter English and so it was modified to fit in with the stress patterns of already existing words like *barometer* and *thermometer*. Because we've now acquired *centimetres*, *millimeters* and so on, many people also say *kilometre*. The problem is that frequently used words often don't conform. Hence, *kilometre* is still for many the more usual pronunciation. In addition, the pronunciation *kilometre* fits better with the general trend for stress to fall on the third last (or antepenultimate) syllable. Should we therefore expect *centimetre* or *millimetre*?

L-drop

One very unstable consonant is the lateral sound – 'l'. For a start, it will change radically depending on where it appears. At the end of words like *pill* or before consonants as in *milk* it has a back resonance, with the back of the tongue slightly raised. Occasionally, it even turns into a 'w' sound, as in pronunciations 'piw' and 'miwk'. Sometimes 'l' drops out altogether and its disappearance in words like *vulnerable*, *million* and *Australia* is a source of great concern for some speakers. Those of you who might be tempted to see this as a linguistic disease of the laterals of today might be comforted to know that this little sound has a long history of instability. And I'm not talking just about the peculiarities of proper names like *Cholmondley* and *Dalziel*. The history of 'l' is one of spectacular disappearances, and equally of spectacular arrivals in unexpected places.

For a start, 'l' has a history of disappearing between vowels made in the back of the mouth and consonants made either with the lips (like 'm' or 'f') or with the back of the tongue (like 'k'). Conveniently, our spelling is conservative and preserves evidence of the earlier pronunciation. Think of words like *calm*, *calf* and *walk*. These 'l's started to disappear some time around 1500. We can guess this from spellings of *walk* as *wauk*. Even so, well into the 1700s people were still recommending the 'l-ful' pronunciations as the correct ones. Our 'l-less' pronunciations today were described as 'negligentius' – in other words slovenly. Or, as one writer of 1662 put it so delightfully, 'A, . . . sometimes drowneth the l'. In fact, 'l's were being drowned all over the place, and not just by 'a' but by many other sounds.

Occasionally written English threw out a life jacket and a number of 'l's were revived. Because of the importance we now place on writing, we tend to pay more attention to spelling and this can affect pronunciation. Words like *salt*, *malt*, *bolt*, *almost* and *walnut* got their 'l' back this way. Some 'l' sounds even snuck into words where they had no place. This was the result of overzealous writers – people keen to show off their etymological erudition. Words like *fault, assault* and *vault* were among those to get a fancy respelling. The reasoning behind this remodelling was that the Latin equivalents have 'l'. The trouble is, these words were borrowed into English directly from French, and the French words didn't have 'l'. *Fault* came from French *faute* and not Latin *fallita*. At the time it entered English it would have rhymed with *thought*. But once again the increasing influence of writing meant that these spurious 'l' sounds eventually came to be pronounced. So you win some, you lose some – this sort of tinkering made up for a few of the laterals we lost.

Third, what about the nouns *res**ear**ch* and *dis**pute***? These are currently showing the effects of a stress change – emphasis is shifting to the first syllable. The verbs *to res**ear**ch* and *to dis**pute*** retain the original stress on the second syllable. Until Shakespeare's time all such noun and verb pairs had stressed second syllables, but then in the 1500s the nouns started to do their own thing. As Chen and Wang's study shows, the first to shift to initial stress were ***out**law*, ***re**bel* and ***re**cord*. This marked the start of a new role for stress – a handy device for distinguishing nouns and verbs. We now ***pro**duce pro**duce***. The problem is, change is very slow. Four hundred years later fewer than two hundred words have been affected, and there are still around a thousand to go. Nouns like *mis**take***, *dis**like***, *oc**cult***, *re**port*** and *ad**dress***, for instance, still show the original stress. This is very typical of the messy reality of language change. Different words are affected at different times. But all signs indicate that ***ad**dress* will be the standard pronunciation in the future.

Finally, the *con**tro**versy* about *con**tro**versy*. *Con**tro**versy* is the older pronunciation and the stress shift to the second syllable might well have been triggered when people stopped pronouncing the second 'r'. If there are two consonants before the *-y* ending, then the stress typically falls on the first syllable, as in ***dif**ficulty*. In countries like the United States where *r* has been retained, the pronunciation ***con**troversy* remains. But loss of the 'r' in other varieties means that there is only one consonant before the *-y* ending. The pronunciation *con**tro**versy* brings it in line with similar words like *a**po**logy*. *Con**tro**versy* also falls into the more expected pattern of stress on the third last syllable. As New Zealand linguist Laurie Bauer describes, this seems to be where English is heading in the matter of stress. Watch out for words like *metallurgy* – will it change to *metallurgy*?

Clearly stress, like any aspect of language, is subject to change. In everyday speech we don't usually notice the changes. It's just that in the public discourse, especially on radio and television, they become more obvious – and people usually react against them. That's not surprising; most of us are conservative about language. Pronunciation, after all, is an important part of our identity. But once we start noticing these things, especially in the media, it's too late. Once a new pronunciation has snuck into that fairly formal setting, the change is clearly here to stay. But remember, no one bats an eyelid now about similar shifts from *character*, *convenient*, *replica*, *bitumen* and hundreds of others. Let me quote Samuel Rogers on changing stress patterns in his day: 'The now fashionable pronunciation of several words is to me at least very offensive: contemplate is bad enough; but balcony makes me sick'. Samuel Rogers was a writer in the late eighteenth and early nineteenth centuries – the pronunciations he would have been familiar with and wanted restored were *contemplate* and *balcony*.

Readin', 'ritin' 'n' 'rithmetic

Many speakers are critical of the kinds of short cuts we make in speech. But shortening words can enrich vocabulary, and over the years it's made some very interesting contributions to our lexicon. We all know about abbreviations like *fridge*, *flu*, *phone*, *ad*, *maths*, *gym* and recent newcomers like *bio* from *biography*. But things get more interesting when the long and short versions of a word part company; for example, *grotty* from *grotesque*, *stroppy* from *obstreperous*, *loony* from *lunatic*, *razz* 'to make fun of' from *raspberry* (as in blowing a raspberry) and *hussy* from *housewife*. The different contexts of use mean that the long and the short versions can end up as two radically different words with quite different meanings – and no one but the most ardent etymologist would ever connect the two.

Probably no one but a word historian would make connections between pairs like *fence* and *defence*, *cute* and *acute*, *ticket* and *etiquette.* These examples are interesting because they show the deletion of weak syllables from the front of the words. Generally, the beginnings of words are more strongly articulated and are therefore more stable. Mind you, occasionally both the beginning and the end get lopped. In fact, words can be mutilated into virtual fragments of what they once were. Take, for example, the expletive *darn* from *eternal.* Now, you'll need a bit of phonological imagination here, but the transition goes something like this. From *eternal* you lop the first syllable and you get *ternal*, or its variant *tarnal.* You then lop the end and this gives you *tarn* which in turn gets remodelled to *darn* under the influence of *damn.* Another favourite of mine is *twit.* This little word is all that remains of a very respectable Old English verb *aetwitan* meaning 'to reproach'. It's a combination of the prefix *aet* and the verb *witan* 'to know'. In this case, of course, the shortened form *twit* outlives its parent.

The precedence that writing is taking over speech has meant that a lot of earlier shortenings have now vanished. The word *nuff* from *enough* once appeared in dictionaries but has since dropped by the wayside. *Stablish* has disappeared and so has *postle* and *pistle* – nowadays they appear only as *establish*, *apostle* and *epistle.* In fact, once upon a time people became so worried by shortenings that they actually created long forms that never ever existed. The word *avail*, for instance, replaced *vail* – presumably the 'a' was tacked on to give the word more respectability. Some went even further and spelt it *advail*! The 'a' in *astound* and *astonish* doesn't belong, either. It's extra, like the 'd' in *adventure.*

So, why do we shorten? Generally speaking, short cuts help us achieve fluency and seamlessness in speech. Words like *arithmetic* and *escape* are likely to be pronounced as *'rithmetic* and *'scape*, with the initial unstressed vowels omitted. These sorts of reductions are part and parcel of natural, smooth-flowing speech. But some shortenings are more deliberate. In taboo areas they can be a kind of euphemistic disguise, as in clippings such as *jeeze* for 'Jesus' and abbreviations like *S.O.B.* and *pee.* Shortening can also create a situation of intimacy, indicating that something or someone is endearing to the speaker. We always make short cuts when we're in familiar territory; so that frequently used everyday words are particularly prone to reduction.

Clearly, we've been shortening words for ages. And we've been sneering at shortened forms for ages, too. Words like *bus*, *cab*, *taxi*, *wig* and *pants* were all once slangy versions of the more respectable *omnibus*, *cabriolet*, *taximeter*, *periwig* and *pantaloons*. But they sound quite proper now. Language change is only ever odious when it's happening under your nose.

Maroon – how do you pronounce it?

Many people have queried the pronunciation of the word that describes a certain brownish-crimson colour. Is it 'merone' or 'meroon'?

The etymology is quite straightforward. *Maroon* entered English during the sixteenth century, originally from Italian but, like so many of our colour words, via French. The word in French is *marron* and in Italian *marrone*, both meaning 'chestnut'. You would imagine the word came into English with the pronunciation closest to the French or Italian original and that the 'meroon' pronunciation you now hear in most of the English-speaking world is the result of sound change. Certainly, there was a vowel shift that changed long 'o' to 'oo' (as happened to *goose*). According to this scenario, the pronunciation 'merone' would be closest to the original before the shift began, and would therefore be some sort of dialect relic form.

Not so. As plausible as this theory sounds, the chronology is all wrong. Recall that the word *maroon*, along with others like *cartoon*, *balloon* and *pantaloon*, came into English at the end of the sixteenth century or later. This was **after** that particular sound change had taken place – 'o' had already shifted to 'oo'. Sound change is a bit like an epidemic. It slowly works its way through the vocabulary of a language, but eventually peters out. Words that enter the language later won't undergo that previous change – it's too late.

According to people writing about pronunciation in the sixteenth and seventeenth centuries, French words spelt 'on' were pronounced 'oo' at that time. So 'meroon' is an earlier pronunciation. But this doesn't solve the puzzle: where do some English speakers get the pronunciation 'merone' from? If it were the outcome of some sort of odd spelling pronunciation you would expect the same people to say, instead of *balloon* and *cartoon*, 'ballone' and 'cartone'. After all, these are spelt the same way. But there's no hint of this pronunciation for these words. So spelling pronunciation seems an unlikely explanation. There is no neat solution to this puzzle. Like the origin of 'she', the plural *dwarves* and the disappearance of 'firkytoodling' from our vocabulary, the pronunciation 'merone' is just another of those many linguistic mysteries that help to keep linguists like me in business.

So what is meant by 'fulsome praise'?

Facts of life are never straightforward – neither are the little words we use to describe them. The word *fulsome* and its complex history gives us a good illustration of this. Its earliest recorded sense, from the thirteenth century, was 'abundant, full, good'. This sense continued for some time – in the sixteenth century, for example, people were still writing of *fulsome fieldes habundaunt of frument* and *good fulsome sheaues* of corn. It was clearly positive. But by late Middle English there were already signs of deterioration. Negative senses to do with 'over-abundance' and 'excess' had begun to attach themselves and it wasn't long before the meaning 'offensive, nauseous, disgusting' had become dominant. It's this negative sense that many people still retain today – although it's usually used now in the context of language or behaviour. Something which is *fulsome* is generally understood to be 'offensive to good taste' or 'overdone' as in *fulsome flattery* or *fulsome praise*.

So why did the word deteriorate this way? There are probably two reasons. For a start, *fulsome* was undoubtedly influenced through its similarity with the word *foul*, which in Middle English would have had a similar pronunciation. (There may even have been a word 'foulsome' which would have been pronounced the same as *fulsome*.) But even without this association, the shift from 'characterized by abundance, good' to 'characterized by over-abundance, offensive' is a predictable one and is well attested. The word *sad* shows a similar development, from an earlier meaning 'full' or 'satisfied' to 'causing sorrow' or even 'deplorably bad'. It's not a coincidence that *sad*, *satisfied* and *satiated* share the same initial syllable. For more recent examples, look at *fed up* or *chocker* (at least in varieties of British English where *chocker* means 'disgruntled' – in Australian English *chockers* hasn't shifted yet). You might compare it with *bellyful*, as in *I've had a bellyful of you*, and the expression *I've had it up to here*. It does seem there's a very fine line between having your fill and having too much.

The problem is that nowadays *fulsome* is on the move again. It's in the process of doing a complete about-face and returning to its first positive meaning; that is, 'abundant, full, good'. Once again, one of the reasons it's shifting is through association, but this time the association is with positive words like *full* and *wholesome*.

Some find this recent change unacceptable and argue the word should mean what it used to mean. But if this is the case, those who use *fulsome* in the sense of 'abundantly good' have got it right. This, after all, was the earliest recorded use. But then we would have to argue the same way for *sad* and *fed up*. In that case, 350 million native speakers have got it wrong!

In 1868 someone used the expression *this fulsome world* and he followed it with a note – 'I use the word fulsome in the original sense'. He was using the term in the sense of 'abundantly good'. Writers around this time couldn't stop the meaning of *fulsome* shifting to 'offensive, loathsome' any more than writers today can stop the meaning from shifting back. As offensive as this might seem to some, the meanings of modern words depend on how speakers are using them now. Inevitably, there will be periods of confusion. Indeed, it's sometimes difficult these days to know exactly what people mean by *fulsome praise*. But then, try figuring out what Chaucer meant by 'sad courage' or what Shakespeare meant by 'sad mortality'. Semantic change is a fact of lexical life.

Singular 'they'

I want to report a usage I increasingly encounter in students' essays these days, and that is the form *themself*. For example, *The speaker must speak of things with reference to themself*. Sentences like these are commonplace. It's an interesting usage because it shows that 'singular *they*' is well integrated into the pronoun system.

Before you leap up and down and howl about declining standards, may I point out that *themself* has, in fact, a long and respectable pedigree? It was standard usage in English until about the mid sixteenth century when it was replaced by *themselves*. We are dealing here with something called reflexive pronouns, and they have quite an untidy history. In the standard language the *I*, *we* and *you* forms are now created on the basis of the possessive: *myself*, *ourselves*, *yourself* and *yourselves*. Here the word *self* is treated like an ordinary noun and therefore you would expect a possessive. Dialect forms like *theirself* and *hisself* fit this pattern, but they're not considered standard. Curiously, they sound perfectly fine in literary English when an adjective intervenes: 'their own sweet very selves', for example. But *theirselves* without the intervening adjectives doesn't quite make it. Forms like *himself* and *themselves* and even *themself* are different. They have as their first element the object pronoun and not the possessive. A form like *meself* fits the pattern too, and would make things more regular, but it is also not considered standard – yet. Remember, today's non-standard is often tomorrow's standard.

Singular *they* and *themself* have the advantage of being gender-free. They are a natural solution to our problem of finding a gender-neutral pronoun to replace clumsy *s/he* and *her/him*. Now, I know that this is difficult for those who have learnt generic 'he' as a kind of immutable rule of English grammar. But in fact this rule was formulated quite recently by prescriptive grammarians, and for ideological rather than grammatical reasons. Early grammatical treatises that pushed the generic masculine argued on the basis of so-called rules of nature: 'Let us set the man before the woman for manners sake', 'The worthier is preferred and set before' and so on. Generic *he* was supposed to have virtues of naturalness. It was these same early prescriptive grammars that outlawed singular *they*.

Some people may well be worried by the fact that singular *they* and its reflexive partner *themself* appear grammatically incorrect. Admittedly, a formal analysis of the English system of pronouns reveals that *they* is plural in meaning. On the basis of formal criteria, however, masculine 'he' should also be judged incorrect when it is used generically. But pronouns aren't that inflexible. We shouldn't expect a perfect match, a one-to-one correspondence, between form and meaning here. Plural *we* can just as easily refer to a singular hearer, as in 'Let's eat up our spinach now, shall **we**, Betty?' (a kind of condescending hospitalese or nurseryspeak). *You* can be used to refer to people in general, as in 'Chocolate is good for **you**' (this is preferable in my variety of English to indefinite *one* – 'Chocolate is good for **one**' sounds a bit over the top). In special cases of extreme politeness, third person forms *he* and *she* can be used to refer to the hearer in a kind of distancing technique; for example, 'If Madam so desires, **she** might have the pavlova without the whipped cream'. In fact, I can use these forms to refer directly to all of you out there – if I'm being polite, that is: 'The astute reader (that's you!) will notice that pronouns often stray from their central meanings and he/she will accommodate them accordingly'.

So why worry about using *they* as a gender-neutral singular pronoun, as in 'If anyone wants it, **they** can have pavlova with extra whipped cream'? The argument that this is grammatically incorrect because a plural pronoun shouldn't refer back to a singular word is linguistically unfounded – clearly, English has many examples where pronouns depart from their core meaning. Furthermore, the form *you* is historically plural. So if you object to singular *they* on the grounds that it's really plural, then you should also return to *thou* and *thee* for singular and retain *you* for plural. Start arguing this way and you quickly impale yourself on your own argument.

Double 'haves'

I want to defend another construction that has attracted a fair amount of bad press lately. This is the so-called 'double *have*' that you find in sentences like *if I **had have** seen her I would have told her*. Those who feel a tad squeamish about such usages might feel marginally happier with something like *Had I have seen her*. It's the double *have* here that causes the steam to come out of some people's ears. It's been labelled 'a barbaric usage of our time'. Fowler describes it as 'an illiterate blunder and easily shown to be absurd'. The kindest descriptions I could find are: 'incorrect'; 'not found in careful speech'; 'a redundant use of have'. It often appears in literature to depict non-standard speech or dialect. There's a lovely line in *Dubliners* where Joyce writes: 'She was a little vulgar – sometimes she said "If I had've known" – but what would grammar matter if he really loved her'.

It is an unusual construction because you would expect after the verb *have* to find the past participle; in other words, *had had*, not *had have*. By behaving this way *have* is fitting in with the pattern of other verbs like *would*, *should* and *could* – for example, I *would/should/could have gone*. There is a lot of evidence that *have* should be treated as one of these verbs, but I'll spare the gory details.

Let me instead tackle some of the criticisms. First, the notion that it's a barbaric usage of our time. Certainly, it's not confined to modern times. This is an abomination of long tradition, dating back to the early fifteenth century in fact. One early example is: 'Had not he have been, we should never have returned'. Second, it's certainly not confined to vulgar dialects of English. You frequently encounter it in Standard English varieties and all around the world. Third, the criticism that it's redundant. The auxiliary verb *have* has many uses, but all seem to have in common some sense of 'unreality' or projected action. Increasingly in English 'have' is coming to mark unfulfilled conditions and this seems to be its use in the 'double *have* construction'. In 'if he **had have** lived a little longer' (instead of 'if he had lived a little longer') the second *have* stresses that the proposition is unfulfilled.

There are several ways this construction could have evolved. Some have suggested it developed from sentences like *if he had a written*. This *a* was left over from a little marker that signaled completed action. We were in the process of losing this prefix; so confusion could have set in and *have* could have crept in in place of the reduced prefix *a* via a kind of overcorrection; in other words, *If I had have written* rather than *If I had a written*. Verbs like *would/could/should* probably also had a role to play. They all signal non-reality, and *would* (like *had*) also reduces to *'d*; for example *I would have/I'd have*. It's not surprising that *have* should have joined their ranks.

Since today's informal usage frequently becomes tomorrow's formal usage, we might expect that this *had've* construction won't even raise an eyebrow in a few years time. Mind you, it's been in the language since the early fifteenth century – it's about time it got some recognition. There's another interesting little wrinkle, too, although it's possibly even more controversial than the 'double *have* construction'. In spoken English we often find *of* in place of unstressed *have*; for example, 'I should of written it', rather than 'I should have written it'. (This 'of', by the way, has also been around for a lot longer than you might imagine.) Reinforced by expressions like *kind of* and *sort of*, this *of* looks like it's in the process of becoming another marker of unreal conditions. Dare I suggest, another linguistic flower out of place?

Our Untidy English

The blind swipe of the pruner and his knife
Robert Lowell, 'Waking Early Sunday Morning', 1965

Many of the tidying-up activities of speakers involve a process called analogy – this happens when a piece of language changes to become more like another piece with which it is somehow associated. Like pruning and cutting back, analogy trims away unkempt straggly bits and dead-heads constructions that have had their day.

I deepfroze or deepfreezed the pizzas?

If *froze* is the past tense of *freeze*, should we say 'I *deepfroze* the pizzas' or 'I *deepfreezed* the pizzas'? We're dealing here with a class of rather awkward verbs in English that are traditionally called 'strong' verbs. These verbs are irregular, like *eat-ate-eaten* and the verb in question, *freeze-froze-frozen*. Once much more common than they are today, they made up one of the two major verb classes in Old English. An inherited Germanic feature dictated that verbs fell into either the so-called 'strong' or 'weak' class. The strong verbs indicate past time by modifying their vowels – as in *freeze-froze-frozen*. The weak class add some kind of ending – so *sneeze-sneezed*.

It's ironic that we use labels like strong and weak here – the weak verbs have much more muscle. Despite valiant efforts by those within the 'Society for the Preservation of Old English Strong Verbs', who have done their best to resuscitate forms like *raught* for *reached* and *clomb* for *climbed*, fewer than 60 of the original 350 strong verbs remain – and this number includes some rather doubtful ones such as *heave-hove*, *glide-glode*, *beseech-besaught*, *cleave-cleft-cloven*, *beget-begat-begotten*, *chide-chid-chidden*, *slay-slew-slain* and *smite-smote-smitten* which are hardly common-or-garden variety. The past millennium has seen the slow but sure demise of these strong patterns. *Heave-hove* changes to *heave-heaved* on analogy with regular verbs like *jump-jumped*; in other words, *heave* is to *heaved* as *jump* is to *jumped*. This is the way of analogy – it wanders through the language nipping off forms that appear outdated.

Anyway, back to the initial question – 'I *deepfroze* the pizzas' or 'I *deepfreezed* the pizzas'? When irregular verbs like *freeze*, *take* or *light* occur in compounds, they tend to be regularized and join the weak verbs. Take the more established example *highlight*. *Highlight* is a fused verb, fused in the sense that *high* and *light* are blended together in pronunciation and meaning. We therefore treat it differently from the verb *light*. So 'I *lit* the lamp', but 'I *highlighted* paragraphs', not 'I *highlit* paragraphs'. Similarly, we have *freeze-froze* but *deepfreeze* is its own verb and therefore is treated differently from *freeze*. This is why *deepfroze* may sound weird. Hence *babysit-babysitted* is more common that *babysat*, and *stocktake-stocktaked* sometimes occurs rather than *stocktook*. It can happen that new compounds fall into a kind of inflectional no-man's-land. Probably in the case of *stocktake*, and perhaps also to some extent *deepfreeze*, the compounds aren't fused to the point that we can treat them entirely differently from *take* and *freeze*.

The golfer taw off?

Somebody once posed an interesting question via the Internet. It went something like this – 'SEE is a verb; TEE is a golfing verb. In my capacity as a naive native speaker I seem to have far less of a problem analyzing SEED as a badly made past tense of SEE than I do analyzing TAW as a badly made past tense of TEE'. Why is this so?

Here is another excellent example of the 'pruning' activities of analogy – the past of *see* becomes *seed* on analogy with the regular verbs of English like *jump* and *climb*. The question is, why can't *tee* borrow its past tense from *see* and produce *taw* on analogy with *saw*?

For a pattern to extend it has to be productive; in other words, lively. The *-ed* ending is, and this is why we understand children when they come up with forms like *seed* and *bringed*. Moreover, any new verb entering the language will also develop this ending. The past of the newly minted verb *screeze*, meaning 'to cut your tongue while licking envelopes', is *screezed* (not *scroze*). We have a regular rule for forming past tense and any irregular pattern like *see* and *saw* has to be stored individually in the memory. Should memory fail, the regular rule steps in and we get *seed*. But we readily understand the form when this happens, because we're dealing with the default rule. You wouldn't extend the pattern *see-saw* in this way because, even though *see* is a very common verb, the pattern itself simply does not occur frequently enough to have stuck in our brains. How many verbs can you think of that follow the *see-saw* pattern?

Another example is the group of verbs *speak* (past *spoke*), *seek* (past *sought*) and *reek* (past *reeked*). All of these verbs sound similar because they end in 'eek', but only *reek* shows the regular past ending *reeked*. We can perfectly well understand the child who says 'I speaked' and 'I seeked'. But what about a child who says 'I spought' and 'I rought' on the pattern of *seek*, or 'I soke' and 'I roke' on analogy with *speak*? You wouldn't expect to find these forms because irregular patterns just don't generalize in this way.

OK, you might be thinking, what about *bring-brang-brung*? Surely, here's an example of an irregular pattern that has extended? Well, analogy does move in mysterious ways and some irregular patterns occasionally do gain new recruits. In this case we have a number of verbs (single syllable and usually ending in a nasal) that pattern this way and what's more they are common ones like *sing*, *drink* and *begin*. Hence *brang*, although incorrect, can be understood, and moreover has a chance of catching on, just as *stick-stuck*, *fling-flung* and *string-strung* have caught on. These new strong verbs now sound perfectly fine. The *sing-sang-sung* pattern does seem a particularly tenacious one and has been successful at resisting being dragged across to a regular pattern of *sing-singed* – so successful, in fact, that it has been able to poach new verbs. Mind you, whether *bring-brang-brung*, or even *think-thunk*, *clink-clunk*, *skim-skum* and *eat-ut*, will catch on remains to be seen. Certainly, Antipodean English *skin-skun* (in the context of skinning a rabbit) has triumphed, at least in some parts of Australia. And *sneak-snuck* is winning out over *sneak-sneaked*. But the point is this: an irregular pattern might every now and again win new recruits, but it's not productive. Were we for example to coin a new verb *ching* (to refer to the noise of clanging change in the pocket), you can be sure that this new verb would have the past tense *chinged* and not *chang* or *chung*!

Shoen, kneen and treen

Forming the plural in English is a straightforward process. Nouns simply take 's'; hence one *dog* and two *dogs*. There is a handful of exceptions, however – common-usage words like *foot* and *child* that are badly behaved when it comes to plurals.

As was the case with eccentric verbs like *sing-sang-sung*, these irregularities are the leftovers of past regularity. Removing them from our noun system involves the same process of analogy. The plural of *eye* (earlier *eyen*) becomes *eyes* on analogy with the regular nouns like *dog*. Once again, only lively patterns win out in this way. This is why we can also understand children when they come up with forms like *mouses* and *foots* – we're dealing with the default rule.

What we are seeing here is a case of linguistic steamrollering by that egregiously successful little ending *-s*. This flourishing suffix has single-handedly wiped out many different plural endings. Here's a potted history. A thousand years ago there was no plural ending as such. Nouns all fell into different classes and had different ways of marking plural. This incredibly elaborate system involved other grammatical properties like gender (nouns fell into the masculine, feminine or neuter class) and case (to mark the function of nouns). By medieval times this whole complex arrangement had been completely obliterated. For the first time we had a plural marker – the problem was, there was more than one. For example, you would refer to one *scip* and two *scipu* 'ships', one *word* and two *word* 'words'; one *hand* and two *handa* 'hands'; one *eye* and two *eyen* 'eyes'; one *stan* and two *stanas* 'stones', and so on.

'Well hanged' or 'well hung'?

What about *hanged* versus *hung*? According to style guides, the difference between these forms lies in whether you are hanging a person or a thing. To hang a person is a method of execution. It takes the past form *hanged* as in *He was* ***hanged*** *for murder.* To hang something takes the past form *hung* as in *The carcass was* ***hung*** *from the rafters.* In reality this distinction is rarely observed. For most people (and that includes me) *hung* is the all-purpose past, used as much to speak of someone having been *hung from the rafters* as *a carcass.* But I'm in good company. All around the world there are signs that *hanged* is giving way to *hung*. Here again, analogy appears to be working in the opposite direction. *Hanged* is the regular and also the older form. So the change here is towards irregularity – a weak becoming a strong verb. Why? It's those verbs like *bring* again. For single-syllable verbs ending in a nasal sound, the pattern of vowel change in the past has occurred so frequently that it actually attracts new verbs like *ring-rung* and *hang-hung*.

But the *hanged-hung* question is instructive in another respect. It often happens that older forms don't disappear entirely but enjoy a kind of afterlife. They might be relegated to marginal functions or else preserved in certain fixed expressions. The reason *hanged* survived for so long in the context of executions was because the form continued to be used in legal English. In many respects, specialist varieties like Legalese work a bit like linguistic formaldehyde. The specialized content encourages a more rigid style that then fixes over time and so preserves forms long since ousted from ordinary usage. *Hanged* also survives in idioms such as *I'll be hanged if . . .* But in more modern idioms, of course, *hung* wins out. He's not *well hanged* – but *well hung!*

For a while it looked as if today we would be forming our plurals with *-en*, for this was emerging as a hot favourite in the south of England and moving northwards. Indeed, we came very close to saying two *shoen*, *kneen* and *treen*. But then *-(e)s* (always

Why children?

We have a few truly eccentric plurals that are doubly marked. *Children* incorporates two plural endings – the 'r' of the *childer* (originally *childru*) and an extra 'en' for good measure (like *ox-oxen*). *Brethren* (originally *brothru*) has the same 'en' plural with an additional mutated vowel (like *tooth-teeth*). *Kine* (the *cows* of poetry) is the same. These forms appeared when the old plurals were on their way out and 'en' was enjoying its brief moment of popularity before the triumph of the 's' ending.

In some words, speakers extended this 's' ending, but again appeared reluctant to give up the original plural form. For example the word *breeches* shows a mutated vowel and an 's' – originally it was one *broc* or 'trouser' and two or more *brec* or 'trousers'.

more popular in the north) suddenly took off and by the end of the fourteenth century it had bulldozed its way right through the country and the noun system to win out as our regular plural marker. How this was managed is a bit of a mystery. A problem of analogy involves trying to figure out why certain patterns prevail and others don't.

Sometimes curious things happen and irregular patterns do surprising things. We are dealing with language, after all – speakers often play with these patterns. The playful plural of *spouse* is now *spice*, on analogy with *mouse-mice*, but with the extra piquancy that *spice* brings. My current favourite is a proposed plural for *Kleenex*. What else but *Kleenices*!

Platypi, platypoi, platypodes or platypuses?

English has other exceptional plurals that come from outside, like *forum-fora*. At the time I was first writing this piece, newspapers seemed full of these problematic plurals. There was talk of new sports *stadiums* – or should that be *stadia*? Universities were extending their *campuses* – or *campi*? There was news of forthcoming *referendums* – or *referenda*? And when there's lots of them, how should we refer to the *platypus* – *platypi*, *platypoi*, *platypuses* or just plain *platypus*?

Words like *forum* are Latin loans. Most of these have now been regularized – *forum-forums* and *stadium-stadiums*. In scholarly or institutional contexts you might still get the Latin plural (*fora*, *stadia*, *curricula*, *millennia* and so on), but even there most people seem to prefer the English plural. *Campus* belongs to another group, ending in *-us*. Actually, these are the trickiest of the lot. Once again they are usually Latin loans, but then it becomes complicated. One subgroup takes an *-i* plural ending: *stimulus-stimuli*. English plurals do seem slower to catch on here. Linguist Pam Peters suggests that it has to do with the concentration of 's's at the end – *stimuluses* sounds simply awful. Nonetheless, I don't think anyone would be tempted to say *circi* as the plural of *circus* or *campi* as the plural of *campus*. Another group of *-us* nouns has a characteristic *-ra* ending for plural: *corpus-corpora*. But be careful not to confuse these with yet another bunch of *-us* nouns that have no plural: one *apparatus* and two *apparatus*. And if this isn't complicated enough, there is yet another group that isn't Latin at all but Greek disguised as Latin. This group includes our old favourites *platypus* and *octopus*. So what is the plural of *platypus*? This word comes from the Greek *platy* 'broad' and *pous* 'foot' (later Latinized to *pus*). This Latinizing encouraged the idea that the plural should be *platypi*. But really if you want to be impressive with your plurals then strictly speaking you should refer to *platypodes* and *octopodes*. Frankly, I'm quite content with *platypuses*, although I notice conservationists and naturalists who are into such things tend towards *platypus* as the plural.

Occasionally, foreign plurals get reanalysed as singular nouns. *Media* and *data* are examples of this. We end up not pluralizing them. Hence, examples like 'The media is responsible'. In fact, what we have here is a split. *Media* refers to mass communication; it's a collective singular referring to newspapers, radio and television. These are now all separate *mediums*. Splits of this kind also occur in the plurals. *Stadiums* might refer to sporting facilities and *stadia* the stages of a disease in medical contexts; *antennas* on TVs and *antennae* on bugs.

Brainchilds or brainchildren?

If you had more than one inspirational thought, would they be *brainchildren*? Surely not, but then I'm not sure that *brainchilds* is very much more elegant. It is the same problem as when we *deepfroze-deepfreezed* the pizzas.

While the majority of nouns happily fall in line, some tenaciously cling to their earlier plural forms like *children, lives, leaves* and *teeth.* But when these occur in compounds, they tend to be regularized. For example, *lives* versus *still-lifes, leaves* versus *cloverleafs* (if we're talking about freeway intersections) or *Silverleafs* (white poplars). Then there are the famous *Maple Leafs*, the Canadian ice-hockey team (known affectionately as the *Leafs*). If we were to form the equivalent hockey team here in Australia they would have to be the *Gum Leafs*, not the *Gum Leaves. Tooth-teeth* of course, but *Sabretooths* (a kind of tiger) and probably also *sweet-tooths*. There are *Pink Foots* (a type of bird), *flatfoots* (policemen), *Micky Mouses* and *computer mouses* too.

So back, then, to the problem of more than one brainchild. Perhaps it's because these brilliant products of thought so rarely occur in the plural that both *brainchilds* and *brainchildren* sound equally maladroit. But if you are fortunate enough to have more than one idea at a time, might I recommend that you speak of brainwaves.

Now, if you're someone who is disturbed by language change and insist, for example, that *data* and *media* remain plural, then you'd better be consistent. Strictly speaking, so should *agenda* and *stamina*. Where then do you draw the line with your scholarly plurals – *traumata* as the plural of *trauma*? Argue this way and before long you're once more in deep water.

Wharfs – wharves?

Yet another plural problem: is it *wharfs* or *wharves*? This is not a straightforward question, and as with most things to do with the wharf, English-speaking nations appear pretty much divided on the issue.

But let's begin at the beginning. Here we have a group of exceptional nouns that show an alternation in the final consonant of their singular and plural stems. Examples like *leaf-leaves; oath-oaths* and *house-houses* all show a voiceless final consonant in their singular forms and a voiced consonant in their plural forms. (Unfortunately our spelling does not always reflect this alternation.) Once again we're dealing with leftover rubble, this time of a previous pronunciation in Old English. Once upon a time, voiceless sounds like 's' and 'f' always became voiced when they were flanked by vowels. This rule is no longer a living part of our language. So what we've been doing over the past few hundred years is regularizing these forms so they fit in better with what is now the usual rule for plural formation. The plural of *cliff*, for example, is no longer *cleves*. We are starting to hear *oaths* and *paths* now with a voiceless 'th'. People even talk about *halfs* rather than *halves*, although generally speaking with a different meaning in mind. *Halfs* can refer to reduced-price tickets, for example. We can say something like one and two halfs (= one adult's and two children's tickets). Sometimes this sort of thing triggers a split – *wolves* are aggressive, erect-eared dog-like mammals while *wolfs* are of the human variety.

OK. So where does that leave us with *wharf*? The plural would originally have been *wharves* – but, like other words where the consonant in question occurs after an 'r' sound, the regularizing took place very early. Forms like *wharfs*, *turfs* and *scarfs* have been around for several centuries. Again it's analogy – *wharf* is to *wharfs* as *cough* is to *coughs*. The important thing about analogical change is the elimination of untidy irregular forms like *wharves* and *cleves*. It's one of the most powerful forces behind grammatical change.

According to the usual direction of analogical change, regular forms like *wharfs*, and also *turfs* and *scarfs*, should win out over *wharves*, *turves* and *scarves*. But in Australia at least, *wharf* has done a bit of a U-turn and *wharves* now appears to be gaining ground. This kind of about-face is interesting. Even more interesting are forms that go completely against the predicted path of change as in the case of *dwarf*. The plural of *dwarf* was always *dwarfs*. The original form of *dwarf* was *dwerg*, which was pronounced with a final guttural 'ch' sound. With sound change we lost this sound and in words like *dwerg* it changed to 'f'. But this change took place well and truly after we had lost the pronunciation rule that changed 'f' to 'v' between vowels. Hence, the plural of *dwarf* was always *dwarfs*, pure and simple. So how come *dwarves*? Good question. The rule that gives us the *wharf-wharves* pattern is dead and buried – it shouldn't gain new recruits this way. *Dwarves* is going directly against the predicted path of change. One suggestion is that *dwarfs* changed because of words like *elves* and *wolves*. As Hans Hock has pointed out, we read about *dwarves* in fairytales, in the same context as we read about *elves* and *wolves* – perhaps we feel these irregular plurals are particularly appropriate for fairytale or fantasy characters. Tolkien must have felt that way for *dwarves* is how he chose to refer to the ancient people in his tales, even though as a philologist he knew this was historically wrong.

Linguists are always trying to impose some order and restraint on analogical processes, and are forever dreaming up laws to govern the ways in which languages can change. They have been successful, but only up to a point. Every now and again the language does its own thing and meanders off in completely the opposite direction. It's the human factor again. As a kind of 'wild card' in the game of change, it makes it impossible to predict the paths (should that be *paths* or *padhs*?) of development, even one as well-trodden as the path along which our plurals are regularized.

So back to my original question: what is the plural of *wharf*? Well, at the risk of sounding feeble: either will do. The tug of war between *wharves* and *wharfs* has been going on for centuries. At the moment it looks as if *wharves* might have a bit more rope, but who knows?

Hunting plurals!

Occasionally, bits of old linguistic rubble get a new lease of life. Take, for example, those exceptional nouns like 'sheep' that take no ending at all in the plural. This is the so-called 'zero plural' – one *sheep* and two *sheep*. Zero plurals were once much more widespread, but like other irregular plurals have gradually been eradicated. Oddly though, one group of nouns suddenly went right against this trend, abandoned their regular *-s* ending and joined the *sheep* type nouns. Whereas once we talked about *fowls* and *boars*, they now usually appear with no ending at all – *fowl* and *boar* are both singular and plural. It seems this is a hangover from a kind of 'huntingspeak' of late medieval and Early Modern English. These exceptions are animals that are, or can be, hunted. For example, even though most of us thankfully aren't likely to, we might imagine saying something like 'I shot six elephant'.

As the linguists Hock and Joseph argue, the model for this change was probably the word *deer*. It never took a plural ending, and being in the past the quintessential animal of the hunt, it seems to have been able to attract others – zero plural became a grammatical routine that came to be associated with hunting jargon. Bear in mind, too, that it was during this time that curious collectives appeared like *a skulk of foxes* and *a pride of lions*. Most of these colourful terms grew up in the context of hunting and, like the zero plurals, also became an earmark of huntingspeak. Hunting was, after all, associated with the British gentry – commoners were excluded – and linguistic curiosities helped define the gang. Nice evidence for this theory is the fact that the words *deer* and *fowl* once had very broad meanings. *Deer* referred to animals of any kind and *fowl* to all birds. Both have narrowed to mean specifically animals of the hunt.

But what about *sheep* and *swine*? They don't take a plural ending, but they're hardly animals of the hunt. These words have an inherited zero plural – they never took an ending; they're survivors. The question is, why weren't they levelled and brought into line with the other plurals? Maybe it's because we don't think of them individually, but as collections; so *sheep* and *swine* get lumped in with collectives like *cattle*. A more serious exception is *fish*. The plural *fishes* was found right into the seventeenth century. So why do we now eat six *fish* for dinner, not six *fishes*? Perhaps it's simply that fishing is a type of hunting; so these creatures pattern like *deer* and *fowl*. They also swim in schools and are often caught collectively in a net; so they might also pattern like cattle.

The tale of requited love

Jack Winter in the piece 'How I Met My Wife' begins his torrid tale of requited love thus:

It had been a rough day, so when I walked into the party I was very chalant, despite my efforts to appear gruntled and consolate. I was furling my wieldy umbrella for the coat check when I saw her standing alone in a corner. She was a descript person, a woman in a state of total array. Her hair was kempt, her clothing shevelled, and she moved in a gainly way. I wanted desperately to meet her, but I knew I'd have to make bones about it, since I was travelling cognito. Beknownst to me, the hostess, whom I could see both hide and hair of, was very proper, so it would be skin off my nose if anything bad happened [. . .] Only toward and heard-of behaviour would do.

The humour here derives in part from words like *shevelled*, *gruntled* and *kempt* – words that exist in Modern English only in their complex forms; in other words, with some sort of affix attached. These all appear to be negative: *dishevelled*, *disgruntled* and *unkempt*. In fact, this may not always be the case. Negative markers can be intensifiers (as in *impassive* and *inflammable*). The *dis-* of *disgruntled* is an example. This word comes from the verb *gruntle*. Originally based on the noise of a pig, it meant quite literally 'to make a little grunt', like a small pig. In the late sixteenth century *gruntle* meant 'to grumble, complain' and the *dis-* in *disgruntled* had an intensifying force. If you were *disgruntled* then you were truly *gruntled*; in other words, really cheesed off.

For some reason the simple forms, like *gruntled* without the affix, occasionally drop out of the language. Take the wonderful word *gormless*. It derives from the original noun *gorm/gaum* meaning something like 'understanding' – hence *gormless* meant 'lacking understanding'. Once upon a time you could do all sorts of things with *gorm*. For example, you could *have gorm*; you could *gorm* or 'stare vacantly'; you could even be *gormlike*, 'having an intelligent look', as in 'She were a poor friendless wench but honest and gaumlike'. Similarly, people once could be *kempt*, that is, 'nicely groomed'. They could be *corrigible*, 'able to be corrected'. People were once replete with *ruth* or *list*; in other words 'full of compassion' or 'full of desire'. And energetic people were those with loads of *ert*, in which case they were probably *wieldy* ('agile') too.

Occasionally you find complex forms like *inept* or *dishevelled* that never had their simple counterparts *ept* and *(s)hevelled*. It might be that we borrowed the words wholesale, say from Latin or French, and their negative prefixes *in-* or *dis-* were part of the package. *Ept* is one such word. It derives from Latin *ineptus*, meaning 'unsuitable, tasteless'. Similarly, Old French *deschevele* meaning 'stripped of hair' came into English intact as *dishevelled*, meaning 'without head-dress' and later 'unkempt, untidy'. Neither of these words had a simple positive form in English. So people then sometimes invent a word to fill this vacancy. It's a kind of backformation – analogy working in the opposite direction. If there's a negative, then surely there must be a positive. And if there isn't, well, let's create one. Some time during the middle of the nineteenth century speakers took *inept* and created the positive counterpart *ept*. However, they took their time about it: this was about four hundred years after *inept* first made its appearance in English. But now we have people who are *ept*; in other words, 'competent, adroit'. I've also occasionally heard speakers use *shevelled* to mean 'neat, tidy'. This hasn't yet made it into the dictionaries, but one term that has gained acceptance is the verb *dishevel*. If there is an adjective *dishevelled*, then surely there is the related verb *to dishevel*. So we use backformation to fill the vacancy.

And you can be sure this tidying-up process will continue. Now, some speakers might make bones about it. It's probably evitable, it's true. There may even be two ways about it, too. But one thing's certain and that is – whenever it happens it'll be skin off someone's nose.

Sound Symbolism

That which we call a rose
By any other name would smell as sweet
William Shakespeare, *Romeo and Juliet*, Act II, sc. ii

Words are symbolic. There's no natural or necessary connection between the shape of a word and its meaning. Shakespeare was right: 'that which we call a rose, by any other name would smell as sweet'. Yet, over time, symbols can stop being symbolic. Recall the story of a little girl who, on seeing a pig for the first time, exclaims just how fitting the name is for such a filthy creature! It is as if the word 'pig' has somehow come to communicate the essential nature of this animal. When speakers make associations between the sounds of words and meaning, they then start to extend this connection to other areas. Again, it has to do with our sensitivity to untidiness in the language garden.

Ugh! Blah! Eek! Uh-oh! Phwoaaarr!

English is full of words that try to copy noises in the exterior world. Look at brand names on cereal packets – *crunchies*, *puffs*, *pops*, *smacks*. They sound crisp. A rooster's crow is remarkably similar across the languages of the world. English roosters go *cockadoodledoo*, German *kikeriki* and Japanese something like *kokekokko*. These sorts of words are largely limited to imitations of natural sounds. Yet, even these so-called natural sounds are often just as conventional as ordinary words. English frogs go *ribbit ribbit* or *croak croak* and German frogs go *quak quak* – so much for imitation!

Words symbolic of sound also include those imitative words known as 'interjections', or what we once called 'ejaculations'. These refer to words that stand for those involuntary noisy responses we make to express some sort of emotion. They include a range of well-bred, dignified utterances like *oh*, *tut-tut*, *ho-ho*, *hoorah* and *bravo* – ones that are likely to make it onto the lists of interjections you find in grammar books. They also include less dignified curiosities like *ugh*, *blah*, *eek*, *uh-oh* and *phwoaaarr* of which comic books are treasure troves.

Clearly, outbursts like *ugh* and *phwoaaarr* don't fit the normal pronunciation patterns of English. So these words always start life as rather inadequate attempts to represent in writing the actual sound being made. If you think about it, *ho-ho*, *yuk-yuk*, *guffaw* and *tee-hee* don't sound much like actual laughter. *Fie*, *faugh*, *bah*, *pish*, *pshaw* and *humph* don't sound like the noises we make when we're annoyed or disgusted, either. But over time, as these written forms become more and more familiar, they are conventionalized as ordinary vocabulary items. So, when we encounter *ha-ha* or *haw-haw* in a text, it seems a perfectly normal representation of laughter. *Yackety-yak* seems a perfectly good way to represent someone talking. These words then start functioning as ordinary nouns and verbs. For example, 'They *ummed* and *ahhed*'; 'She *hemmed* and *hawed*'; 'He *pooh-poohed* my memo'. Words like *burp* and *hiccough* started life this way – written representations of our automatic noises (genteel or otherwise) that then became regular parts of speech.

Once these expressions develop their own spelling pronunciations, these pronunciations can remove them even further from the original noises they're supposed to represent. *Tut-tut* and *tisk-tisk* don't sound much like the curious clicking noise we make to express impatience or disapproval. Yet *tisk-tisk* now seems a reasonable way to represent this noise. What's more, so completely do we come to accept these as somehow natural, they then become the actual noises we make. We might say *tisk-tisk* when we're ticking someone off. Some of us actually do say *yum* when eating something mouth-watering, even though this word is nothing like the sound of smacking lips. Many of us say *ouch* when we bang our thumb with a hammer – probably along with a few other less well-bred vocalizations. *Ouch* started life as a rather inadequate representation of the shriek or squeal we make when we're in pain, or probably what a German might make in pain, since *ouch* is assumed to be borrowed from German.

When you consider the range of bizarre noises we release in response to emotional situations, we could never hope to represent them accurately with speech sounds. Yet, somehow with time, these sounds come to be quite appropriate.

'They seem to fill my head with ideas'

Individual sounds aren't supposed to have meaning, but we behave as if they do. We are always looking for some sort of meaningful connection between sounds and the outside world. We constantly make associations between sound and sense.

It often happens, for example, that we start to associate certain sounds or sound sequences with particular meanings, and these are then used in the formation of new, similar words. The term for these sound sequences is 'phonestheme'. Phonesthemes are either the beginnings of words, like 'tw-', or their rhymes, like '-ash'. They symbolize a certain meaning, although sometimes it's difficult to pin down exactly what it is. Just as Alice said on hearing the poem 'Jabberwocky' – 'Somehow it seems to fill my head with ideas, only I don't exactly know what they are'. For instance, recently I had cause to check the thesaurus for synonyms for 'unchaste, wanton'. Is it a coincidence that so many of these words began with 'l' – *licentious*, *lascivious*, *loose*, *lubricous*, *lecherous*, *libidinous*, *lustful*, *lickerish* and *lewd*, to name a few? Somehow this luscious, liquidy *l*-sound seems well suited to convey the sense of wantonness. Words commonly group this way, sharing both meaning and a vague resemblance of sound. So the sounds we use to stand for things might start off being arbitrary, but over time the arbitrariness often falls away.

Look at words that rhyme with *stodge*: *splodge* (as in trudging through mud), *podge* (short, stout, thick-set), *wodge* (a bulky lumpy mass). There's something about this *-odge* rhyme. All these words denote something solid, bulky, lumpy, and this has been the inspiration of many new words – like *stodge*, in fact. How beautifully *stodge* conveys the thick, heavy, stiff, starchy, lethally fattening food so well known in English cuisine. Don't get me wrong – I'm a fan of stodge. In a world of low-fat, low-cholesterol, lite-this and diet-that, stodge has a special place in my heart. It's also a wonderful example of how we manipulate language for our own ends.

English has lots of these phonesthemes. The following verbs show a characteristic *-ump* rhyme and seem to denote 'heavy fall': *bump*, *clump*, *dump*, *flump*, *jump*, *slump*, *thump*. Nouns with the same rhyme denote some sort of 'round protuberance': *bump*, *chump*, *clump*, *dump*, *hump*, *lump*, *mump(s)*, *rump*, *stump*. An initial 'sw-' conveys a meaning something like 'a smooth, wide-reaching movement, probably in an arc formation': *swagger*, *swash*, *swat*, *sway*, *sweep*, *swerve*, *swig*, *swill*, *swing*, *swipe*, *swirl*, *swish*. The 'gl-' words often convey brightness and light: *glare*, *gleam*, *glimmer*, *glint*, *glisten*, *glitter*, *gloss*, *glow*. *Fl-* conveys 'sudden violent movement': *flame*, *flap*, *flare*, *flash*, *flop*, *flounce*, *flurry*. *Sn-* conveys something unpleasant, although it's often hard to pinpoint the nastiness (you'll notice many of these words have associations with the nose, too): *snaffle*, *snout*, *snag*, *snail*, *snake*, *snare*, *snarl*, *snort*, *sneak*, *sneer*, *sneeze*, *snipe*, *snivel*, *snot*, *snoop*, *sneeze*, *sniff* and so on – I think you get the idea.

Sometimes it's possible to find reasons for these sound-symbolic associations. For example, many languages show a strong connection between sounds produced with the tongue high in the mouth (like 'ee') and the meaning 'small'; by comparison sounds made with the tongue low in the mouth suggest 'largeness'. Contrast words like *teeny-weeny*, *itsy-bitsy*, *wee* and even *little* with words like *large*, *vast* and *grand*. A *chip* (of wood) sounds smaller than a *chop*. So does a *slit* when compared to a *slot* – or a *dint* compared to a *dent*. 'Many a mickle makes a muckle' is an old saying that's virtually disappeared. While we mightn't know what a mickle is any more, I'm sure most people feel it's smaller than a muckle. Is it a coincidence that when we want to make *little* sound even smaller we make it *leetle*; that is, we raise the tongue even higher? This is the sound that crops up in stereotypically female names, too (think of the rather overly feminine *Mimi* and *Fifi*) and is part of the diminutive ending in pet names like *Shelly* and *Katie*. When we produce that 'ee' sound we only have a very tiny opening in the mouth and this matches its meaning. Some have suggested that this connection has come about because small vocal tracts are possessed by smaller, weaker and less threatening beings.

Finally, there is one context where speakers will always sense a link between certain sounds and what they stand for: the area of taboo. When it comes to tabooed expressions, speakers behave as if there were a very real connection between the physical shape of the words and their taboo sense. This is exactly why taboo terms are often said to be unpleasant or ugly-sounding, and why they are miscalled 'dirty words'. It also explains their remarkable ability to 'chill the blood and raise gooseflesh', as Henry Wyld writing early last century put it. These words are felt to be intrinsically nasty, and that's what makes them so very powerful.

Jupes, jumps and jumpers

Someone once asked me where the word 'jumper' comes from. Is it associated with the verb *jump* meaning 'to spring clear of the ground'? And why is it that *jumper* refers to different items of clothing in different parts of the English-speaking world?

The original word was *jupe*. It comes from the earlier Spanish word for some kind of long woollen Moorish garment and would originally have been Arabic. *Jupe* came into English via French during the Middle Ages (late 1200s). When it first appeared it referred to a loose-fitting jacket or tunic, probably made of wool and worn by men. This word *jupe* is now obsolete, but you could still find it well into the nineteenth century. The Oxford English Dictionary has a reference to 'frightful men clad in jupes of coarse wool'.

Some time during the seventeenth century a remodelled version of *jupe* appeared in competition – *jump*. So, why might speakers have felt moved to change *jupe* to *jump*? Unfamiliar-looking words are often remodelled to look more familiar, and there is no doubt that English is full of *-ump* words like *bump*, *clump* and *hump*. Perhaps this was the motivation. Certainly, *-ump* nouns typically convey 'roundness' of some sort. Could it be that the sound of the word *jump* was felt to be appropriate for such a baggy, loose-fitting sort of tunic? It seems feasible that a bit of wordplay might have been involved here. Around that time the word also appeared in the plural and could mean something more general like 'clothing' – one's Sunday *jumps* were one's Sunday best. It was extended as well to women's undergarments, where it referred to some kind of bodice fitted to the bust. The Oxford English Dictionary has references to 'slatterns in jumps'.

The word *jumper* as we know it today didn't appear until the nineteenth century. At that time it still meant a kind of loose outer jacket of the type worn by seamen and labourers. A kind of smock, it became the distinctive garment of the early Australian gold-miner – perhaps you've encountered poetic references to the generous hearts of Australian diggers beating beneath mudbespattered jumpers. Presumably, the word shifted to mean the kind of woolly pullover that we think of today when the clothing item itself changed. In the United States interestingly, it didn't shift and *jumper* still refers to a kind of pinafore or smock. But the question is: having changed the word from *jupe* to *jump*, why did speakers then change it again from *jump* to *jumper*. Could there have been a link with the other *jumper* – one who jumps? Possibly. After all, we do have *rompers* or *romper suits*. I wonder, too, whether *trousers*, *knickers* and *bloomers* mightn't have been an inspiration. Admittedly, these are usually pairs of things (and jumpers don't come in pairs). Nonetheless, the extension of *jump* to *jumper* could easily be a case where an unusual word is remodelled to bring it in line with other associated words.

There is still, of course, the *jumpsuit* without the *-er* ending – a kind of outer garment covering both body and legs, close-fitting if worn by adults, but more baggy if worn by children. It's tempting to trace this directly back to the original *jump* or the *jump coat* of the seventeenth century; in other words, a relic of original French *jupe*. But our modern-day *jumpsuit* derives directly from the verb *to jump* – the original *jumpsuit* was just that, a parachutist's one-piece garment. This is not to be confused with *jumper suits* which **can** be traced back to *jupe*. It is all very confusing, as you can see.

Even the simple verb *jump* is a mystery. Most dictionaries suggest it's simply onomatopoeic; that is, involving the 'ump' rhyme again. But what was its inspiration? As it so often turns out with etymology, even the most mundane-looking little words can have obscure and complicated histories.

Cosmetic 'dead-heading'

Speakers sometimes change the pronunciation of expressions simply so they resemble other words which are somehow associated in meaning. Our English word *father* is an example. Originally it was *fæder*, but since the sixteenth century we've been pronouncing it *father*. Why? On analogy with related words like *brother*, 'd' changed to 'th'. Similarly, early English *femelle* was replaced by *female* under the influence of the word *male*. The curious little word *yep* from *yes* was remodelled to be more like *nope*, the emphatic form of *no*. Modern English *groin* should really be *grine* – but *grine* was contaminated by the body part *loin* and accordingly *grine* was changed to *groin* to be more like it.

This kind of change is extremely common with anything naturally occurring in a list or sequence. Numerals are particularly susceptible. English *four* should begin with 'wh', but the word changed in anticipation of the following number *five*. It's not only English speakers who do this sort of thing. The Latin word for 'five' should be *pinque*, but it comes out as *quinque* because of the preceding numeral 'four' – *quattuor*. Examples like these occur in languages all around the world.

It can happen that a number of words are affected in the same way and end up forming a family of similar-sounding words that then attracts new members. Remember the *-odge* rhyme? Words like *podge*, conjuring up something solid, bulky and lumpy, have been the inspiration for new words like *stodge*. For the sort of thick, heavy indigestible food epitomized by the pork pie and lardy cake, *stodge* is made to measure. Already existing words that have something of a bulky sense then change to form part of this '-odge' family. Look at *wodge* and *bodge*. Both words changed their shape: *wodge* probably grew out of *wad* and *bodge* out of *botch*. So much for arbitrariness!

Speakers can also shift the **meaning** of words because of the way they sound. We can sympathize with the child who describes *flagrant* as 'the way flowers smell'. And some sounds seem particularly well suited to certain meanings. For example, *hoi polloi* (from Greek) means 'the rabble', but many younger speakers now understand it to mean the opposite, or 'aristocratic persons, the high born'. This shift has presumably come about through association with words like *high*, *haughty* and *hoity toity*, meaning something like 'supercilious'. It's interesting that the meaning of *hoity toity* itself changed in precisely this way. Derived from repetition of the now obsolete verb *hoit* 'to behave boisterously', *hoity toity* originally meant 'riotous giddy behaviour', which is nothing like the meaning we have for it today. It shifted to mean 'stuck up behaviour' because it collided with *haughty*. And now it's influencing *hoi polloi* in precisely the same way.

In the case of *titivate* and *titillate* we again have two similar-sounding words that, not surprisingly, are clashing. *Titivate* originally meant 'to tidy up', but some dictionaries now give the additional meaning 'to tickle, excite agreeably' (although they label it incorrect). Clearly, *titivate* is in the process of taking on the meaning of similar-sounding *titillate* 'to excite'. It's not surprising which way the transfer goes, as *titillate* is by far the more common word. But, probably more importantly, *titillate* has strong associated meanings to do with exciting bodily lust (with the reinforcement of *tits*). If there is one law of semantic change, it's that risqué meanings will come to dominate and drive out other meanings.

These shifts start life as malapropisms, where speakers mix up words because of similarities in pronunciation. An inappropriate word is used in place of another that resembles it in sound or spelling (there might be a vague similarity in meaning). A journalist writing in the *Saturday Age*, for example, described how speculation was 'ripe' about the return of former ministers to the front bench. What the writer meant, of course, was 'rife'. In this case the sense is vaguely similar – *rife* meaning 'of common occurrence, well provided with' and *ripe* meaning 'ready to reap, fully developed'. A famous malapropism occurs in the Watergate tapes where Nixon is talking to Ehrlichman about the possibility of dumping John Dean. Ehrlichman suggests spreading the word that Dean is 'a piranha'. As a Washington newspaper editorial later noted: was he really suggesting that Dean was a particularly voracious South American freshwater fish, or did he mean a *pariah*, 'a person rejected or despised'?

The term malapropism comes from Mrs Malaprop, a character in Sheridan's famous play *The Rivals* (from *mal* 'ill' + *a* 'to' + *propos* 'purpose'). Mrs Malaprop had a chronic problem with

Until stocks last!

Some changes are the result of a compromise between two or more competing forms. Sometimes they occur as one-off slips of the tongue; sometimes they are more long-lasting. When a speaker says *irregardless*, the word *regardless* has been influenced by the word *irrespective*. It can happen with longer expressions, too – a speaker might say for instance *near miss* (which is a kind of blend of *close miss* and *near hit*). A shop in my neighbourhood frequently has the rather curious sign in its window 'Until stocks last' – presumably a blend of the two competing phrases 'while stocks last' and 'until stocks run out'.

words and was famous for coming out with outlandish examples like 'as headstrong as an allegory on the banks of the Nile'. Such mixups are commonplace in everyday language: *mitigate* for *militate*, *prodigy* for *protégé*, *prostate* for *prostrate* and *economically depraved* for *economically deprived*. Sometimes the mistake is driven by linguistic snobbery: the desire to use a more impressive-sounding word like *enormity* instead of the more mundane *enormousness*. The result can be a shift in meaning. Compare what is currently happening to *epicentre* (used in place of *centre*).

If you are incensed by these misuses, you might like to pause for a moment and think about golden oldies like *fortuitous* and *fruition*. *Fortuitous* originally meant 'occurring by chance' but shifted to its current meaning of 'fortunate' because of its similarity with the word *fortune*. *Fruition* comes from the Latin word for 'enjoy' and originally meant 'enjoyment'. The association with fruit changed all that.

It all goes well

Folk etymology is the name given to a specific kind of malapropism. This type stems from a desire to make more familiar a word or an expression that for some reason has become unfamiliar. We replace opaque words (perhaps foreign in origin or just plain obscure) with something similar but more transparent. Usually there's some meaning connection too; in other words, an added semantic motivation. What we're doing is getting rid of bits of language we consider meaningless. More dead-heading!

Take an expression like *it augurs well* 'it promises a good outcome'. In our English, *augur* doesn't mean much of anything any more – most of us have given up the habit of interpreting omens by the appearance of entrails or the behaviour patterns of birds. So it's understandable that we replace this expression with something more familiar-looking, such as *it all goes well.* Nowadays, we're more likely to *wind our way home* than *wend our way home.* The verb *wend* 'to go' has dropped out of general use, so we replace it with a more familiar verb (justified because of an association with *winding* roads). *Running the gauntlet* has nothing to do with mailed gloves or gauntlets. The phrase was originally *run the gatlop*, a ghastly kind of punishment where prisoners stripped to the waist had to run between two rows of soldiers, forming a lane or gat, while being struck with knotted cords or sticks. *Gat* is the same word that appears in placenames like *Highgate*, but it fell out of use. Of course, *lope* 'to run' isn't all that usual either. So, by the time it reached bullying English public school speakers, the expression had been remodelled into *running the gauntlet* – reinforced, presumably, by the brutality of the medieval tournament.

Our language is full of such examples: *short shift* for *short shrift*, *flaunt the law* for *flout the law*, *one foul swoop* for *one fell swoop*, *tenderhooks* for *tenterhooks*, *wrecking havoc* for *wreaking havoc.* These are all expressions containing curious words that have otherwise disappeared from ordinary usage. So we turn them into something that makes more sense to us. And we can usually justify it on the basis of meaning: *chaise longue* to *chaise lounge* (because we lounge on it), *coleslaw* to *coldslaw* (it *is* a type of cold salad), *Alzheimer's Disease* to *Old Timer's Disease* (a mental deterioration generally occurring in old age), *angnail* to *hangnail* (well, they do hang!) and there was the student in my classes who came up with *rope learning* for *rote learning*, probably on the basis of *learn the ropes.*

Sometimes people do this deliberately for humorous effect, as is probably the case with the Australian expression *cast nasturtiums (on)* 'to slander'. This is a remodelling of the phrase *cast aspersions (on)*. The name for the orange-yellow flowers is probably more user-friendly than the word *aspersions*, but it creates a comic image too. To indicate just how complicated things can become, speakers have further manipulated this expression and created *tossing flowers* as in *Don't toss me no flowers*, or 'don't cast a slur upon me'! Without knowing its history, etymologists attempting to reconstruct a motivation for this phrase would have a difficult time of it.

Occasionally speakers reinterpret the boundaries within words to give their structure more meaning. This can have quite an impact on the vocabulary. Australian English provides a nice example with its innovative *chino* (*ccino*?) compounds. It so happens that the first part of the Italian word *cappuccino* collides, at least in pronunciation, with English *cup*. This is all the encouragement local speakers need for a bit of inventive restructuring. Cafes all over the place are now advertising, in addition to *cappuccino*, *muguccino* (cappuccino coffee served in a mug), *frothucino*, *bubaccino* or *bambinoccino* (for children – milk froth with chocolate on top), *chococcino* (frothy hot chocolate), *melloccino* or *malloccino* (a giant *latte* topped with marshmallow froth) and *skinnyccino* and *caroccino* (for the health conscious). Some cafes now go as far as offering a *cup o' chino*. This kind of word gaming is also a type of folk etymology. In this instance, speakers have rewritten the history of *cappuccino* (from Italian *cappuccio* 'hood') and in a sense provided it with a new etymology.

You might well laugh at these innovations and write them off as linguistic gimmickry, but speakers have been doing this sort of thing for centuries. Take one of the golden oldies like *hamburger*. We borrowed the word *hamburger* from German (as the adjective formed from the placename Hamburg). The first part of the word happens to correspond to a type of meat in English and the word was 'misinterpreted' as a compound *ham* + *burger* (even though there was never any ham involved). This false analysis has given rise to a spate of new compounds like *Aussie lamburger*, *eggburger*, *cheeseburger*, *chickenburger*, *steakburger*, *vegeburger*, even *burger bits* (for the dog). Similar examples are *spamwich* and *eggwich*, though they haven't caught on in the same way – maybe because they don't have quite the same culinary caché.

Christmas blunders

Mistletoe is a parasitic plant that grows on trees, particularly oaks. It was especially revered by the ancient Druids, and later came to be hung as a Christmas decoration. During the seventeenth century a custom developed whereby those caught standing under the mistletoe had to kiss. The word has absolutely nothing to do with toes, even though this might seem a reasonable assumption given the look of the plant, especially when it's hung as decoration. *Mistletoe* in fact derives from an Old English compound made up of the word for the plant *mistel* plus *tān* 'twig'. There are no sound laws which will change *tān* into *toe*. Speakers simply did it, no doubt justifying it on the basis of the appearance of the plant.

You might even think the word *reindeer* has something to do with *reins*, the long narrow straps used, for example, to guide Santa's reindeer. You'd be right now, of course, because we've remodelled it to make it look like that. But it comes from the Scandinavian word for this animal, *hreinn* in combination with *dyr* 'deer' (originally, *deer* was a general word for 'animal').

Folk etymology, like so many linguistic processes we see, stems from our desire to make more familiar any word or expression that seems to us unusual. Once again, we're simply nipping off the awkward bits.

As a final example, consider what we have done with the word *bikini*. It derives from the name of a Pacific Ocean atoll, but the first part of the word coincides with the prefix *bi-* in English meaning 'two'. The swimsuit also happens to be made in two pieces. This subsequently inspired speakers to form new creations like *monokini* or *unikini* (a single piece bathing suit), *dental floss kini* (one held together by something resembling dental floss), *tankini* (two piece with a tank top) and the old *high-cut kini*. (I owe my knowledge here to Professor Barry Blake, who over the years has made a keen study of the 'kini morph'.)

What is Correct English?

A proper garden might be known
Geoffrey Taylor, *Some Nineteenth-Century Gardeners*, 1951

Linguists view language as a natural phenomenon – something that evolves and adapts. Others may view it as an art form – or as something to be preserved and cherished. No wonder different camps approach English in different ways. Gardeners of the eighteenth and nineteenth centuries also fell into two groups over the question of the 'proper garden'. Was it a work of nature or a work of art? Underpinning this question is the assumption that there exists some accepted measure or standard by which we can recognize what is proper – an assumption that might be applied to types of etiquette, but not to gardens and certainly not to languages.

'Perplexity to be disentangled'

For centuries people have been trying to clean up English and stop it from changing. But it's probably the eighteenth century that will go down as the golden age of linguistic control, of prescription and protection. In 1755 there appeared the first real English dictionary. Its maker, Samuel Johnson, was clear in his aim: to rid the language of 'barbarous corruptions, licentious idioms and colloquial barbarisms'. Like others of his time, he couldn't help contrasting English with the Classical languages of Greek and Latin – and certainly by comparison English did seem unregulated and unrefined. Of course, these Classical languages existed purely as written languages, which meant that they lacked the natural flux and variance of living, breathing languages like English. Against these ossified paragons of linguistic virtue, poor old English did come across badly. Not one ever to mince his words, Johnson described his language in the preface to his dictionary as being 'copious without order, and energetick without rules [. . .] perplexity to be disentangled, and confusion to be regulated'. The cry was up at this time for some sort of academy to do a bit of regulating, polishing and refining and to prevent the language from slipping into further decline. Writers fretted that their works would not be understood by future generations, if they couldn't stop the changes. Countries like France and Italy had their academies – English looked even more unruly without one.

Jonathan Swift, author of *Gulliver's Travels*, was responsible in 1712 for what is still one of the greatest pieces of complaint literature of all time: *A Proposal for Correcting, Improving and Ascertaining the English Tongue.* He was one of the most passionate proponents for a regulating body to be set up to 'ascertain' the English language; in other words, to determine correct usage and settle the language for good. He wrote: 'if [the English tongue] were once refined to a certain Standard, perhaps there might be Ways to fix it forever [. . .] I see no absolute Necessity why any Language should be perpetually changing.' Despite enthusiastic support for such an academy, nothing ever came of it. Nonetheless, large numbers of regulating handbooks did start to be published, setting out how the language should and should not be used. Following Johnson's dictionary came more dictionaries, and in the second half of the century grammar books abounded. Notions of 'right' and 'wrong' in English grammar became hot topics, and we owe many of our current prescriptions to the grammatical debates of this time.

Certainly, writers like Swift were correct in one thing. There is a real drawback to language change and that is that wonderful literature of the past does become difficult and, given enough time, even unintelligible to us. The language used by characters in a Jane Austen novel may not be strikingly different to ours, except perhaps in the matter of style, but Shakespeare – well, that is another matter. His prose and verse take work, and there are pitfalls. Some of the language might look familiar but must be understood quite differently. We must know that when Romeo says of Juliet 'I am too fond', he doesn't mean that he was devotedly attached to her, but was foolish. When Shakespeare writes in one of his sonnets of 'sad mortality', we have to know that *sad* here doesn't mean 'causing grief' but something like 'steadfast' or 'constant'. As for Geoffrey Chaucer – even the well-known lines from the Prologue of *The Canterbury Tales* appear quite foreign to us now.

> Whan that Aprille with his shoures soote
> The droghte of March hath perced to the roote
> And bathed euery veyne in swich licour
> Of which vertu engendred is the flour.

And from a thousand years ago a simple remedy for joint pain is totally incomprehensible: 'Wiþ lið wærce genim culfran tord and gate tord'. It's not even recognizably English. Perhaps we don't particularly need to be able to read a tenth-century remedy, especially one that recommends rubbing excrement of dove and goat into the painful limb. But something like the great epic poem *Beowulf* is good literature, and this we might want to read. You can understand why writers like Jonathan Swift were so hell-bent on establishing an academy. But would you want to stop the changes, even if you could? Stop the language, or fix it forever (as Swift put it), and you also stop the kind of imaginative manipulation and wondrous creativity that we marvel at in the work of writers like Shakespeare. You can't have it both ways.

Whose standard?

Are there dialects that are linguistically superior? Our culture certainly tells us that Standard English is the best form of English. Non-standard dialects are the varieties that don't quite come up to scratch. They don't confer the same social prestige or status as the standard 'language', and they lack the backing of any army or navy (to adapt a description attributed to Max Weinreich, referring to the arsenal of prescriptive texts like dictionaries and grammars). On purely linguistic grounds, however, all dialects are equal. All have the same potential, at least, for complexity and richness of expression. Let me give an example where Standard English could gain from its non-standard relatives. (I should probably begin with some sort of linguistic health-warning – some of the pronouns that follow may shock or offend!)

Some time ago I received an interesting inquiry from someone who drew my attention to a sentence in 'The Australian Food Standards Code'. It read in part: *Concentrated orange juice* ***whose*** *volume has been reduced by the removal of water to a volume not exceeding one half of the original [. . .]* It was the pronoun *whose* in particular that the inquirer objected to. Many people dislike and therefore avoid *whose* when it refers to something inanimate. However, the only alternative Standard English can offer us is something like *orange juice, the volume of which has been reduced [. . .]* Most of you would probably agree this construction is very formal, and really quite inelegant. Perhaps you'd write it, but you certainly wouldn't say it. We've hit a little flaw in Standard English.

Our vernacular English, on the other hand, finds several ways around this tricky problem. One is the *that its* construction. For example, *orange juice* ***that its*** *volume has been reduced [. . .]* But there's another, and probably more commonly heard construction: *orange juice* ***thats*** *volume has been reduced [. . .]* *Thats* uses the regular formation of the possessive by adding *-s* to the pronoun and it nicely fills the awkward gap in our standard language.

On the matter of *orange juice that its volume has been reduced*, or alternatively *orange juice thats volume has been reduced* – it's probably no comfort to know that any squeamishness you experience on hearing these constructions has no linguistic basis at all. Both constructions are also already well attested in informal speech in Scotland, Ireland, the United States and in Australia. Quite probably they will eventually form part of the repertoire of acceptable constructions in our Standard English of the future. Our language is changing – just as it always has done, and will continue to do.

Overcorrection

Most of us trot out our 'best language' on special occasions, much as we might trot out our best china and cutlery. The notion of correct usage is very ingrained; so ingrained, in fact, that it frequently triggers something called hypercorrection. This is where speakers overuse a pattern, say, a pronunciation or a construction, and in particular one that they consider to be more proper than others. In other words, they overuse a pattern of language that has more social clout, using it in places where it isn't appropriate.

Take a simple example. Let's say you're told that dropping your aitches is a bad thing. In an effort to improve your speech you might stick an 'h' in words that have never had one, as in *hever* for *ever* or *hextra* for *extra*. You may remember Eliza Doolittle here – 'In Hertford, Hereford and Hampshire hurricanes hardly **hever** happen'. Curiously, it wasn't until the eighteenth century that dropping one's 'h's was considered improper. The new regard for 'h' would have coincided with the spread of education and the increasing importance of writing over speech. Suddenly people started to feel that if something appeared in the spelling, then it should be pronounced. This is exactly how the word *aitch*, as the name of the letter, came to get its own aitch; in other words, *haitch*. It's also how the French words we now pronounce as *herb* and *hotel* got their 'h'. In French, the 'h' would never have been pronounced. Yet people worried so much about dropping aitches that they hypercorrected and inserted them here too.

You also find this sort of thing in grammar. Many of us, as kids, would have been admonished for saying something like *Fred and me* – 'Don't say Fred and me, say Fred and I'. But it's rather more complicated than our parents let on, and there are all sorts of constructions where *Fred and I* is just not appropriate. For example, 'They saw Fred and me' or 'They gave it to Fred and me' are what the grammar books recommend. 'They saw Fred and I' or 'They gave it to Fred and I' are hypercorrections. In going out of our way to avoid the pronoun 'me' in sentences like 'Fred and me went to town', we overdo it. Hypercorrection can have historical effects, and in many varieties of English these have become usual usage.

A very clear example of this is in our current pronunciation of words like *talking* and *swimming*. In Early New English the pronunciations *talkin'* and *swimmin'* were acceptable and very widespread. Early pronunciation dictionaries make this clear. Cooper, for example, writing in 1685, states that *coughing* and *coffin* are pronounced the same (as 'coffin'); also *coming* and the spice *cummin*. Poets rhymed these words too. Swift in his rhyming couplets would rhyme, for example, *fitting* and *spit in*. Shakespeare spelt words like *napkin* and *cushion* with a final 'g'. Indeed, this pronunciation was considered acceptable right into the early 1900s. The pronunciation we now have for *talking* and *swimming* arose through hypercorrection. Presumably, it was through pressure of spelling that 'dropping g' like 'dropping h' became a bad thing. (I should emphasize we're not really dropping a 'g' here – what we're doing is changing the nature of the final nasal sound which in spelling is represented 'ng'.) Nonetheless, a dread of dropping these 'g's has caused some linguistically insecure types to even correct nouns like *chicken* and *kitchen* to *chicking* and *kitching*.

There's another kind of hypercorrection that occurs with foreign words, a sort of hyper-foreignization. Certain sounds or words can acquire exotic significance for speakers and they overuse them. The pronunciation (observed since the 1930s) of *coup de grace* as 'coo do gra' is a good example. This expression in French means literally 'blow of mercy' and in English means something like 'the final blow'. French does indeed drop consonants at the end of words; hence the pronunciation of *coup* as 'coo'. The word which follows it, however, is spelt *grace*. It has a final vowel **not** a final consonant, and so should be pronounced 'gras'. As Hock and Joseph point out, if you say 'gra' not 'gras' then you're actually pronouncing the French word for grease – so the blow of mercy becomes the blow of grease!

Linguistic perfection

If only life could be as simple as E. S. Weiner sees it in the introduction to his Oxford *Miniguide to English Usage*. 'The perfect use of language', he wrote, 'is that in which every word carries the meaning that it is intended to, no less and no more'.

If only the interpretations of hearers (or readers) and the intentions of speakers (or writers) could be a perfect match. But even the best, plainest and most simple of words can never guarantee this. Hearers and readers often attribute to wording all sorts of meanings that were never in the minds of the speakers or writers. As the linguist Fred Householder once observed, 'nothing can be so clearly and carefully expressed that it cannot be utterly misinterpreted'.

Language is not a precise notation like logic. Not all our linguistic contributions are simple propositions that can be evaluated as true or false. Words aren't symbols, either, with a fixed and constant designation. Language has to be much more flexible than that. Firstly, it has to cover a huge range of social behaviour. There is much that goes beyond literal meaning and is never subject to precise definition. I'm sure you are painfully aware of the inadequacy of language when it comes to expressing thoughts and feelings. This is one reason why our speech is full of approximating phrases or hedges like 'kinda', 'like', 'sorta', 'ya know', 'I mean'. These expressions aren't just the stuff of teen-speak!

Another problem: speakers speak using minimum effort. They do what they have to and they get away with what they can. Hearers listen with minimum effort too. They listen with half an ear. They make inferences. Readers read selectively. This tug of war between the players brings into a language many of its indeterminacies. There is a human 'wild card' element that will eventually undermine even the most perfectly constructed language.

Of course, none of this has ever stopped people from trying to devise a perfect linguistic system: a logical, consistent and transparent language that matches thinking and replicates reality. Over the years there have been many attempts at artificially constructing a language. None has ever been very successful. But even if one of these scientifically engineered languages were somehow to succeed and become the first language of a group of speakers, it would eventually be struck with similar linguistic infirmities as beset English: the same contradictions, the same vagueness, indeterminacy, variability and ambiguity that plague all natural language systems. There is no doubt that faults like these are a real nuisance for functional languages like Insurancespeak or Legalese, but it wouldn't be possible – in fact, it wouldn't even be good – to eradicate them. After all, it's these same imperfections that give us irony and metaphor. It's these features that provide what Anthony Burgess once described as 'the harmonics of the complicated music of literature'. Or, as T. S. Eliot marvellously put it: 'Out of the slimy mud of words, out of the sleet and hail of verbal imprecisions/There spring the perfect order of speech, and the beauty of incantation.'

You're probably thinking, given the variability and indeterminacy in language, how on earth do we ever communicate? Whether it involves an everyday conversation or an insurance policy, we've got to cooperate with each other. Language exchanges will only ever succeed if all the players mutually recognize that a set of ground rules governs their use of language and also their interpretations of the use of language by others. Even our everyday conversations operate according to 'utmost good faith'.

'All grammars leak'

Some time back an interesting query was put to me regarding the phrase *all of a sudden*. Surely, *sudden* is an adjective, a describing word. So what's it describing – a sudden moment, a sudden movement? Where's the noun it describes?

This person was quite right to pose the question. My first thought was that this was perhaps one of those fixed expressions where the noun has simply disappeared over time. This can happen. For example, in slang people talk about *the ready*; in other words *the ready **cash*** or *the ready **money***. The whole meaning of the noun gets dumped into the adjective, which then takes on all the noun-like qualities. But *sudden* is different. In this case we're really dealing with an adjective disguised as a noun. Once upon a time English could do this with much more ease, but today adjectives used as nouns are confined to those which stand for classes of persons, like *the good, the bad and the ugly/the rich and the poor* – or else they stand for abstract notions like *the mystical/the impossible*. These look like nouns because they appear in the positions where you expect nouns to appear. But if they are nouns, they are lousy examples of them because quite simply they don't do the things nouns should do. You can't add an 's' and make them plural, for example. And they can't be modified by things that modify nouns. Sure, you can say something like *the very poor* – but *very* is an intensifying word that's used to modify adjectives, not nouns.

The word *sudden* falls into a subclass of this group of nouny adjectives, one involving fixed expressions headed by words like *of*, *in*, *on* and *for*. They include examples like *in the nude*, *on the sly*, *for the good*, *out of the ordinary* and so on. Words like *nude*, *sly*, *good* and *ordinary*, like *sudden*, are not clearly nouns, but they're not clearly adjectives either. Their status can change with time, too. *Sudden* used to look much more like a noun than it does today. It was once possible to modify it as in *all upon a very great sudden*. But nowadays the nouny *sudden* simply occurs in that fixed expression *all of a sudden* and you can't modify it in any way. A shame really, *all upon a very great sudden* has a rather lovely ring to it.

Words are often stripped of their properties like this when they're on the way out. Take a noun like *umbrage*. Once this was a very ordinary noun and carried all the trappings of a very ordinary noun. You could modify it – *sweet umbrage*, *cloudy umbrage*, *my umbrage was great*. You could *dispel umbrages*; in other words make it plural. You could derive the adjective *umbrageous* or adverb *umbrageously*. We still call it a noun, but it doesn't have any of these noun qualities any more. It's restricted to the fixed expression *to take umbrage*. Now, all you can do with *umbrage* is take it.

It's unfortunate that grammar books like to give the impression that categories like nouns, adjectives and verbs are all clear cut. This is not the case. Not all the members of a class will necessarily have all the identifying properties. Membership is really a matter of degree. As we've seen, there are adjectives that behave more like nouns and there are nouns that behave like adjectives. There are adjectives that look awfully verb-like too – and there are even verby nouns and nouny verbs. As one linguist put it, categories are 'squishy'. In this regard, grammar is no different from the real world. Categories like noun, adjective and verb are much like the mental categories we have of things like vegetables, chairs or sport. As you know, there are prototypical vegetables like *carrots* and *potatoes* and not-so-vegetably vegetables like *bean sprouts*, *chilli peppers* and *edible flowers*. There are prototypical chairs; these have four legs, are probably made of wood, have a back and we sit on them. But there are less chair-like chairs too, such as *sofas*, *pews* and *benches* – these are marginal chairs. There are straightforward sports like *football* and *cricket* and then there's *darts* and *synchronized swimming*. Human categorization is rarely in terms of sharp boundaries. And so it is with the categories we set up in the linguistic world: there is always irregularity and fluidity. Languages are not completely regular systems (as grammar books pretend). Grammar is not a precise, logical or mathematical system – it has fuzzy edges. Or, as the linguist Edward Sapir once neatly put it, 'all grammars leak'.

Dictionaries, Style Guides and Grammars

Who loves a garden loves a greenhouse too
William Cowper, *The Task*, 1785

Those who love language generally enjoy dictionaries, style guides and grammars. In some ways, these are like gardeners' glasshouses. Endangered constructions, words, meanings and pronunciations sit warm and snug in the protective environment of these linguistic nurseries – even our writing and its spelling system provide some of the artificial heat. And just as tender greenhouse plants don't survive if placed out into the garden, these prescriptive texts are the life support systems that keep alive features that haven't survived in ordinary usage.

Keeping words alive

We all get very excited about new words. But what about dead and dying words – words that even as I write are quietly shuffling off this lexical coil? Well, that's the thing – most of the time we just don't notice. Dictionary editors, of course, have to be more aware. They need to make decisions all the time as to whether to classify a word as *archaic* or *obsolete* or even to include it at all. It can be a difficult decision. Words may be no longer relevant for modern speakers; yet we may need to know them when we're reading texts from the past. Influential texts like the Bible provide additional conservatories and greenhouses for rare plants.

Certainly, dictionaries are treasure troves of forgotten words. These can provide wonderful windows into earlier values and attitudes of society. Recently I was thumbing through various collections hunting for obscure words describing food. I came upon a truly extraordinary lost lexicon of gastronomy. Of course, there were many names of now unknown dishes like *pottage*, *mortrews*, *buknade* and *civet* (all porridge-like substances). The necessity in medieval times to smash, pulp and spice food beyond recognition makes many early dishes appear now quite unappetizing. Small wonder these disappeared. But what happened to the *flurch of flampoints*, I want to know, the *licious lozens*, the *fitchet pies*? The descriptions under these throw flashes of light on past luxurious banquets, gastronomic galas and superb cooks. Among these forgotten terms are *opsophagist* 'frequenter of pastry shops'; *symposiast* 'one of a drinking party, banqueter'; *pabulous* 'abounding in food'; *eubrotic* 'good to eat'; *orectic* 'characterized by appetite or desire'; *esculent* 'good to eat'; *deipnetic* 'fond of eating'; *pamphagous* 'omnivorous'; *coenaculous* 'fond of suppers'; *gulch* 'to swallow hungrily', and *pinguedinize* 'to make fat'. The entries under *pabulous comessations* and *dapatical ebrieties* say it all. Many such valuable and interesting words have vanished. I've grown attached to *smellfeast* 'the uninvited dinner guest' and *shotclog* 'the companion tolerated because he or she pay for drinks'. *Potvaliant* is a wonderful word for someone who's courageous through drink. However, my current favourite would have to be *supernaculum*, a word referring to the act of drinking the very last drop from a glass or bottle. How can we do without it?

To give a hint of what we've lost in the way of vocabulary, here's a wee story that tells of a dieter at one of these gastronomic orgies. I've kept the grammatical bits and pieces in Modern English, but have replaced all other words with ones from our lost, or at least endangered, lexicon.

She was the groak whilim as they gulched and guttled. Mephitically alliaceous, steatopygous, ventripotent fopdoodles and slubberdegullions, she mussitated. She fibulated, piddling moliminously at the jejune and unsaporous grots tofore her. Fackins! She was an opsophagist, coenaculous and cuppedous – pabulous comessations were an ephialtes for the deipnetic. It was a niminy gulosity, she wiste it, but they begat swilk an increment in her recrement, a cupidity that was ineluctable – it was the flurch of post-jentacular flampoints and licious lozens. Thilke trogalions she yissed avidulously. She could but gorm esuriently at the ashet. She fimbled her falbala aganacticiously. They were swa gustful, swa opimely ambrosial. In hér mulligrubs, she oculated her embonpoint, but it was nugatory, frustraneous – achrestrous. She underfong an ereption and there was no wight to threap or objurgate – to fillip her opisthenar. The ashet of sugrative and eubrotic flampoints evanesced swith, dagma by dagma. She didn't wamble. But oscilant and gotchy, she recumbed. And unwarrocking her femoral integuments, she pandiculated dapatically and trutinated the ineluctable costnung of mangery.

It's always sad when words die. But we probably shouldn't distress ourselves. After all, with well over a million words, and gaining new ones all the time, the English lexicon is in a pretty healthy state.

Hothouse words

Hothouse words are those that in a sense have never really existed. They're planted in dictionaries, but usually are never placed out into the garden beds. Often they're the product of the fertile imagination of the dictionary makers themselves. Many such hothouse sprouts were cultivated in early English dictionaries, especially those of the seventeenth century. Inventive lexicographers at the time nurtured in their dictionaries a number of erudite-sounding words with classical roots – perhaps they felt these should exist in the language, or perhaps they were just anxious to show off their knowledge of Greek and Latin. Some of them you could imagine would be quite handy – *dentiloquist* 'someone who speaks through the teeth', *dentiloquent* 'speaking through one's teeth', *doctiloquent* 'speaking learnedly'.

Occasionally, hothouse products arose because of a blunder: an error by an early English scribe perhaps, a printer or even a dictionary editor. This sort of thing can happen very easily. A lexicographer imagines a word to exist and so pops it into the dictionary even though it's never been used. One lexicographer by the name of Allen Read included the entry *vanute* in his collection on Britishisms. The example read: 'They vanuted a somewhat uneasy sophistication'. As it turns out, *vanute* was a misprint for *vaunt*. This one perished. But as you can imagine, once in the protective environment of a dictionary these words can survive. Quite simply, people think it's got to be a word because it's in the dictionary. Hothouse words may then be picked up by other dictionaries – and authority after authority repeats the blunder, until no one would dare doubt the word's provenance.

Probably the most famous hothouse product of all time is the word *dord* that appeared in the 1934 (second) edition of the Merriam Webster's Dictionary. Its source was a file of abbreviations, one entry of which read 'D or d', meaning a capital D or a small d. These were abbreviations of the word *density*. Now, somehow this abbreviation got detached and came to be included in the main alphabet. The letters were then run together to give the word *dord* meaning 'density'. It was given a phonetic transcription and allocated a part of speech. By this stage, of course, it was starting to look like a thoroughly respectable word. So *dord* made it into the dictionary and subsequently into others. In 1939, however, the impostor was discovered – much to the embarrassment of the editors. Some (probably the embarrassed editors) have claimed that the ghost word was included to deliberately trap any would-be plagiarists – a likely story!

Editors of the Oxford English Dictionary once had a query: how do you describe people who drink their own bathwater? Quick as a flash and in the great hothouse tradition of the seventeenth century they offered *autoloutrophilist* 'one who drinks one's own bathwater', as opposed to *alloloutrophilist* 'one who drinks another's bathwater'. This would mean that couples who drink each other's water could be described as *alleloloutropinic* pairs. Hard to imagine these particular hothouse words coming alive, unless of course the practice of drinking one's own bathwater, or anyone else's, becomes particularly fashionable.

Christians and cretins

How often have you heard people argue that the verb *aggravate* can't possible mean 'to annoy' because it comes from the Latin *gravis* meaning 'serious'? Therefore, so the argument goes, *aggravate* can only ever mean 'to make worse'. Or how about those talkback callers who vent their spleen on air complaining about a sportswriter's use of the verb *decimate*. How can we

Hothouse products from science

Scientific terminology from the seventeenth, eighteenth and nineteenth centuries really did change the nature of English vocabulary for all time. With the discovery of the world, suddenly people had to come up with scientific names for new plants, elements, stars and objects. Roy Porter, a medical historian from the Wellcome Institute, gives a nice example. During the eighteenth century, the astronomer William Herschel discovered a new planet. Apparently, he wanted to call it after King George – but could you really call a new planet George? Not surprisingly it ended up with the thoroughly respectable Latin name Uranus.

The new terminology from this time was overwhelmingly classical in origin, drawing especially on high-bred affixes from Latin and Greek. Literally thousands of classical coinages flooded into the language. This did enrich our vocabulary with a new source for lexical inventiveness, but it also bred a real linguistic snobbery. As early as the sixteenth century people were coming up with over-the-top scholarly coinages. Large numbers of rather pedantic inventions based on Latin replaced what was regarded as vulgar native English vocabulary. *Deruncinate* in place of common-or-garden 'pruning', *carbunculate* 'burn', *diffibulate* 'unbutton', *pistate* 'bake (a cake!)' Even though people grew critical of this scholarly vocabulary, a number of terms managed to survive: *impede* (though not its partner *expede*), *dismiss, disabuse, disagree, transmit, dexterity* and *absurdity* to name a few.

It's interesting that with the huge number of words now appearing in the sphere of information technology, there doesn't seem to be the same dependence on classically inspired terminology. Look at words like *boot, bite, bug, input* and *interface*. These are borrowed from ordinary language and move right away from the scholarly tradition for technical terminology. But there is still a real power and prestige attached to Classical vocabulary. Why else would the hamburger industry opt for terms like *autocondimentation* (as opposed to *precondimentation*). It's an economical means of distinguishing a client's right to salt his or her own hamburger, to be sure. But more importantly, it confers upon the industry a certain dignity and complexity, qualities that come from the Graeco-Latinate linguistic paraphernalia. Now, I'm not sure what's involved in *calibrating a milkshake*, but it sounds damned impressive!

decimate the opposing cricket team, complains John of Claremont, when *decimate* originates from the Latin word *decimus* meaning 'tenth'. If you decimate the team then surely you knock over only one in ten of the opposing batsmen, just as the Romans put to death only one in ten of a group of prisoners. This was decimation! This sort of thinking is something that has been dubbed the 'etymological fallacy'. It is the idea that the etymology of a word – that is, the original root meaning of a word – is somehow its correct or true meaning. To be fair, this is partly the fault of the word 'etymology' itself which has as its root the Greek meaning 'true'. Originally, etymology did make reference to the true sense of the word.

The wrongheadedness of this thinking shows up when you consider doublets, words with the same origin that have diverged significantly in meaning. Perhaps they began as pronunciation variants which for some reason then parted company and went down (in some instances) spectacularly different paths. Take the extraordinary doublet *cretin* and *Christian*. If you can believe it, these two words are historically the same. This remarkable split probably came about via the idea of the holy simpleton. In early times mental illness could be considered to place you closer to God and set you above ordinary human beings (if you were unlucky it was thought to be the work of malicious devils and brutal treatments were prescribed). The original cretins were probably those that were touched; in other words, touched by the hand of God.

Showing a somewhat similar development is the pair *daft* and *deft*. Historically the same word too, these have diverged to the extent they now have opposite meanings – *daft* 'simple-minded' versus *deft* 'skilful'. Both *daft* and *deft* go back to a word which in Old English meant 'gentle, meek, humble'. The Virgin Mary, for example, was described as 'that defte meiden'. At that time it would have been pronounced with an 'æ' sound as in the word 'hand'. The different pronunciations *daft* and *deft* grew out of this. A shift from 'gentle, humble' to 'apt' and then to 'skilful' is understandable. But what about 'gentle, humble' to 'foolish'? The explanation here lies in the additional senses *daft* took on as 'unlearned, lacking knowledge' (in other words, ignorant, but in a neutral sense). This is a shift we've seen before. Expressions suggesting a lack of education often end up terms of disapproval. Recall the fate of *lewd* and *uncouth*.

One of my favourite pairs is *noise* and *nauseous*. What could possibly connect these two? In this case we have to start out from the Greek word meaning 'ship'. *Nauseous* way back meant 'ship-sickness'. We don't tend nowadays to think of the noise of sea-sickness, but as the great word sleuth Eric Partridge pointed out, it must have been incredible. These words provide us with a nice little window into what it must have been like on board a tiny vessel in ancient Greece in the middle of a storm. Imagine it – the groans, the moans, the retchings of the poor sods on board, plus the creaking, the wind howling, waves battering the sides. Conjure up this and a meaning shift from 'sea-sickness' to 'noise' seems quite reasonable.

Clearly words aren't like maths symbols. They don't have a fixed designation – and they're 'sprouting' new meanings all the time. As fascinating as dictionary etymologies are, clearly they have little status in the subsequent history of words.

Can we rescue them?

I was reading something the other day written by Peggy Noonan, a journalist and former speech writer for Ronald Reagan. It was a piece on political correctness and Noonan was lamenting the loss of words – words she claims have been hijacked by various groups who then twist their meanings. 'I wish we could rescue them', she writes,'and return them to their true meanings'. This notion of a word's true meaning is a curious one. Peggy Noonan's complaint suggests there is something true, natural and inevitable about her own use of language. But then perhaps this is what most of us feel.

It's understandable that people like Peggy Noonan get upset. Even laid-back linguists have to concede that losing distinctions between *imply* and *infer* or between *disinterested* 'impartial, unbiased' and *uninterested* 'without interest' can cause confusion while the shift is in progress. Mind you, it's not clear to me we've ever kept *disinterested* and *uninterested* apart. The Oxford English Dictionary gives the earliest use (1662) of *disinterested* as 'without interest' and the earliest use of *uninterested* (1646) as 'impartial, unbiased'. That's nearly four hundred years ago! But yes, meanings shifts can create confusion – they always have. When 'want' was shifting in the early 1700s from meaning 'lack' to 'desire', what did speakers mean when they said 'I want this'? Did they desire it or did they lack it? And a real problem that the English language has **never** sorted out is what 'next Saturday' means if you're uttering the phrase, say, on a Tuesday. Half the population understand it to be the first Saturday coming up (the English sense) and for the rest it's the Saturday following (the Scottish sense). I'd like the language to sort that one out. What do people now mean when they say 'minimal accuracy is required'? Do they mean 'the least possible accuracy' or do they mean 'at least some accuracy'? And what about *instep?* Most people now understand it to mean the underneath part of the foot. However, many dictionaries still insist it means the arched upper part of the foot, between the toes and the ankle. For half the population *several* means a number around five or six. For the rest it means a proportion of what you start out with. For those people *several* can be as high as four hundred if you start off with one thousand. For many Australians, *a couple* now means more than two. Is this misuse? If it is, then there's a lot of it about.

The problem is: when does misuse become use? Do 350 million native speakers of English misuse the word *sad* because really it means 'content'? When one or two people start using *a couple* to mean more than two then it's clearly misuse, but you can't prosecute them (as my local baker would like to). And when many people start using the word this way, what do you do? Unfortunately, there's no magic instant when misuse suddenly becomes use.

In truth, Peggy Noonan probably didn't want to return those words to their true meanings. When most people argue they want words to mean what they used to mean, they don't really want the words to go back to their original senses, just back to the meanings that were around a generation or so ago; in other words, the meanings that they grew up with and are familiar with. Besides, what on earth is a word's true meaning?

Quotation

We all quote. Quoting behaviour, it seems, is universal. So why do we do it? Well, it's comforting to see that there are others around with the same thoughts as our own, and at the same time a quote lends credence to these thoughts. What's more, we are usually giving them a far more brilliant, more catchy manner of expression than we could manage alone – and perhaps too we convey an impression of being well read. For example, I might have started this section by saying something like: As linguist David Crystal says, 'a quotation is a fragment of socially embalmed language – language placed on a pedestal'. Frankly, Crystal says it much better than I could.

But quotes can offer protection too, a kind of verbal escape hatch for those moments when you might want to distance yourself, when you don't want to take full responsibility for your words, particularly if those words might cause offence. You know – you were only quoting someone else. Your words 'dirty scumbag' were actually encased in inaudible quotation marks. But in fact this depersonalizing aspect of quotations can provide an important safety valve. In the everyday life of many societies outside our own, quoting behaviour is used as a means of social control, and can be quite crucial in times of dispute. A quote from the Bible in communities like the horse-and-buggy Amish and Mennonite groups in North America, for instance, can resolve a conflict in a non-threatening way. In some societies quotes are used as precedents, much like prior cases are used in our own legal proceedings.

You would imagine therefore that quotes would remain fixed. They are, after all, quotations – specimens protected within the safe environment of a set text. But no! Once released into the world there's the Chinese whisper effect: quotes can be remembered wrongly. Alexander Pope's original was not 'a little

knowledge is a dangerous thing' but 'a little **learning**'. Sometimes we make them shorter, more catchy. Then they become more like a proverb, a snippet of traditional wisdom. Nowadays, we talk of 'gilding the lily'. It's a tad more tripping than Shakespeare's original 'To gild refined gold, to paint the lily'. Most of us now understand by gilding the lily the idea of trying to artificially enhance natural beauty. Lilies aren't gold of course; so we interpret the phrase differently to try to make sense of it. We also talk about escaping 'by the skin of our teeth', by which we mean we escaped by the narrowest of margins. But when Job originally used it he meant he escaped with only the skin of his teeth, everything else was taken away from him. The original in Job 19, verse 20 reads 'My bone cleaveth to my skin and to my flesh and I am escaped with the skin of my teeth'. Ask people now what they understand by 'hoist by his own petard' (a remodelled version of Hamlet's original 'hoist with his own petar') and most will have an idea of someone being hung by their own rope. In fact a *petard* was an unreliable explosive device often used in blowing up walls, and frequently it blew up the person who was using it.

So how do someone's words become a quotable quote? Well, the expression has to be memorable somehow, perhaps poetic, witty, brilliant, or interesting in sound and metaphor: good ideas clothed in well-turned-out phrases. They have to delight, or irritate for that matter. Look in a book of quotations. Many will be novel, but inevitably many will be very familiar too, bordering on common idiom. Most of us don't think of Milton's *Paradise Lost* as the origin of the common expression 'All hell broke loose'. And we have no thought either for General Sherman, the originator of 'Hold the fort'. Shakespeare has contributed many: 'to play fast and loose', 'to be cruel only to be kind', 'at one fell swoop', 'tower of strength', even 'It's Greek to me'. These quotations are all so familiar to us now that they are part and parcel of our modern idiom, perhaps to the point of being so overused they border on cliché. But then – cliché is in the eye of the beholder!

'If you lay down with dogs'

A prescriptive approach is one that tells you how you ought to speak. Prescriptive grammars comprise a hodgepodge of dos and don'ts about sentence structure, word meaning and word usage. A rule that says 'don't use *lay* as an intransitive verb' is a bit like a rule of etiquette. This is language doing the right thing: the sort of language that wipes its feet before it enters a room and that leaves the room before it breaks wind.

We all make value judgements about language. As Deborah Cameron argues in *Verbal Hygiene*, it's an integral part of our linguistic behaviour, as basic as vowels and consonants. A sense of linguistic values is built into our social structure and it's always been this way. So 'rules' in language are inevitable. But not all rules are good rules. Take the example of the notorious *lay-lie* rule. This would have disappeared long ago if it hadn't been kept alive in linguistic greenhouses like Harry Blamires' *The Queen's English*. Books like these condemn sentences like 'If you lay down with dogs, you will get up with fleas' (to quote an example I encountered recently) as 'incorrect', 'dialectal' or 'illiterate'. According to linguistic inspectors like Harry Blamires, it shows a failure to master a feature in English known as transitivity. Transitive verbs are those that can have something following them; the action transfers across to some other entity. *Lay* is transitive: *hens lay eggs*. *Lie* is intransitive: you can't *lie anything down*. So, 'to lay down with dogs' instead of 'to lie down with dogs' demonstrates you haven't mastered this basic feature of transitivity. But in fact many English verbs can be both transitive and intransitive and no one condemns these.

Linguist Dwight Bolinger has outlined some of the problems of the *lay-lie* rule in his book *Language the Loaded Weapon*. Let me mention some of them here. These two verbs *lay* and *lie* share forms. The past tense of *lie* is *lay*. The verb *lie* also has a whole host of different meanings including 'to fib'. So we need to add *down* if we mean 'to assume a recumbent position'. Instead of 'If you lie with dogs' you must say 'If you lie **down** with dogs'. Problems occur if you then put this in the past. It becomes 'If you lay down with dogs'. In normal fast speech the 'd' of *down* transfers to the end of *lay* and you get *layd*. So really is it any wonder that speakers confuse the verbs and arrive at 'If you lay down with dogs'! The basic units of language are distinctive sounds and words and for effective communication they must be kept distinctive. *Lay-lie* fails in this requirement. As

Bolinger concludes, the price of maintaining this rule is just too high.

Yet, because of the way our society operates, rules like this one continue to matter. They become social passwords for the elite – the more impractical, the more difficult, the better. To master the *lay-lie* distinction takes a time, effort, proper schooling. If you've survived all this, you're not going give up the rule easily. For many people, too, it's not so much cleanliness that's next to godliness, as good grammar – and good grammar means knowing the distinction between *lay* and *lie*. Despite our current era of equal opportunity and equality for all, many are still discriminated against for using non-standard dialects and low-status accents. Sentences like 'If you lay down with dogs, you will get up with fleas' can place people at a disadvantage. Even my apparently laid-back-anything-goes first year students frequently come out with outrageous statements about other people's language. Linguistic prejudices never seem to be challenged.

Urges to cultivate and tidy up the language are clearly part and parcel of the solidarity and separating function of language. All this edging, staking, cutting back, keeping bugs at bay is clearly about social status too. So, teachers must continue to give students access to these rules – if they choose to break them, so be it, but this should come from a position of knowledge not from ignorance. However, let's not put the prescriptive cart before the usage horse. Clearly many of the rules handed down to us are impractical, unjust and often simply wrong-headed. They don't allow for language change. They don't allow for stylistic variation. Many have even been artificial for English from the start, stemming from a time when regulating English meant making it look more like Latin. Rules are inevitable, yes, but, let's make them sensible.

To apostrophize or not!

Some time ago I bravely suggested that English would be better off if it abandoned the apostrophe to signal possession and retained it only for its other functions. The hate mail flooded in. Public flogging seemed too lenient a punishment for my crime – well, at least in some people's minds.

Now is my chance to outline why I think this way. Let's start with history. The apostrophe was introduced in English only in the sixteenth century. Originally borrowed from the French, it started life as a marker of omission; for instance, to show when vowels had been omitted as in *think'st thou*. But the Golden Age of the Apostrophe didn't come until the eighteenth century. Suddenly, pages were strewn with apostrophes supposedly marking omissions, some real but many not. *Has* was spelled *ha's* on the mistaken belief that *has* was an abbreviation of *haves*. People then started using them to mark possession, arguing that possessive *s* was originally *es* and therefore the apostrophe would mark the missing vowel. (The fact that the vowel had disappeared centuries ago didn't seem to matter.) There were also some who believed there was a missing pronoun here: they derived *father's car* from *father **his** car.* The reasoning behind the possessive apostrophe was shaky from the start.

During the eighteenth century it marked singular nouns and during the nineteenth century it came to mark plural possessives as well (although inconsistently). This was the heyday of prescription. People had started to lay down rules left, right and centre and many tried to do the same with the apostrophe. But this was difficult because no one had ever agreed on when to use it. Many argued it should only mark true possession; in other words, you wouldn't expect it in something like *today's announcement* or *the book's cover* because we're not dealing here with real owners. There was also a lot of inconsistency. For example, it wasn't used with pronouns, except for *one's*. Then there was the general problem: how do you tell whether actual possession is involved? Something as straightforward as *the boy's photo* could involve possession, as in 'the photo the boy owns', but it could also have various descriptive meanings such as 'the photo of the boy himself'. And what about something like *travellers(') cheques* – do the travellers own the cheques, or is *travellers* descriptive here, too? Most style manuals recommend omitting it from expressions of time and space like *five weeks time*, but none are consistent on this point.

In short, what we have is a saga of confusion, inconsistency, flux and wild imagination, ever since the apostrophe made its appearance in the sixteenth century. Small wonder people today are unsure about when and where to place the apostrophe.

Worldwide, you find instances of 'greengrocer's apostrophe' (as it's now called). On the Internet recently, linguists from every corner of the English-speaking world painted the same picture – the global proliferation of apostrophe 's'. On menus in South Africa you can choose from 'Pizza's, Hot Dog's and Taco's'. In the United States, signs like 'Plea's flush the toilet' and 'The Ladie's' occur. A Newcastle market advertises 'Deliciou's Fruit' and the sandwiches and spuds in a Whitley Bay cafe boast 'Variou's Filling's'. A sign in a shop window in Melbourne reads 'Canva's Hat's'. But don't think that aberrant apostrophes are limited to the ignorant. 'Nomination's for Director' appeared in a publication from the National Art Gallery of Victoria. It seems the apostrophe is entering a new phase in its history, a more flamboyant and artistic phase. Decorative flourishes replace the older, more mundane structural function!

The question is – and I pose this with great trepidation – do we really need it? In the case of obvious omissions, as in contractions like *it's* for *it is*, it probably serves a useful function. But my suggestion was only ever to remove it from possession.

In the case of the possessive apostrophe, what we have is a long history of bewildering and inconsistent usage. I am not denying the importance of standards and values (as people suggested in their letters of outrage). Rather, I am proposing that we assess the merits of these standards being invoked. Of course, if a case could be made that the apostrophe speeds up mental processing, for example, as at least one person has suggested, then there would be a good reason to hang on to it. But that case has yet to be made, at least to my knowledge. If a rule offers no advantages (which I suspect is the case here), then why keep it?

The fate of (h)aitch

Whatever happened to the pronunciation of the sound at the start of words like *which* and *what*? Once upon a time this was pronounced something like it's spelt – 'wh'. (In fact the spelling was originally 'hw' – 'hw' changed to the 'wh' we know today some time after the Norman Conquest.) According to linguists who spend their time researching these things, the change in the pronunciation from 'wh' to 'w' started in the south of England as far back as the Middle Ages. Apparently, though, it didn't spread much during this period. We can be pretty sure of that because the pronunciation that went across to America in the seventeenth century was 'wh'.

However, in the course of the eighteenth century 'w' began to gain ground. It even started to creep into the speech of the educated, who before then had considered it a vulgarism. By 1800 'w' as in *which*, *white* and *what* was the norm. So *which* and *witch*, *whether* and *weather* became homophones. Today the pronunciation 'w' is universal in England and Wales (except Northumberland). True, some elocution manuals still insist on 'wh' and are acting rather like artificial life support systems for the pronunciation. But its days are clearly numbered. In Scotland and Ireland, however, there's no need for life support systems – here 'wh' is thriving outside the greenhouse. In the United States, the 'w' pronunciation appears to have started in New York and Boston where it was probably introduced from England. Since then it has also spread rapidly there, and according to some American reports on the Internet recently, 'wh' is confined to a handful of 'old fogies'.

The disappearance of 'wh' is in fact part of an ongoing trend. Once upon a time, 'h' clustered with a number of consonants, not just 'w'. *Loud* was pronounced 'hlud', *ring* was 'hring' and *nick* began with an initial 'hn' (a bit like a sniff) – the word was *hnecca*. The only surviving cluster is the 'hy' at the beginning of words like *Hugh* and *human*. Mind you, some speakers have jettisoned this cluster, too. For these speakers, the name *Hugh* and *you* are pronounced the same as 'yew' – in other words, *Hugh* has lost its 'h'.

In general, the sound represented by the letter 'h' is really on its last legs. Not only is it weakly articulated, but in terms of the symmetry of our consonant system we can predict its demise. Languages tend to align their consonants in pairs – voiceless sounds are usually matched with voiced ones across the board. All of our voiceless consonants like 'f', 's' and 'th' have now acquired voiced partners except for poor old 'h', which stands by itself without a voiced mate. As a kind of neatening process you'd expect 'h' to either get a mate or drop out – as it's already done in dialects like

Cockney. In fact, it probably would have dropped out long ago except that 'dropping one's h's' became a bad thing, and there was considerable social pressure to hang on to it. This has been the case now for a number of centuries. As a commentator in the 1800s wrote, 'Few things will the English youth find in after-life more profitable than the right use of the aforesaid letter *h*'. Curiously, this wasn't always the case. Before the eighteenth century no one gave two hoots about h-less pronunciations; even the poshest people dropped their aitches. A new spelling-awareness then restored the 'h' in words like *hopeless*. But somehow the missing 'h' in words like *vehicle* and *which* escaped attention.

Spelling pronunciation

Once upon a time, we wrote as we spoke. Speech was primary, and writing was there to represent it visually. Nowadays, writing has taken centre stage, and speech we seem to view more as its oral representation. More than ever before, writing is affecting pronunciation; in particular, by way of retarding, perhaps even reversing, the normal processes of change.

Spelling can influence pronunciation a number of ways. Firstly, it can be conservative. In everyday day speech it's usual to drop unstressed sounds or run them together. In normal connected speech, most of us would pronounce strings of words like *fit you* as 'fitcha'. These sorts of short cuts are an inherent characteristic of ordinary casual speech. They needn't have any long-term effect, but often they do. For example, our 'ch' sound in *chin* and *cheese* (Old English *cinn* and *cēse*) began life as exactly this sort of fast speech phenomenon. But such changes occur much more easily if we have no notion of the written word, and will slow down with a knowledge of spelling. Having a visual image of a word like *government* probably means we are less likely to pronounce it 'gubment'!

Secondly, spelling can be retrograde. A consciousness of spelling can lead to the reversal of a sound change, thus restoring an earlier pronunciation. A number of lost consonants and vowels have been restored in this way. *Often* now frequently receives a spelling pronunciation rather than the 't-less' pronunciation typical of the eighteenth and nineteenth centuries (compare *soften* and *glisten*). Some of you might recall Major-General Stanley's question to the Pirate King in Gilbert and Sullivan's *The Pirates of Penzance* – 'When you said "orphan" did you mean "orphan" – a person who has lost his parents, or "often" – frequently?' Clearly, this joke could soon be lost on modern audiences.

Finally, spelling can be radical. During the Renaissance period, 'h's were inserted into the spelling of borrowed words like *throne*, *theatre* and *thesis*. This supposedly brought them closer to the original Greek. It didn't seem to matter that many weren't actually Greek in origin – this was a way of making English appear more respectable. Because people placed so much importance on writing, eventually the *th*'s came to be pronounced. Words like *fault* and *vault* also got fancy respellings to make them look more impressively Latin. At the time they entered English, both words would have rhymed with *ought*.

The primacy of writing has meant that ordinary speech has become rather neglected – even devalued. For quite a while now, the written word has been holding a pre-eminent place. You can understand why this is. It's the medium of literature, the source of standards of linguistic excellence, it has permanence, authority, worldwide circulation. All these things give writing a special place in our society. Understandably, speech now plays second fiddle. We've just seen how pronunciation has been made to follow the standard written forms. We're all expected to 'say the h' and 'not drop the g'. Even the rules of grammar – those which come down to us in the form of traditional grammar, that is – are largely based on written texts. But writing and speech should never be made to confront one another. Speech is not 'spoken writing', any more than writing is 'speech written down', and to judge one in terms of the other is something like – well, judging a pavlova in terms of whether it makes a good cheesecake or not. Both are two different systems of communication and each has capabilities of expression that are simply not available to the other.

Our spelling – how bad is it?

English spelling has been evolving for over a thousand years and the complications we encounter today are the consequences of many different linguistic and social events that have taken place over this period. Problems existed from the very beginning. Quite simply the 23-letter Roman alphabet was not adequate for the 35 or so sounds that were distinctive in English at that time. Modifications had to be made. Complications were then introduced by French scribes, who imposed several of their own spelling conventions. With the first printing presses came more complexity. Many of the printers were European and they imposed further spelling conventions from their respective native languages. William Caxton himself introduced Dutch spellings like 'gh' in *ghost* and *ghastly*. Printers also used flexibility of spelling to solve the tricky problem of justifying lines. Instead of varying word spaces, they could shorten or lengthen words by swapping an 'i' for a 'y' or adding an extra 'e' here and there. When at last spelling settled down, there came subsequent massive sound changes. The result – thousands of words with spelling closer to the pronunciation around in Chaucer's time. If the printer Caxton had been born a couple of centuries later, or if these sound changes had occurred a couple of centuries earlier, our spelling would be much truer to pronunciation.

There were some early attempts to rationalize spelling. Scholars changed *coude* to look like *would*, *delite* to look like *light* and *rime* to look like *rhythm*. They added 'b's to *debt*, *subtle* and *doubt* to show their Latin origin. All interesting ideas, to be sure, but ones that hardly make for a consistent spelling system! Inconsistencies continue to appear with every linguistic alien that comes into the language with an unEnglish-like spelling.

So it is from this haphazard evolution that we end up with the spelling system we have. Plagued from the start with an inadequate alphabet, language change, imaginative respellings, borrowed words and spelling conventions, it's surprising it's as regular as it is. So should we reform it? It's a thorny question generally for speakers – unless they happen to be Dutch. Remarkably, the Dutch seem to cope with serious spelling reforms every few years. Everywhere else, people remain vociferously opposed. We might love to whinge about English spelling, but reforming it is another question. Perhaps it's simply because people associate being able to spell with education. How would you feel about spelling *you* as 'yu' or *tongue* as 'tung'? These spellings make a lot of sense, but seem just too strange to the eye. And, of course,

Spelling blunders

Over the years there have been a number of quite startling blunders made by printers, scribes, even dictionary editors. A few have stuck. Some of my favourites concern the letters 's' and 'f'. Once upon a time, 's' had three different shapes depending on where it occurred in the word. One of these was so-called long 's'. It looked very like a modern 'f', except if you looked very carefully the stroke didn't continue through to the right of the letter. This symbol continued to be used until the end of the eighteenth century – despite the fact that people kept confusing the symbols. The 'f' in *fnese* was misread as 's' and *fnese* turned into *sneeze*. So Chaucer's 'he speketh in his nose and fneseth faste' became 'he speaks in his nose and sneezes strongly'. This misreading was probably assisted by the abundance of 'sn' words in English that are connected with the nose, like *snout, sniff* and *snot*. It probably also didn't help that there weren't many 'fn' words left in English. In fact, there's only one left – *fnast* 'to pant, snort'. You'll still find *fnast* in some dictionaries. It's being kept on a lexical life support system probably because it's so weird.

The letters *u, v, i, n* and *m* were once written in a very similar fashion and once again this was the source of considerable confusion, particularly in the case of 'n' and 'u'. A number of errors have stuck, like the word *gravy*. This has its origin in an Old French word, either *graine* 'meat', or *grané* 'grain of spice'. We should really pronounce this word as if it were spelt *graney*, but it came into English as *grav(e)y* because someone goofed in translating a French cooking book in the fourteenth century and misread the 'n' for 'u' or 'v' (the letters 'u' and 'v' were interchangeable at this time). This determined the pronunciation of *gravy* we have today. Another scribal blunder gave us the word *syllabus*. It comes from Greek *sittybas*. Corrupted readings in Greek were then copied into Latin and subsequently came into English.

Other favourites of mine are those fake antique names like 'Ye olde Englishe fishe shoppe'. There are all the final 'e's of course – nice hyperarchaisms! And then there's *ye* instead of *the*. The confusion arose from the original spelling of our modern 'th' which was earlier written with an ancient runic symbol called 'thorn'. Over the years people started to get rather careless writing this symbol, and a sloppy thorn starts to look awfully like a 'y'. The symbol continued to be used for words like *the* and *that* into the nineteenth century, by which time people had forgotten it represented 'th' – and so it came to be pronounced 'ye'.

writers make use of precisely these sorts of conventions to indicate a lack of education.

Yet, the simple fact remains: English spelling is neither totally consistent nor globally standardized. There is certainly scope for some sensible reform to take place. Not wholesale change, though. This is out of the question. Imagine revising the entire corpus of English writing from the past several hundred years. Besides, which system would you choose? Many people argue that a regular correspondence between the spoken and written word is optimal. The problem is, such a correspondence is doomed to break down. Once upon a time we had something along these lines and look what then happened – large-scale shifts in vowels and consonants that had a profound effect on the relationship between sound and symbol.

Whose dialect would you choose, anyway? Think of the enormous variation that exists, especially with respect to vowel sounds. For many New Zealand dialect speakers, *cheer* and *chair* are pronounced the same. Should they be written that way? For some Americans, *father* and *bother* rhyme. So do *cot* and *caught*. In Atlanta, *boil* and *sky* sound more like 'bahl' and 'skah'. Then again, in terms of sheer numbers of speakers, perhaps the new spelling system should be based on Indian English pronunciation. There are more speakers of English in India than anywhere else in the world.

But how bad is our spelling system really? If you look at it closely, it does in fact have a lot going for it. It's not simply a rotten letter-to-sound system full of inconsistencies. One positive feature, for instance, is that it's grammatically representative. In

To enquire or inquire?

An interesting problem came up at my university concerning the naming of a new school within the Faculty of Humanities and Social Sciences. Should it be *The School of Communication, Arts and Critical Enquiry* – or *Critical Inquiry*?

On this matter, it seems English speakers (not only those within faculties of Humanities and Social Sciences) are quite divided. And, you'll find, so too are the authorities. In the Webster's, Oxford and Macquarie dictionaries both are listed as accepted spellings, but priority is given to *inquire* and *inquiry* (with *enquire* and *enquiry* as alternatives). Fowler's *Modern English Usage* recommends both, but gives different meanings: *inquire* 'to investigate' (*inquiries* might entail official investigations) and *enquire* 'to ask' (as in an informal sort of query). This is probably why some authorities claim *inquiry* as a higher style. Its formality probably arises from its use in bureaucracy. *Enquiry* involves simple everyday questions. This divided usage, however, is more usual in the United Kingdom.

In the United States and Australia, most speakers prefer *inquiry* for the noun. According to Pam Peters, *inquiry* is the more usual form in written texts, outnumbering *enquiry* in the Macquarie corpus more than ten to one. Newspapers here use only *inquire* and *inquiry*, whereas in British corpuses (corpora, if you prefer) they are more evenly matched. Curiously, in Australia, it seems to me *enquiry* has a more formal ring, rather than *inquiry* as in the United Kingdom. The database bears this out. *Enquiry* seems largely confined to academic and bureaucratic prose, while *inquiry* appears in a wider range of different styles. Oddly though, when it comes to the verb forms in the Australian corpus, *inquire* and *enquire* are more evenly matched. The verb *enquire* is more usual here than its noun *enquiry*.

Imported words with the *en-* prefix came from French and those with *in-* from Latin. *Inquire/enquire* derive from *enquerre*, but the word was Latinized during the fourteenth and fifteenth centuries. First, the stem vowel changed from 'e' to 'i' and we got *enquire*, which is sort of half Latin and half French. Then the prefix was Latinized and 'en' was changed to 'in' and we got *inquire.* The trouble is, half Latin-half French *enquire* stuck around, and as so often happens with spelling splits of this kind, some speakers started to assign different meanings to the different spellings. This is also what happened with *insure* and *ensure.* In Australia and the United Kingdom, *insure* means 'to take out insurance to compensate for loss or damage'. *Ensure* has the broader meaning of 'to guarantee'. But this difference is only about one hundred years old, and in the United States *insure* and *ensure* simply remain alternative spellings.

Which brings me back to the naming of the new school. So, what was eventually decided upon? Well, in the beginning it looked quite firm – 'Communication, Arts and Critical Inquiry'. Perhaps it was the unfortunate acronym CACI (pronounced 'cacky') that triggered the sudden about-face, but it has now been settled at 'Communication, Arts and Critical Enquiry'. Or should that be 'Communication, Arts and Critical *En*quiry', with the stress on the first syllable? *En*quiry would fit better with the general stress pattern of Modern English, and has the added bonus that with the stress on the first syllable you can actually hear the intended vowel. That is, of course, if you think the distinction between *inquiry* and *enquiry* is something worth maintaining.

groups of words like *sign-signal* and *electric-electricity-electrician*, the relationship between each of the words is preserved despite the different pronunciations. Our spelling is one that preserves the shape of words and this has advantages. Primarily, it's impervious to change. It's also handy when it comes to dialect differences.

In short, ours is a system which combines being phonetically representative and grammatically so. Sure, it's not optimal. Fourteen different ways of spelling 'sh' is hardly ideal. But it's not as bad as people like to make out. Reports that *foolish* can be spelled 613,975 different ways are clearly exaggerated. In fact, over eighty per cent of words are spelt according to regular patterns. So wholesale change is not what we want. But certainly modest adjustments could be made without any major upheaval. We could get rid of horrors like *haemorrhage* and *diarrhoea* (America has already done that). We could also promote more-regular spellings wherever they're already familiar as alternative spellings. To introduce the *-or* spelling across the board would be a painless reform, especially since it only affects about thirty words. A few sensible reforms like these would help tidy up the system considerably.

But it's doubtful whether reforms (as sensible as they appear) like *filosofy* will ever catch on. Whenever spelling reform boards start pushing for these sorts of changes, reactions are immediately hostile. Can you imagine psychologists ever agreeing to spell their profession *sikology*? You can only go so far with simplified spellings.

Personal Names

What's in a name?
William Shakespeare, *Romeo and Juliet*, Act II, sc. ii

Some gardening books extol the virtues of hardy perennials like *Convolvulus arvensis*. Others advise the continued application of Dutch hoes and sprays to eradicate the horribly invasive *bindweed*. It's the same plant. What's in a name? Well, a great deal, it seems.

Names are everything

'People always grow up like their names. It took me thirty years to work off the effects of being called Eric. If I wanted a girl to grow up beautiful I'd call her Elizabeth'. These are the words of George Orwell – originally Eric Blair.

Most of the time our names carry clear masculine and feminine connotations, and their structure, it turns out, is very revealing. In 1990 three English researchers, Cutler, McQueen and Robinson, carried out a study of nearly 1700 different names. Here are some of the most interesting of these findings.

Firstly, it seems there are significant differences in the matter of length. Whereas about a quarter of men's names are only one syllable (like John and Mark), there are fewer one syllable female names, less than ten per cent in fact. Female names tend to be much longer – nearly forty per cent are three syllables or more. Names like Elizabeth and Rebecca are typical, but male names of this length are rare, especially among the very popular names.

Apparently, ninety-five per cent of male names have a strong initial syllable like William and Richard. In fact, it's hard to think of male names that don't show this pattern. Examples like Tobias, Matthias, Adolphus and Jerome don't spring easily to mind and they certainly never make it to the lists of the year's most popular names. By comparison, many female names have a weak initial syllable, especially the most popular like Patricia and Michelle. Moreover, female names often include a strong, high front vowel like 'ee'; for example, Lisa, Tina and Maxine. It's much harder to find male examples with this vowel sound. On top of this, many female diminutive names also show the familiar cuddly *-y/-ie* ending – for example, Judy, Suzie and Margie. Pet names for males are more likely to be single syllables like Bill and Bob. That doesn't mean names like Tommy and Jamie don't exist, of course, but they're not common and they usually don't continue into adulthood.

Finally, female names tend to end in a vowel, and not just this *-y/-ie* diminutive (or fondling) ending either. Look at very popular names like Deborah, Mary and Sarah. If they don't end in a vowel, then it's often a vowel-like consonant; in other words, a consonant that has a sonorous quality, one that can be sustained. Nasal sounds are also particularly common, and names like Susan, Jane and Sharon are typical. So are names ending in 'l', such as Rachel, Carol and Nicole. By comparison, male names are more likely to end in short stopped sounds like 'b' and 'd' as in Bob, David and Frank. (It's precisely these sounds that crop up repeatedly in swear words, and particularly at the end of these words.) So does my name, Kate, sound more masculine than Kath or Katie? Probably.

It's not unexpected that so few names work for both sexes. These trends do strongly reinforce the sex dichotomy. As these three researchers conclude, 'a Rose by any other name might be Christine, Elizabeth or Michelle. A Ross by any other name, however, is most likely to be James, Mark or Donald'. It's these sorts of names that appear among the top ten in the most popular names lists. One American survey of men found Christine to be the sexiest female name. Christine, you'll notice, has all the right attributes: a reasonable length, an unstressed first syllable, a strong 'ee' vowel and a vowel-like sound at the end. It's probably not surprising George Orwell was so attracted by Elizabeth. It scores quite highly, too. So what's wrong with Eric then? Well, maybe it's not as clear-cut masculine as Bob, but for George Orwell there must have been specific sound-symbolic associations for the name to affect him so badly!

As Oscar Wilde put it, 'Names are everything'. Consider how often in a day you identify yourself by name, and how often you refer to others by their names. Names are much more than a tag or a label. They're shorthand indicators to our personality, to those qualities and attributes that define us as individuals. More than that, names are a proper part of us. And perhaps George Orwell was right – our names do influence our character. Would my behaviour be different if I'd been called Sabrina or Josephine, names whose sound patterns seem so quintessentially female?

The magic of names

Some time back, Keith Allan and I explored the powerful magic of naming. Many societies, past and present, have fear-based taboos surrounding personal names (that is, 'true names'). Just as malevolent magic can be wrought with someone's bodily effluvia (their spittle, nail parings, blood, hair clippings, for example), so too can it be wrought when someone is in possession of another's true name. In this context a personal name is regarded as a proper part of the name bearer – not just a symbol, but the verbal expression of the personality. Indeed, in many languages you find names are assumed to be an inseparable part of the body, a bit like spirits or souls, and this is reflected even in the way names are treated in the grammar. Moreover, because 'true' names are so closely associated with their name bearer, in some societies there are strict taboos preventing two living persons from going by the same name. Sometimes they're even kept secret, and euphemistic names are necessary for public naming and addressing.

In ancient Egyptian mythology, Isis gained power over the sun god Ra because she persuaded him to divulge his name. In European folktales we read of an evil character variously called Rumpelstiltskin (in Germany, parts of England), Terry Top (Cornwall), Tom Tit Tot (Suffolk), Trit-a-Trot (Ireland) Whuppity Stoorie (Scotland) and Ricidin-Ricdon (France). In all the stories the same

Jack?

As Gwendolen (a good female name) said to Jack (a quintessentially masculine name) in *The Importance of Being Earnest*, 'There is very little music in the name Jack, if any at all, indeed. It does not thrill. It produces absolutely no vibrations . . . I have known several Jacks, and they all, without exception, were more than usually plain.'

The name Jack has a long history of unfortunate associations. Indeed, some uses made it so offensive that at one time those in polite society refrained from using it, even in ordinary expressions like *jackass*. In his eighteenth-century *Dictionary of the Vulgar Tongue* Captain Grose gives the expression *Johnny Bum* as a euphemism for *jackass*, to be used by 'polite and modest ladies who would not say Jack because it was vulgar, nor ass because it was indecent'.

So how did *Jack* acquire this unfortunate reputation? Originally, it was simply a pet form (or as Gwendolen put it 'a notorious domesticity') for John. Personal names often extend to become ordinary words, but in the case of *Jack* its extended uses are remarkable. *Jack* appears in well over one hundred different words and phrases and most are negative, ranging from the slightly disparaging to the wildly offensive.

For a start, since the Late Middle Ages it's been used as a common noun for lad or chap, usually an ill-mannered one – *a jack* was 'a low bred knave'. This gave rise to particular jacks like *Jack Adams* (a fool), *Jack Sprat* (a small fellow), *Jack Sauce* (an impudent fellow), *Jack Strop* (an obstreperous fellow), *Jack Weight* (a fat fellow), *Jack Tar* (a sailor), and *Jack Ketch* (the hangman). *Jack* still appears in a number of extended expressions like *I'm alright Jack*, *jack-of-all-trades*, and our peculiarly Australian the *jack system* (= utter selfishness). Of course, you can *jack up, be jack of something* or *jack it in*. There's also *before you can say Jack Robinson, Jack the lad, Jack in the office, jack-in-the-box, jack o' lantern*, *Jack Frost* and many more.

Jacks are also various contrivances or tools taking the place of a human. There's the *car jack*, *smoke jack* (that turns the spit), *jack roll* (a kind of winch), *boot jack, bottle jack, roasting jack, jackhammer* and *jackstay*. *Jack* also has diminutive force. It's used for things that are inferior or smaller in size. Think of the *jack* in the game of bowls (the small bowl to serve as the marker), *jack timber/jack rafter* is shorter than the full length, a *jack brick* is smaller in size, as is the *jack flag* (jack flags are small versions of national flags; the Union Jack should be the Union Flag). The *jack* in plant names typically refers to undersized plants like *jack in the pulpit, jumping jacks, jack by the hedge, jack go to bed at noon* and *little creeping jack*. *Jack* appears in many animal names too – *jackass, jack rabbit, jackdaw, jack salmon, jack mackerel* are just a few.

Then there are the many euphemistic uses of *jack* in the context of bodily functions and secretions. In fact, I don't think there's a single tabooed bodily function and secretion that doesn't have an expression featuring *jack*. *Jack* has a long association with lavatories (replaced more recently by *john*). It was also used for 'semen' which gives us *jack off* and similar expressions. *I've got jack* was an old euphemism for menstruation, *jacksy* for copulation and *jack-in-the-box* was old rhyming slang for the 'pox' or 'syphilis'.

Despite this deplorable history, *Jack* is making something of a comeback now as a popular name. Perhaps its sound-symbolic associations are enough to override its unfortunate historical baggage. In terms of its structure, *Jack* does score very highly as a clear-cut masculine name: single syllable, the right vowel quality and a final stopped consonant. These are the three magic ingredients of the quintessential masculine name. Even so, rarely do words that have been degraded in this way come back from the abyss after they've lost their negative senses. *Jack* is unusual.

occurs – the discovery of the villain's name destroys his power. Even in English, when we say of Bill Jackson's son Eric that 'Eric's a real Jackson', we speak as if the surname itself carries the genes that make Eric 'a chip off the old block'. The same is true of phrases like *make a name for oneself, have a good name, bring one's name into disrepute, clearing one's name* and so on. Even in our society we speak as if the name carries the properties of the name-bearer, which is why personal names sometimes lose their capital letter and enter the general lexicon as ordinary words.

Boycott, for example, was originally an agent for an earl in Ireland who refused to reduce his rents and was boycotted by his master's tenants. Ned Lud, who destroyed two knitting frames in the late 1700s, gave us *Luddite*, the forerunner of the modern-day technophobe. These expressions are called eponyms – people either give their names to something or others give it for them. And, of course, once they enter English they behave like any other word in the language. Through our various word formation processes they can extend in many ways. Take the example of Thomas Bowdler, who in the early nineteenth century set about to expurgate Shakespeare. Bowdler gave us the so-called *Family Shakespeare* and also the verb *bowdlerize* and nouns *bowdlerism* and *bowdlerite*.

It's been estimated that English has about thirty-five thousand eponyms. This figure would have to be conservative. It doesn't for example include the sort of eponymic phrases like *throw a Sarah Bernhardt* or *be in like Flynn*, not to mention the rhyming slang eponyms like *Germaine Greer* for 'beer' or pairs like *Brahms and Liszt* for 'pissed'. It also doesn't include the ones that are created daily in newspapers and magazines. You might remember back in June 1992 when Lorena Bobbit cut off her husband's penis. Suddenly the verb to *bobbit* appeared in newspapers around the world to describe this and similar events. Dictionary editors seem to agree it's too early to speculate on the future of the word, but the associate editor of the Oxford English Dictionary has stated that: 'if "bobbit" turns up in several different stories over a period of time, this suggests it should go in the dictionary'. Then again, the word might just drop by the wayside like the hundreds of eponyms that crop up all the time in areas like sport, science, technology and the arts.

Whether these words survive or not, they do give us an interesting insight into the way our culture promotes personal names. It's a striking contrast to those traditional societies where there are strict taboos on naming and where true names always remain secret. How different this is from the media-conscious Western world in the twenty-first century where everyone is out there striving to *be a name*.

Nicknames

Typically, nicknames express intimacy or at least a positive or friendly attitude, and they're most commonly found in close-knit groups. People who get them tend to be good friends or family. They can be enemies too; perhaps people in authority or in the public eye – but somehow they must be special. For some groups, nicknames can be crucial for identification. Among conservative Anabaptist groups in North America (the Old Order Amish and Mennonites) first names derive from the Old Testament and there's a limited number of family names. In the small village of St Jacobs in Ontario, for example, there are around forty-five David Martins registered at the local post office. So people usually have a distinguishing nickname.

Tom, Dick and Harry

Our personal names really do become verbal expressions of our personalities, and because of this special force they often enter ordinary language as a generic label for a certain 'type'. *Sheila*, Australian slang for 'young woman', stems from the generic use of an (originally Irish) proper name. At first it applied to any young Irish woman, much like Paddy for Irish men, but then extended to include all women. Or take the name Tom – it's been used to denote the 'man in the street' since as early as the 1300s, possibly even earlier. The striking thing about some men's names is how quickly they develop connotations of stupidity, like *tomfoolery* and its related forms *tomfoolish* and *tomfoolishness*. The original *Tom Fool* for 'half-witted person' has been around since at least the early fourteenth century. In fact, there seem to have been loads of foolish Toms about in those early times – Tom Cuny (the simpleton), Tom Doodle (the blockhead), Tom Farthing (the simpleton), Tom Towly (another simpleton), Tom Tug (rhyming slang for 'mug'), Tom Bedlam (the madman), Tom Long (the tiresome storyteller) and so on. These are predecessors of the modern-day *charlie* or *wally*. (In the United Kingdom a *wally*

has additional connections with stupidity through its association with cucumbers pickled in brine – compare the word *dill*, both 'a fool' and 'a pickle'!)

Australian English has its *ocker* (from Oscar). The original *Ocker* was a TV character played by the comedian Ron Frazer. In the 1970s the name began to be used generically for any character of that type; in other words, cheerful, unpretentious, not overly intellectual, dressed in *stubbies*, *Chesty Bond* singlet and thongs – and usually supporting a generous verandah over the toyshop! He has now made his debut in the *New Shorter Oxford English Dictionary*, which defines him as 'a rough, uncultivated, or aggressively boorish Australian man (esp. as a stereotype)'. In many ways he is like *Norm*, the creation of Phillip Adams for the *Life. Be In It* campaign in Victoria in 1975. Designed to spur us all into athletic pursuits, Norm is the supreme couch potato – slumped in front of the TV, wrapped around a tinnie [of beer] and watching sport. Although he retains his initial capital, Norm is certainly well along the path of commonization.

We know who Ocker was. But who were the original Sheila and Tom? Plenty of candidates have been suggested over the years, but it's probably simply that the most popular names get used to refer to the archetype of normality. Ironically, their immortalization in idiom almost guarantees they will quickly drop out of fashion as children's names, at least until the taint wears off.

In many communities nicknames become associated with certain surnames – *Spud* with *Murphy*, *Nobby* with *Clarke*, *Chook* with *Fowler*. Some first names also have standard nicknames, like *Chuck* for *Charles* (at least in the United States), but typically they're based on physical attributes; for example, *Baldy*, *Ginger*, *Four Eyes*, *Tubby*. In Australia these names frequently have an ironic twist to them: *Shorty* (for someone exceptionally tall), *Curly* (for someone with dead-straight hair) and, of course, *Blue* or *Bluey* (for someone with red hair – the colours red and blue are about as distinct as you can get).

Nicknaming generally is an important part of Australian lingo. We give informal names to just about anyone or anything – from

God (as in *Send 'er down, Hughie*) to the ABC (known nationally as *Auntie*). Politicians are often renamed, of course. Menzies was known as *Ming the Merciless*, Bob Hawke as *The Mild Colonial Boy* and *The Silver Bodgie*, Gareth Evans acquired *Biggles* when he was appointed attorney-general in 1983.

But Australians love abbreviations and many of our informal names end up being simply truncated forms of first names, usually shortened so they end in a consonant like *Man* for *Mandy*, *Rach* for *Rachel*, *Ness* for *Vanessa*, *Tone* for *Tony*. Some of these get an extra bit added on the end – *Tez* for *Terry*, *Gaz* for *Garry*, *Baz* for *Barry*. Names like *Jules* for *Julie* or *Marz* for *Mary* show that this is actually an ending – it's not that we're changing the 'r' of *Terry* or *Garry* to a 'z'. It's probably the same ending you find on pet names like *Cuddles*, *Ducks* and *Toots*. Like most cuddly endings, this one creates a warm, friendly feeling; it indicates that something or someone is endearing to us. These typically Australian abbreviations are more affectionate than the more usual *Bob* or *Deb*. They're also quite different from English pet names like *Debbie* or *Sherry* with the other fondling ending. *Debs* and *Shaz* indicate greater familiarity, greater solidarity. Of course, we've got the option of further extending these abbreviated names with another fondling ending. Let's not forget *Shazza*, *Bazza* and *Gazza*. There's a great deal of informality in these names and perhaps even more of that casual laid-back toughness that crops up in so much Aussie argot. There's no doubt we fiddle with people's names to show our affection – and the more we like someone, the more we fiddle. Think of *Ocker* from *Oscar*, *Macca* from *Mackenzie*, *Ecca* from *Eric*.

Even standard pet names can end up sounding very different from the longer names they're supposed to derive from: *Dotty* from *Dorothy*, *Betty* from *Elizabeth*, *Tony* from *Anthony*, *Kate* from *Kathryn*. These are old names and, in fact, retain early pronunciations that have long disappeared. During the Renaissance, those keen to show off their etymological erudition introduced 'h' into the spelling of a number of words, supposedly to reflect the original Greek. The 'h' in *Kathryn* isn't original but was introduced and the short forms *Kate* and *Kit* preserve the earlier pronunciation. Similar spelling pronunciations introduced 'th' into names like *Anthony*, *Dorothy* and *Elizabeth*; so *Tony*, *Dotty* and *Betty* are conservative. Curiously, *Thomas* got a 'th' in the spelling, too, but this didn't change the way people pronounced it. The original 't' pronunciation remained. And, of course, British English speakers didn't go for the 'th' pronunciation of *Anthony* either. They continue to pronounce it with 't'.

Finally, what about *Jack* as the pet name for *John*? Most likely it comes from the diminutive form of *John* – something like *Johnkin*. You need a bit of phonological imagination, but drop a few sounds, change a vowel and you can get from *Johnkin* to *Jack*. *Richard* or *Rick* to *Dick* is a bit trickier. Some claim it's come about because of the inability of English speakers to pronounce the Normal French 'r'. Good story, but highly unlikely. It's probably simply another example of the kind of playful remodelling that gives us *Bob* from *Robert*, *Peggy* from *Margaret* and *Polly* from *Mary*. Our language is notorious for short cuts and spectacular sound shifts, but nowhere is this more obvious than in names. It's almost as if the more severe the pruning and the more excessive the sound change the more affection we show.

What happened to Dalziel?

The consonant 'l' has a history of disappearing and many names reflect this – curiosities like *Rafe* in place of *Ralph*. Even *Walter* and *Malcolm* lost their *l*'s for a while. *Walter* would have rhymed with *water* but its 'l' made a comeback. *Malcolm* must have been pronounced something like 'mawkim'. Only one 'l' was restored. But what about the name Dalziel, as in the police drama *Dalziel and Pascoe* – how can a name spelt *Dalziel* get pronounced 'Diyel'? It's not only lost 'l' but also 'z' and a vowel. It all revolves around the curious little letter 'yogh'. Yogh looked a bit like a fancy 'z' with a tail and would have been pronounced either as a 'y' sound (as in *yell*) or 'ch' (the guttural sound in Scottish *loch*), depending on where it appeared in the word. The symbol was given up in the Middle Ages and replaced by other letters like 'y' and 'gh', except in Scotland. People in England who no longer used yogh not surprisingly misread it as 'z'. So the spelling pronunciation 'Dalziel', that you hear as well, is the result of a misreading of yogh. And, of course, 'Dalziel' also restores the lost 'l'. The name originally would have been pronounced something like 'Dalyel'. By the way, it's also little yogh that's behind the mystery of *Menzies* and *Mengis* or *Minges* as different pronunciations of the same name.

To my Succulent Tasty Lamb

Throughout the history of English there has always been a strong food/eating metaphor for sex, with both sexes depicted as edible objects. Food and love, after all, have a long and healthy association. Nowhere is this more obvious than in the St Valentine's Day notices published in the newspapers. Let me report on what one day's trawling through these notices revealed.

The range of food types covered was extraordinary. There were the usual suspects – women as buttered buns and crumpets, men as meaty bites and beef cakes. But every conceivable comestible was covered. Breakfast Cereals – *You are my Snap and Crackle love Lizzy Pops; dearest Honey Smacks.* Under Pies and Casseroles – *Punkin Pie; your Tuna Casserole* and how about *to My Darling Patti Plumb Poo Pie love Snutchums.* Fruit, Vegetables and Nuts were well represented. Now, I'd never thought of pumpkin as sexy and mashed potato never held much erotic significance for me, but references to these two vegetables abounded – *Will you be my Chunky Pumpkin; I love you Mashed Potato.* Frankly, I can't think of vegetables less likely to provoke passion. There were plenty of cheeses and the meat metaphor was of course very strong – *to Chicken Skin; Plum Chicken; your Spunky Chicken; your little Ham Sandwich; your Baby Lamb Chop, love Chicken Legs; my Succulent Tasty Lamb.* Needless to say, women called Rosemary got great mileage out of this lamb metaphor – *my cute little Lamb Chop let me spice up your life.* Cakes and Biscuits – there were lashings of them in these notices: cherry pies, patty cakes, scones (including pumpkin) and plenty of muffins. Finally, a curious collection of odds and ends, not the usual foods one thinks of as stirring up bodily lust – pickles, omelettes, cream rice, pizzas, even guacamole.

As you would predict, plenty of expressions of endearment derived from animal terms, too – chooks, budgerigars, hummingbirds, wombats, roosters, rats. Not surprisingly, furry animal nicknames abounded for females – *to Cuddle Kitten; to Snuggle (Bad) Bunny.* There was one *Little Grey Duck* and a *Little Yellow Duck* too – but I'm not sure how thrilled I'd be to receive a Valentine's Day message dedicated to *My Domestos Duck*! Curiously, marine-life also abounded. One letter to *Squid* was signed *Crabstick*; one was addressed to *a precious little Sea Calf* and there were loads of references to fish. Not unexpectly there was an abundance of flowers too – messages to *Petal*, *Rose*, *Sweetleaf* and *Sweetpea*. But most surprising to me was the rich exuberance of insects. Now, I'm not just talking of cuddlebugs and butterflies, but fruit flies, dung beetles, grasshoppers and silverfish. There were 'Happy Valentines' to creepy-crawlies of all kinds, some signed *Bug Catcher* or *Fly Spray*!

Leaving the food and animal world, other notices contained an odd assortment of images. Some contained references to *Roman love slaves* or *pillaging Viking warriors.* Not surprisingly, I suppose, tools were pretty well represented. There were generators, power drills, piledrivers, hammers – and one *The Complete Total Tool.* Given how extraordinarily strong the sporting metaphor is in our lives, I was surprised to find only one Valentine that drew on sport – *To Drop Kick, from your Pretty Left Foot Kick.*

These Valentine's Day messages also contained a treasure trove of cuddlesome endings, with some names carrying as many as three at a time. They teemed with fondling 's' endings – *Snookems; Spunkytrunks; Sweetchops; Lovechunks; Piggy Toes; Little Plopps; Wrinkles; Bubbles; Snuggles* and *WicksyJeffyPoos.* The *-y/-ie* ending was abundant too – *to Pooky love Snoopy and Bubs; Sooty – I love you Cookie; dear Fluffy Bunny love Chopsy.* There were the less-usual diminutive endings *-let* and *-kin* as in *Sprinklet*, *Chicklet* and *Munchkin*, and no end of cuddly reduplication – *Chooka Wooka*, *Col Col Tippy Moo Moo*, *Schnoopy Woopy*, *Snooky Booky* and *Chubchub.* Who said English was light on in fondling endings? Linguists who make such claims are clearly looking in the wrong places.

Dirty Words

Delighteth to wallow in the durt
B. Googe, *Heresbach's Husbandry III*, 1596

Fertilizer, mulch, aged manure, well-rotted compost – since Egyptian times gardeners have known the powerful magic dirt works in the garden. Never doubt the potency of dirt in language either. Just utter a taboo word in an inappropriate context and observe the reaction. As with most things forbidden, dirty words have a special fascination for us. What is taboo is revolting, untouchable, filthy, unmentionable, dangerous, disturbing, thrilling – but above all powerful.

Dirty language

Most of us have experienced a reluctance to talk directly about things that might embarrass us, frighten us, or that are for some reason just plain difficult. To help us cope with the messy and frightening facts of life, we're provided with linguistic escape hatches in the form of euphemism. This is avoidance or evasive language – a deodorant language that disguises stinking reality.

Euphemism involves a very special kind of human mental dishonesty. Just think about it – we can speak of something that's tabooed by using a euphemism, but not a tabooed term. Why is it that a euphemistic expression like *excrement* has fewer unpleasant associations than its corresponding tabooed expression *shit*? Linguist Keith Allan and I explored the subject a number of years ago, discovering that speakers behave as if the form of tabooed words somehow reflects the essential nature of the topics they refer to. This is why expressions like *shit* are described as 'unpleasant' or 'ugly-sounding' and why people label them 'dirty', 'filthy', 'impure', 'grotty', 'unclean', 'bad', 'foul', 'off'. Poor little words, they can't help it! Contact with dirt requires that we wash our hands with soap before we eat or shake hands with others. Foul language was once sanitized in the same way.

Whereas the term euphemism is well known and has wide currency, for some reason 'dysphemism' rarely appears in ordinary language – curious, because there's certainly a lot of it about. As you will have guessed, dysphemism is, roughly speaking, the opposite of euphemism. It includes the verbal resources we have for being offensive, for being abusive or just plain letting off steam. Taboo terms are ready-to-wear dysphemisms, and what makes up much of our dysphemistic vocabulary is whatever happens to be taboo in society at the time. Modern English is full of terms of abuse naming bodily emissions, tabooed body parts and sexual pastimes. Profanity and blasphemy are still fairly potent sources for dysphemism too, though with the increasing secularization of many English-speaking societies, clearly not as potent as it once was.

There is no such thing as everybody's dysphemism, or everybody's euphemism for that matter. Offensiveness is never an intrinsic quality of the word, but of the way it's used and its context. As you know, apparent expressions of opprobrium like *you old bastard* can be used in a jocular, even affectionate fashion, and it has always been this way. Blunt expressions like *cark it* and *croak* between certain individuals can be cheerfully euphemistic. Their flippancy detracts from the seriousness of death, which can make them preferable to more direct terms like *die*. A jocular approach to death is offensive only if it can be expected that your audience would regard it as such. It would not be the thing, for example, for a doctor to inform close family that their loved one had *pegged out* during the night.

We borrowed the word 'taboo' from Tongan. In its original conception, it referred to prohibited behaviour; especially behaviour believed dangerous to particular individuals or to the society as a whole. Violations of taboos were expected to have dire consequences and euphemism could literally be a matter of life or death. Western-style taboos, however, typically rest on traditions of etiquette and are closely linked with social parameters like age, sex, education, social status and the like. The taboo topics we're most familiar with are avoided, not because we believe that any physical or metaphysical harm will come to us, but because their use is regarded as distasteful within a given social context. Here, employing euphemism is the polite thing to do and using offensive language is little more than breaking a social convention. Whether you *micturate*, *powder your nose*, *go to the washroom*, *have a leak*, *a piss* or *a pee*, the choice is a matter of appropriate style.

So on the face of it, euphemism isn't such a major issue in English as it is in more traditional societies. But the differences are more apparent than real. The degree of tolerance shown to taboo-defying behaviour can change over time. We don't have to look far back in history to find dire consequences for people observed violating some of our own Western taboos – imprisonment, hanging, even burning at the stake. And as some taboos relax, others come to replace them. The current 'politicial correctness' regime prescribes the sort of language we may and may not use when talking about differences between humans, especially difference based on race, ethnicity and gender. This has given rise to sanctions against what might be dubbed *-ist* language – racist and sexist language, for example. At the same time, taboos on profanity, blasphemy and sexual obscenity have diminished.

These sorts of shifts are nicely reflected in changes to dictionary-making conventions. The Oxford English Dictionary originally included religious and racial swear words but omitted sexually obscene words. The last few decades, however, have seen mounting pressure on editors to omit or alter political and racial definitions of words. Some might remember the controversy surrounding the opprobrious senses of the word *Jew*. Just as revealing of changing taboos were the activities of self-appointed arbiters of linguistic goodness like Dr Thomas Bowdler, Mrs Mary Whitehouse and the imaginary Mrs Grundy. Take Dr Bowdler. In the early nineteenth century he set about cleaning up Shakespeare and produced the so-called *Family Shakespeare*, from which, as he described on the title page, 'those words and expressions are omitted which cannot with propriety be read aloud in a family'.

Bowdlerism sought to expunge profanity and sexual explicitness. His activities led to the progressive sanitizing of a range of works, including novels by Fielding and Swift. The targets of modern-day Bowdlerites are quite different. They include class, gender, ethnicity and especially race. The activities are the same – only the definition of dirt has shifted.

Handism

There is one type of *-ist* language that rarely cracks a mention – handist language – simple, everyday language that contains a view of the left side as weak, feeble, worthless (at best) and untrustworthy, shameful, even evil (at worst).

In the fourteenth century *a left* was a 'mean and worthless person'. Still today there are many expressions involving 'left' which suggest incompetence and inefficiency: *see with the left eye, work with the left hand, take in by the left ear*, to name just a few. Someone who can't dance has *two left feet*, surfers who lead with the left leg are *goofy-footed. Left-handed compliments* are veiled insults, *left-handed oaths* are not meant to be binding and *out in left field* is in the middle of nowhere. If something is squandered it goes *over the left shoulder*, comic reference is made to *the left-handed screwdriver* – and don't forget the *children of the left hand* and those *left-handed marriages*.

There is also an array of appalling words to describe left-handers. *Molly-dooker* derives from *molly* 'weak worthless fellow, simpleton' and *dook* 'fist, hand'. There's *cackhanded*, of course, and *watty handed* – the list goes on. *Southpaws* doesn't sound too bad, but then where are all the *northpaws*? Perhaps even more disturbing, though, is how once-innocent little words simply meaning 'left' deteriorate over time. *Gauche* originally meant 'left' but has now come to mean 'clumsy, awkward'. *Sinister*, the Latin word for 'left', has become 'wicked, evil'.

The word *right*, by contrast, has all the positive associations of strength, efficiency, skill, correctness, trustworthiness and reliability. The dictionary says, 'that which is consonant with justice, goodness or reason; that which is morally or socially correct'. Things can be *right-side up*, people can be *in their right minds* or show *right thinking*, our spiritual leaders are the *Right Reverends*, there are *Right Honourables* and *right-hand men*. The Latin word for 'right' *dexter* gives us *dexterity* (compared to what happened to poor old *sinister*); the French word gives us *adroit*. If you lack dexterity then you are of course *maladroit* ('not adroit'). Even *ambidexterous* 'able to use both hands' means literally 'having two right or dexter hands'. In the spirit of inclusive language, I propose *ambisinexterous* – well, at least it recognizes both hands.

At a time when we're all carefully tiptoeing around linguistic landmines, you might like to reflect on this under-acknowledged area of linguistic discrimination. It's finally time the left hand knew what the right hand is doing!

P***ks

Nineteen ninety-nine was the year for swear words, well, certainly in Australia. In April that year, former Victorian Premier Jeff Kennett caused quite a storm when – on radio – he used the insult *pricks* to describe those who had flouted the gas restrictions during the Longford crisis the previous year. He defended his use of this word by invoking the spirit of none other than William Shakespeare, who he said used this word 'well and often'. Around the same time appeared a television advertisement using *bugger* to sell the new Toyota Hilux pickup truck. This had followed hot on the heels of a West Australia Lotteries advertisement in which a winner says *bullshit*. Finally, in June the Australia Institute's executive director, Dr Clive Hamilton, was heard to use the 'f-word' during an interview on ABC's *Four Corners*. This was the third appearance for this little word on a *Four Corners* programme that year. So much foul language, and in the public arena!

There are three interesting aspects to the particular insult the premier chose. First, the nature of the idiom. A hundred years ago Jeff Kennett probably would have described these gas cheats as *bounders*, *cads*, *rotters* or *villains*. This category of morally based expression has now disappeared from the language, replaced by more physically and sexually based terms like *bastard*, *bugger* and *prick*. Earlier still, Kennett would have had an array of virulent religious insults at his disposal like *heathen*, *pagan*, *devil* and *witch*. These terms are no longer offensive and have well and truly lost their potency. The focus of insulting language has shifted from the religious to the secular, especially to matters relating to sexual and bodily functions. Sure, Kennett was correct, Shakespeare would have known the word *prick* – but only as a term for the body part. In this sense it has been in use since the sixteenth century. *Prick* was not used as an insult, however, until much later, the 1920s in fact. This metaphorical extension of sexual parts is really very recent.

The second interesting aspect to the former premier's use of *prick* as an insult is that he felt able to use this word on radio. This shows just how much words like *prick* have lost their original intensity. There are two reasons for this weakening. One is a natural bleaching process – abuse terms wear out over time. The other reason is that sex is no longer the great taboo. It's true, sex-related words are still offensive to some who would feel uncomfortable hearing them on radio, for instance. But racial and ethnic swear words are now the true obscenities. Their use is so provocative as to have legal consequences.

Finally, Jeff Kennett claimed he was directing this insult to obnoxious and difficult men and women. I don't believe, however, that speakers anywhere in the English-speaking world generally use *prick* to insult women. And here lies an interesting sexist asymmetry in our use of body parts as insults. Keith Allan is one linguist who has given bawdy body part abuse considerable scholarly attention, and as he points out, in many languages terms invoking the female sex organ have a wider range than those invoking the male sex organ. While *prick* can only be applied to males, female body part terms are applicable to both males and females. Moreover, the female-derived terms are much more potent. So why this imbalance? Well, by convention, a man is abused by ascribing to him the characteristics of a woman. Look at the insult for males in terms like *sissy*, *old woman* and *girl*. Perhaps a woman cannot be abused as a *prick* because women are often not downgraded by being ascribed the characteristics of a man. In fact to say of a woman that 'she's got balls' or 'she's ballsy' is to praise her strength of character. So our language allows us to compliment a woman by using male-associated words, but by social convention a man is downgraded by ascribing to him the characteristics of a woman.

As a final note, many of you may well be using these body part insults without knowing it. Be aware that they sometimes come down to us in heavy disguise. For example, people use the expression 'He gets on my wick' without realizing that this is in fact abbreviated Cockney rhyming slang – Hampton Wick = prick. Similarly, 'He's a real berk' comes from Berkeley/Berkshire Hunt = cunt and 'Cobblers' comes from Cobbler's Awls = balls. Now, those of you who are perturbed by the sexually based idiom of modern swearing might be comforted with the thought that English has lost at least one collection of truly nasty little words; namely, those invoking deadly and disfiguring diseases. Not that swearing is ever meant to be taken literally, of course – most swearing formulas are nonsense. But consider 'A pox on you!' Here's an expression that invokes either bubonic plague or syphilis – either way, we're looking at sores, suffering and (at the time the expression was in use) inevitable death. Many of our linguistic relatives have retained this gruesome idiom in their maledictions, with images of cholera, plague, leprosy and even cancer. I recently attended a conference on changes in the Dutch language where the presenter reported on the increased use of terms for cancer, plague, pleuritis, smallpox, tuberculosis and typhus as expletives in a number of modern dialects. Perhaps we should be more appreciative of the sexually based idiom of our modern-day English expressions.

'That excrement of the mouth'

Daniel Defoe, back in 1697, had much to say on the subject of foul language. 'Swearing, that Lewdness of the Tongue, that Scum and Excrement of the Mouth, is of all Vices the most foolish and senseless. The Grace of Swearing has not obtained upon Good Manners to be a Mode yet among the Women; *God Damn ye*, does not sit well upon a Female Tongue; it seems to be a Masculine Vice, which the Women are not arriv'd to yet; and I wou'd only desire those Gentlemen who practise it themselves, to hear a Woman swear: it has no Musik at all there, I am sure; and just as little does it become any Gentleman, if he wou'd suffer himself to be judged by all the Laws of Sense or Good Manners in the world . . . there is neither Pleasure nor Profit; no Design pursued, no Lust gratified, but is a mere Frenzy of the Tongue, a Vomit of the Brain, which works by putting a Contrary upon the Course of Nature'. In fact, we all swear – even nice girls. So, why do we do it? Well, there are at least three reasons.

Euphemism with attitude?

What do people mean by the expression 'political correctness' or PC? My dictionary defines it simply as 'conformity to current beliefs about correctness in language and behaviour with regard to policies on sexism, racism, ageism etc.'. Indeed most of us probably first encountered the term in the early 1980s, in the context of affirmative action hiring policies, curriculum revision, speech codes and general guidelines for non-discriminatory language. Here in Australia its adjectival phrase *politically correct* quietly took over from the earlier expression *ideologically sound* – a bit like American *cookie* is now quietly taking over from *bickie*. In fact the term *politically correct* is not nearly as recent as most people think. It's been around since at least the 1700s.

When specialist terms end up in everyday parlance, especially when they are taken up by the mass media, meanings can shift a long way from their original precision. It seems to me the expressions *political correctness* and *politically correct* are well on their way to moving outside the political arena. Nowadays, PCdom typically refers to behaviour, especially verbal behaviour, and less so to any political position. For instance, on the electronic mailing list *Linguist List*, someone contributed examples like: 'It is not politically correct to let your dinner hosts wash all the dishes themselves' and 'Sending an [email] memo to the CEO of your company is as easy as sending one to the mail clerk, if not always politically correct'. In examples like these there's the same intention not to offend any person or group, but gone is any reference to a political position, gone is the sympathetic concern for members of minority groups – indeed, gone is any mention at all of a current social issue. This is political correctness as 'doing the polite thing'. 'Incorrect' behaviour is little more than a social gaffe. Apparently, *background actors* is now the politically correct term for 'extras' on a film set. Why on earth do we need a politically correct term for extra actors on a film set? We are certainly a long way from the sphere of sympathetic concern about gender or race. Political correctness seems to be getting completely tangled up with euphemism, to the extent that some people seem to now use the words interchangeably.

In one edition of the Melbourne *Big Issue* (a street magazine sold by homeless or vulnerably housed people), computer programmer Chris Rae was quoted as saying 'I know it's not very politically correct these days but to be honest I wouldn't recommend one' – he was referring here to the Tamagotchi, the virtual reality pet. Now what on earth is PC about Tamagotchis?

First, there's the obvious expletive function of swearing – the use of a swear word to let off steam. Whether we use full-blown swear words or select from among the many euphemistic remodellings like *Shivers! Golly! Gosh!* or *Crumbs!*, swearing is a way of releasing anger, frustration or anguish. It's a kind of catharsis.

There's the abusive function as well, of course – curses, name-calling, any sort of derogatory comment directed towards others to insult or wound them.

There are important social functions, too – swearing as a means of marking social distance, or alternatively signalling social solidarity. Studies of people's swearing patterns reveal very clearly the sociable side of swearing. Generally speaking, the more relaxed a group, the more swearing there is. Of course, there's also plenty of annoyance swearing when things get tough, but what these studies reveal is that when things grow truly stressful, swearing diminishes. Could it be then that swearing actually reduces stress? As linguist David Crystal speculates – do swearers perhaps lead less stressful lives than non-swearers? An interesting idea!

Many communities of the world past and present have what you could describe as ritualized swearing. In Black American English, and urban Australian Aboriginal English, for instance, you find something called cracking on or capping. It's a kind of competitive ritual slanging match, sometimes also called ranking (as in *I ranked him out* 'I won'). The players bait and tease each other, trying to outdo with insults. It's a conventionalized breaking of taboo, another kind of linguistic social safety valve. But it can turn nasty. There are certain boundaries players don't cross. Cracking on about your conversational partner's kin, especially their mother, is definitely out.

All this cracking on is very similar to something called 'flyting' which was around in Anglo-Saxon times, and right up into the fifteenth and sixteenth centuries. Like cracking on, flyting can demonstrate great linguistic skill. Geoffrey Hughes, who has made a study of the evolution of our swearing habits, describes it as 'the fine art of savage insult'. The language can be sophisticated, passionate and highly charged – and, oh yes, very, very foul. In fact, ancient Germanic flyting makes anything that comes out of the modern-day locker room sound like positive politeness!

The unprintable swear word

So where does the word *bloody* come from? Many have argued it derives from the remodelling of the expression *By our lady*, an oath calling on the assistance of the Virgin Mary. At first blush this sounds plausible, especially when you consider the spectacular remodellings that once produced disguised oaths like *strewth* from 'God's truth' (where God is omitted to avoid explicit blasphemy or profanity). But *By our lady* can't be the source of *bloody*. The two terms have different functions. *By our lady* is an expletive; in other words, a type of exclamation that can stand by itself. *Bloody* is what's called an epithet; a term that expresses the quality of something – 'bloody this or bloody that'.

As far as swear words go, *bloody* is comparatively recent. It's been around for only about three hundred years. Captain Grose in his *Dictionary of the Vulgar Tongue* (late eighteenth century) describes it as 'a favourite word used by thieves in swearing'. He gives the example 'bloody rascal'. *Bloody* started life this way, as an adjective, but soon extended to an intensifying adverb as in 'bloody marvellous'. More recently it's become a kind of emphatic sentence particle, as in 'I'm not going to bloody walk', and more recently still an infix, where it's stuffed inside a word, as in 'fan-bloodytastic'. You have to admire its grammatical flexibility!

As to its origin, *bloody* seems to have had two colliding sources. One is simply the idea of blood. The word would always have had unpleasant, violent associations which would make it very suitable as an intensifying word. Compare other graphic intensifiers like *awfully* and *horribly*. Expressions like 'bloody battle' and 'bloody murder' would then give rise to others – and always there would be lurid associations of bloodshed and murder. This is probably also why the word came to be associated with the underworld, and hence its greater currency in Australian English. A second source is the so-called 'blood', the young aristocratic lout of the seventeenth and early eighteenth centuries. In that period you would have heard descriptions like *drunk as a blood*; in other words, *drunk as a lord*. So an expression like *bloody behaviour* would have double significance – objectionable behaviour, something you might expect of a young blood, with the added force of the *bloody* intensifier.

These two origins fit in with the fact that early in its life *bloody* was not considered a bad word at all. In 1714 Jonathan Swift in a letter to a woman friend described the weather as 'bloody hot'. And in later letters he talked about being 'bloody sick', and the weather being 'bloody cold'. Swift seems to be using *bloody* with the same freedom that gentlemen and ladies of good breeding would have used terms like *frightfully*, *vastly* or *dashed*. It couldn't have been an impolite term at that time.

Yet, two hundred years later, *bloody* had become such 'a horrid word' it was necessary to render it in print as *b****y*. Indeed, after Eliza Doolittle's scandalous outburst in Act III of *Pygmalion* ('Walk! Not bloody likely'), the press in 1914 could do no more than hint at it. It was 'the Unprintable Swearword', 'the Word', 'Shaw's Bold Bad Word' – a kind of invisible word. Its unmentionableness triggered a number of euphemistic remodellings such as the expletives *blimey!*, *blast!*, *blow!* and epithets *blessed*, *bleeding*, *blinking*, *blooming*, *blinding*, *blasted*. Many of these, you'll recognize, have blasphemous and profane implications, invoking fires of hell and the wrath of God. These include curiosities like *What the blazes!* and *blighter*. Even our use of *blank* as an omnibus euphemism and the game *Blankety Blank* are obviously playing on this *bl-* cluster too. The *bl-* has become suggestive, a kind of wink-wink, nudge-nudge phonestheme, and even *blue* 'risqué' gets support from this (though some claim the original blue movies were just that – literally blue!). There's also the interesting verb *bleep*, as in 'bleeping out' in a radio broadcast. *Bleep* is obviously the beeping sound, but *beep* gets remodelled to *bleep* once more under the influence of the *bl-* cluster (reinforced by earlier *blip*). And what is it that causes all this bleeping and blipping? Well, *bloopers* of course!

Linguistic xenophobia

All language groups have derogatory expressions for other groups they come in contact with. One particular type of linguistic xenophobia is the use of nationalities as descriptive nouns. Look at the way English uses French and Dutch.

Let's start with the French – 'the nationality', as Geoffrey Hughes describes it, 'most associated in the English mind with sex'. Hughes is right. There are large numbers of expressions in English for things relating to sex, all involving French in some way. For example, *French vice* 'sexual malpractices', *French postcards* 'pornographic pictures', *French kiss* 'a deep kiss', *French disease/French pox* 'venereal disease' (sufferers of syphilis were *frenchified*), *French letter/French tickler* 'condom' (the French have retaliated with *capote anglaise*, literally 'English raincoat'), and of course, there's the excuse for colourful or offensive language – *Excuse my French*. That's been around since the late 1800s.

But what about the Dutch? The list of expressions seems endless, and many are offensive. Here are a few:

Dutch courage   False or temporary courage found by drinking alcohol

Dutch bargain   A one-sided bargain (usually struck during a drinking session)

Dutch feast   The host gets drunk before the guests do

Dutch concert   A drunken uproar

Double Dutch   Gibberish, incomprehensible speech

Dutch auction   An auction where the auctioneer starts off at a high price and then works down

Dutch nightingale   A frog
Dutch shout/to go Dutch/Dutch treat   You pay for yourself (therefore not a treat)
Dutch talent   Something requiring brute strength and no intelligence
Dutch gold   An alloy of copper and zinc (therefore not gold at all)
Dutch wife   Either an artificial sexual partner or a bolster for resting the limbs in bed.

There are also longer expressions such as the phrase (or kind of finishing-off remark) 'I'm a Dutchman'. For example, 'such and such will happen or I'm a Dutchman'. This seems to imply that being a Dutchman is the ultimate disgrace. It means that you have the greatest confidence in the truth of the first statement, because being called Dutch is so unthinkable.

In the seventeenth century the Dutch were the commercial and military rivals of the English. The strong contempt in which the English held the Dutch at this time spawned this huge number of anti-Dutch expressions. Fortunately the strong negative feelings didn't last long. Only a few of these early derogatory expressions survive in ordinary usage today, and those that do certainly don't carry the same malice they once did. The Dutch never retaliated linguistically – or at least, I've never discovered a comparable list of Dutch expressions that sneer at the English in the same way.

Nonetheless, English is certainly not alone here. We might talk about Double Dutch, but for the Spanish nonsense is spoken in Greek and for the French 'it's all Hebrew'. Anyone with poor French is said to speak French like a Spanish cow – a double whammy! Linguistic taunts of this kind are an international pastime.

Taboo Language

Corruption is the mother of vegetation
Old saying

No manure is so rich as taboo. It provides a fertile seedbed for words to flourish – and the more potent the taboo, the richer the growth. Euphemism is attractive mulching. It gives a handsome finish to any garden bed; it covers the dirt and any weed growth as well. But mulch is short-lived, and so is euphemism. Even attractive shredded bark eventually breaks down and rots. Today's euphemism is tomorrow's dirt.

Dirt sticks

When it comes to taboo, speakers do behave as if there were a very real connection between the words themselves and their taboo senses. So real is the connection that this taboo will also affect innocent language expressions. Speakers will avoid certain words or phrases simply because they sound similar to taboo terms. *Regina* makes many feel uncomfortable because of its phonetic similarity to *vagina*. Look at the fate of *feck* 'purpose' and *cunny* 'rabbit'. When *arse* collided with *ass* this caused problems for *ass* 'donkey', which as you've probably noticed is now generally avoided. Some speakers still use *cock* to mean 'rooster', but its shared meaning with the name of a tabooed body part is killing off the use of the 'rooster' sense. There has also been an effect on words containing *cock*. Think of the surname *Alcox* that gets remodelled to *Alcott*. In American English *cockroach* is typically clipped to *roach*. The change *haycock* to *haystack* and *weathercock* to *weathervane* (at least outside of farming communities) was undoubtedly influenced by taboo avoidance, too. *Cockpit* and *cocktail* are still alive and well – perhaps the taboo is no longer as strong.

Sociology claims Knight's Law: 'Bad talk drives out good'. Economics has Gresham's Law: 'Bad money drives out good'. Linguistics has its own Gresham's Law of Semantic Change: 'Bad connotations drive out good'. A simple example is English *undertaker*. The word once meant 'odd job man' ('someone who undertakes to do things') and it was used as a euphemism for a person taking care of funerals. However, like most terms used for something taboo, in this case death, it wasn't long before the meaning of *undertaker* narrowed to the taboo sense alone. It is now being replaced by euphemisms like *mortician* and more recently *funeral director*. Taboo areas of vocabulary perpetually generate this sort of narrowing and deterioration of meaning. For example, words connoting sexual activity like *copulation*, *seduction*, *orgasm*, *intercourse*, *ejaculation* and *erection* were once quite general terms. As soon as they were pressed into euphemistic service, all quickly narrowed to the sexual sense alone. Taboo senses never fail to dominate, and eventually kill off all the other senses. Look how the sexual meaning of *interference* now dominates the interpretation of this word. People won't risk being misunderstood so they avoid these words and seek others. Consider something as innocent as *liaison*. Originally a cooking expression to refer to the thickening of sauces, *liaison* then extended to refer to any sort of association or cooperation. Nowadays, of course, it's illicit sexual association that first comes to mind – University Library Liaison Committees are almost certainly doomed! English *hussy*, originally from *housewife*, shows the same contamination, as do hundreds of expressions referring to women. English has amassed an extraordinary two thousand expressions to refer to 'sexually promiscuous woman'. Many started life as neutral terms and were recruited as euphemisms for 'wanton woman'. The result is an ever-changing chain of words and phrases denoting taboo concepts. And the more severe the taboo, the longer the chain.

Over the years English has also accumulated more than 2,500 expressions for male and female genitalia – now, this is lexical richness!

Clearly, taboo and euphemism are potent forces for word loss and word addition. The protective magic of the sweet-smelling euphemism is only effective for a short time, and all euphemisms eventually degenerate through contamination by the taboo topic. As poet George Herbert so beautifully wrote, 'Sweet rose thy root is ever in its grave, And thou must die'.

Words on the nose

Some of you may recall Patrick Süskind's creation Jean-Baptiste Grenouille, the grotesque character in his novel *Perfume*. Grenouille's gift was his extraordinary sense of smell. Described as 'the finest nose in Paris', and capable of nuancing hundreds of thousands of different odours, Grenouille could differentiate objects by smell far more keenly and more precisely than others could do by sight. Now, for Grenouille the mismatch between his rich world of smells and the poverty of his language was particularly acute. The French language proved totally inadequate for his intense olfactory experiences, even those he encountered on a day to day basis. 'Why should smoke possess only the name "smoke",' he complained. 'Why should earth, landscape, air – each filled at every step and every breath with yet another odour and thus animated with another identity – [why should they] still be designated by just those three coarse words?'

For the rest of us, with our more pedestrian protuberances, the sort of lexical richness that Grenouille was seeking is totally unnecessary. Nonetheless, when it comes to the language of smells, English is also found wanting – but not in the way Grenouille imagined. Just pick up any thesaurus and check out the words and phrases associated with smelling. What is immediately striking about our words for those 'substances which excite the membrane of the nose' is the asymmetry – loads of words to describe bad smells (like *stink*, *stench*, *reek*, *pong*, *niff*) but very few positive expressions (like *fragrance* and *perfume*) and curiously few, if any, genuinely neutral ones. Even the term *smell* has a bit of a whiff about it – its derived adjective *smelly* certainly does. The problem is, words for smells are unstable and very prone to change. What typically happens is that they start off life either with a neutral meaning, or indeed smelling quite sweetly, but after a period of time become tainted and end up smelling a mile off! It seems the shift from 'good smell' to 'disagreeable smell' is a well-worn path.

Take the following eight examples. What I've done is rank the terms, starting with those that have the most unpleasant connotations and ending with those that have the most pleasing – or at least according to my nostrils. The dates are based on the first attestations cited in the Oxford English Dictionary. (I should add that the inspiration for this exercise also came from that wonderful workbook by John Algeo):

stink verb 8th century; noun 13th century
stench noun 9th century; verb 10th century
smell noun and verb 12th century
odour noun 14th century
scent verb and noun 15th century
perfume verb and noun 16th century
fragrance noun 17th century
aroma noun 19th century

There are a couple of things to notice here. Firstly, the longer the word has been in the language to refer to smell, the more offensive its connotations – in short, the older the word, the more disagreeable. *Stench* and *stink* have been around the longest. We've hit an area of mild social taboo here which explains the rapid semantic change.

The most positive terms here are French – *odour*, *scent*, *perfume*, *fragrance* and *aroma*. Using words borrowed from other languages to function as euphemisms is characteristic of many languages. French, together with Latin, has long been a source of deodorizing for English. Of course, just how fragrant these words are will depend on how long they've been pressed into euphemistic service. *Aroma* and *perfume*, as the most recent recruits, are those most sweet-scented. *Odour*, as the oldest of the four, has already started to fester. The deodorizing qualities of the euphemism inevitably fade as the taboo sense asserts itself.

Covering up the dirt

The words *tax* and *toll* have been in the language a long time. There's nothing particularly comfortable or caring about either of them. In an area otherwise rich in weaselspeak and deodorant language, taxes and tolls are dirty words. (By the way, *tax* is the same word as *task* – it grew out of *task* in the same way the pronunciation *aks* grew out of *ask*.)

So how do you put a good spin on taxation? Well, for a start you'll obviously seek out expressions with pleasing associations. Some of you might remember the British Government's use of the expression *community charge* for the local tax introduced into England and Wales in 1990. *Community* – now, there's a caring word if ever there was one. It provides the semantic halo for many expressions and certainly has been a popular modifier with politicians. You'll find it crops up in many officially sanctioned euphemisms like *community care*, *community treatment centre*, *community home*, to name just a few. The expression *community charge* didn't catch on in the United Kingdom, and its synonym *poll tax* won out (although that was eventually replaced too). *Poll tax* has a pretty nasty ring to it now, but it's a tad more pleasing than the earlier expression *capitation tax*. Both refer quite plainly to payment per head, but neither does much to make the tax any more appealing.

If it's camouflage you're looking for, there's nothing like a good foreign expression to blur unpleasant reality. French has been providing us with linguistic fig leaves for centuries. Take even a word like *levy* (from the French meaning 'to raise'). It's an oldie, with us since the 1400s, and its euphemistic sheen is definitely tarnished. Nonetheless, you have to admit it still has a more cheerful ring to it than *tax*. But I reckon we should bring back the French word *gabelle*. This was a word also used back in the 1400s for tax. Or how about resurrecting *octroi* – that comes to us from a French word meaning 'to grant'. Originally this was a tax or toll levied at the gates of a city. It has a classier and certainly more pleasing ring than either tax or toll. And while we're about it, why not prefix it with the word *community*. *Community octroi*, now that would put a gloss on the unsavoury business of road tolls.

But if it's weasel words you're looking for, you can't do better than *voluntary contribution*. This is obviously a piece of out-and-out doublespeak. For most us ordinary folk, *voluntary* means something like 'acting by choice'. Not in this context. For *voluntary* here read 'forced'. I read somewhere that US President Richard Nixon was the first to 'misremember' the meaning of *voluntary*, when in 1971 he imposed his *voluntary wage and price controls*. This shows another effective strategy – conceal the unwelcome under a cover of words, and the more words the better. This is the world of *offsetting measures* and *fiscal adjustments*, and plenty of those *terminological inexactitudes* and *categorial inaccuracies*. Even better if you can throw in a few Latinized abstractions. In the world of tax, *exaction* is a good one; *impost* isn't bad either. But there's the antithetical strategy too – shortening. There's nothing like a good acronym or abbreviation to obscure ghastly reality. Here we enter the world of VAT, PST, FPT and of course GST.

It's interesting to compare what's going on here with more traditional areas of taboo. Taboo originally referred to prohibited behaviour – people avoided words thought to be ominous, evil or somehow offensive to supernatural powers. For instance, they might substitute the original name of the feared powers with some sort of euphemistic appellation in the hope of somehow winning their favour. It's for this reason the elves and fairies of folklore are sometimes referred to as *the good neighbours*. In the world of politics and government, we find the same practice at work, only this time it's the electorate who represent the all-powerful beings whose favours are sought. Politicians must be cautiously considerate and tender of their electorate's feelings – they must avoid words that have unpleasant associations and they must be excessively polite. The twentieth century saw an explosion of descriptive terms for this such as gobbledygook, discombobulation, doublespeak, officialese and bureaucratese – ours without doubt is the golden age of verbal flummery and weaselspeak!

Dressing up the goods

We're surrounded by advertisements. They look good, they sound good. They're full of promise. 'Large Promise', wrote Samuel Johnson back in 1761, 'is the soul of an Advertisement.'

Obviously, advertisers are going to use the sweetest-sounding words to highlight the qualities of the product (or conceal its faults). The word *blend* sounds so much better than *mixture*, and *flavour* so much better than *taste*. Of course, certain adjectives are avoided at all costs – like *small*. Surely you've noticed the decrease in size of your favourite chocolate bar over the years? I certainly have (and I'm positive it's not just that I'm much bigger now). The procedure is to retain the same price and develop a euphemistic *new fun size* or *handy size* which really mean *smaller than before*. *Small* is avoided even for those products that come in more than one size – don't mention *small*, start with *large* and move to *extra large* or *jumbo*.

I once spent a weekend counting adjectives in food advertising in magazines. (And Samuel Johnson described lexicography as drudgery!) The most frequently used adjectives (and they beat the others by a long shot) were *new*, *natural*, *fresh*, *delicious*, *healthy*, *good*, *light*, *creamy*, *Australian*, *easy*, *perfect*. *New* is an interesting adjective. In Chaucer's time our language was full of words for 'new', but they were pejorative. The meaning was something like 'newfangled'. In other words, 'new' was not to be trusted. Nowadays, the adjective *new* is biased overwhelmingly to the positive. It represents an escape from the old. If it's new, it's improved. However, while we might want new, we also reject artificiality, anything that smacks of intervention by humans. We want *natural* – breads made of 'one hundred per cent natural ingredients' and ice-creams with that 'all-natural flavour'. This weaselword also offers the advertiser protection. Who's to say what is and what is not natural?

But it's not just suasive words and expressions we must guard against. Grammatical structures, too, have the power to lead us by the nose, to compel us in one direction or the other. They can even force us to take sides. Children very early on learn the concealed bias of grammatical constructions. The child who says 'the window got broken' has learnt the advantage of the so-called agentless passive construction, especially in combination with a *get* auxiliary verb. The construction conceals the agent and in combination with *get* shifts responsibility to something or someone else. The child then grows up to be the advertiser or the politician who can use the agentless passive to great effect. Recently I came across an advertisement for AUSTRALIAN FRESH orange juice.

> Grown in the lush Murrumbidgee, only the best oranges are selected and squeezed just hours after picking. Nothing added, the juice is then filled into packaging ready to be transported to the supermarket, arriving just as fresh and great tasting as the oranges it's made from.

Every clause here has an agentless passive. There is no mention of who is doing the growing, selecting, squeezing, picking, adding, filling, transporting. 'Natural' is the flavour of the month in food advertising and AUSTRALIAN FRESH orange juice, it seems, comes to us completely untouched by human hands!

Clearly, advertisers will exploit these sorts of constructions that enable them to leave certain things out (usually undesirable of course). Another one that's currently being used to great effect is the comparative construction, but with a missing conclusion. Things are described as being *tastier*, *crunchier*, *bigger*, *softer* – than what, you well might ask. But there is never any standard of comparison provided. One can always be supplied, and that's how advertisers are protected. 'Our oranges are sweeter'. Sweeter than they were before? Sweeter than anyone else's oranges? Sweeter than lemons, perhaps?

Many ads dance on the edge of truth. And the way they can get away with this is ambiguity. This is the safeguard. Ads and labels can be ambiguous. Most probably they're false on the interpretation most favourable to the product, but they can also be true by some other interpretation. Olympic athletes, we are told, drink this product, wear these shoes, even use this sort of deodorant. This could mean all athletes or a small group of athletes (namely, the ones who use the product). Advertisers, of course, want us to imagine all athletes.

Many ads dance on the edge of good grammar, too. Some of their compounds certainly stretch the boundaries of acceptability. I once encountered an ad for a range of designer dinner plates where the quirky cartoon characters were described as 'quasiaggressive-in-a-sweet-way figures'. Who said modern-day compounds weren't a patch on those of Old English? Violations of the rules of grammar are also commonplace. This is perhaps a dangerous strategy. You do risk running foul of the purists. Then again, getting up the nose of the viewer or reader is an effective way of drawing attention to your message. As is the use of the offbeat or wacky. If you can't convince people that your milk is really tastier or healthier than other brands, then go for the high-impact, totally loopy commercial – at least people will remember it when next confronted with the bewildering selection of milks in the supermarket cabinet.

Culinary camouflage – the gastronomic red herring

Metaphorical red herrings are misleading distractions (the expression derives from the early practice of drawing a smelly dried red herring across the path of a hunted animal). It was lexicographer John Ayto who first used the delightful term 'gastronomic red herring' to describe those dishes whose names suggest something they are definitely not. *Bombay duck* isn't duck at all but fish (one that skims the surface of the water, which may be why it's called duck). It's an Indian fish that's generally dried and eaten with curry, but the description *Bombay* is also misleading. This is actually a remodelling of the Marathi term for the fish *bombila*. Bombay was, however, a centre from which this fish was exported – so at least there's some motivation for the name. *Welsh rabbit* is neither Welsh nor is it even rabbit. It was probably a dish which people ate when meat wasn't available and the use of Welsh is a bit of early linguistic xenophobia. Welsh was often used for anything substandard or vulgar. A *Welsh comb* is when you comb your hair with your fingers; a *Welsh pearl* is a counterfeit pearl or one of inferior quality; a *Welsh cricket* is a louse and *Welsh fiddle* 'the Itch' (presumably some sort of nasty skin disease).

In fact, the term gastronomic red herring can be extended to include any sort of deceptive language used in the world of gastronomy. Language that disguises, distorts, deceives, misleads, inflates, obfuscates – language that makes the unpalatable seem palatable, the negative seem positive, the unpleasant seem attractive, the ordinary seem extraordinary. Often herrings are quite harmless. They might, for example, be motivated by the need to make something that is intrinsically unappetizing or embarrassing sound better by giving it a nice name – a kind of linguistic dressing. *Luncheon meat* sounds positively mouth-watering compared to that nasty pink textureless stuff we buy in a tin. *Prairie oysters* sound a good deal more appetizing than *calf's testicles*, something we probably know better as *fry*. In many English dialects *fry* has become a kind of all-purpose euphemism for any embarrassing bit of an animal which we use as food. The label refers to the method of cooking and nicely sidesteps the issue of what bits actually get fried in the dish. In some varieties of English lamb's fries are testicles of young sheep, but in Australian English *lamb's fry* is 'liver'. The name effectively disguises the fact that liver is involved – with all the unappetizing associations of hydatid cysts. And while we're on the subject of linguistic fig leaves, there is also Australian English *flake* and New Zealand English *lemon fish*. For some reason many of us are squeamish at the thought of eating shark, so we talk it up a bit to make it sound more appetizing. Now that 'mad cow disease' has come to light, it'll be interesting to see what euphemisms appear in place of *beef*. What new gastronomic red herring will supplant the Roast Beef of Old England, I wonder?

What are the sources for these red herrings? As it turns out, they involve quite ordinary and commonplace linguistic strategies. There's the hyperbolic herring. Let's turn *Welsh rabbit* into *Welsh Rarebit*, a classy variant of the name that appeared in the eighteenth century. For other examples, just look at the names of pet foods on the supermarket shelves. Tins of cat food have names like *Tuna Flakes Fusion with Whitebait in Tuna Jus* and *Greek Isle Feast with Calamari, Lamb and Rice*. The best examples come from the cosmetics of food advertising. Menuese doesn't do a bad line in the hyperbolic herring either. *Golden Fried Bermuda Onion Rings* – so much more tempting than your basic fried onion!

A close relative of the hyperbolic herring is the figurative herring. Be very wary of a dish that goes by the name *Love in Disguise*. The name screams out linguistic subterfuge. Indeed, who would suspect a calf's heart wrapped in veal coated with crushed vermicelli? Better still is if the herring can be foreign, especially French: *Welsh rabbit prepared en vue of guest.* French suggests to us culinary excellence. How much finer a meal becomes when soup is changed to *potage de* whatever. How much better *casserole* sounds compared to *stew. Paté de foie* against *liver paste.* No comparison! Apple pie with a dollop of ice-cream is so much more chic when it's apple pie *à la mode.* The French definite article *le* often gets plopped on like a bit of linguistic garnish – *Welsh rabbit* becomes *Le Welsh.* Or how about *du jour* for another bit of French dressing – *Welsh rabbit du jour* or *Welsh rabbit au sherry*, to make it truly continental. Of course, *rabbit Welsh* would have the 'je ne sais quoi' word order in the tradition of Tournedos Rossini and Steak Diane! In fact, I'm thinking of calling my own risotto *Risotto Kate* – a risotto with the consistency of Clag glue; the sort of remarkable texture they strove for in the Middle Ages when teeth were shocking and there was no cutlery. 'Not a pretty dish', as the modern critic would say.

The chronologically gifted

Nineteen ninety-eight was the 'Year of the Older Person'. It's an interesting title. Think about it. Just exactly how old is older? *Older* is the comparative form of *old* and generally speaking comparatives express difference along a scale – specifically the notion 'more'. But not here, it seems. In this case *older* is not as old as *old.* This use of comparatives with missing conclusions (*older than . . .* ?) is a subtle euphemistic practice. Compare the *fuller figure.* There are certain things we'd rather not represent too conspicuously and aging and fatness are two of them. Comparatives like *older* or *fuller* work to blur reality and like all euphemisms involve a very special kind of mental dishonesty. Think of that other cagey comparative *the longer living* or *the longer lived.* Its heyday was the 1970s. In the United States in particular, the cry was out to relabel all 'Departments of the Aging' as 'Departments of the Longer Living'.

And here lies the problem – the short life of a euphemism. The effects of the verbal vanishing cream wear off in time. The negative associations quickly reattach themselves. Look at the appalling deterioration of very early words denoting 'old'. Words such as *geriatric* and *senile*, for example, were once respectful terms for one's elders, but became highly contemptuous in the twentieth century. The longer the word's been around, the more negative the associations. *Elderly* has been in the language since the early 1600s and it's well and truly lost its euphemistic sheen. To date, the word *senior*, as in *senior citizen*, has not yet had time to acquire quite the same negative overtones, but the verbal veneer is wearing thin and it's a euphemism ripe for renewal.

Speaking of ripe, there are of course the *golden years* and those *golden agers* who inhabit them. But perhaps these expressions have had their day too – the golden glow has faded, as it has for expressions like *sunset years* and *twilight years.* I used to work in a hospital known as *Sunset.* Other *homes* (now there's a nice euphemism) exploited the same imagery – *Twighlight Home*, *Sundowners*, *Eventide Home* and so on. These sorts of euphemisms are figurative. The taboo topic is paired up with a pleasurable notion. Sometimes chains of figurativeness are established. Those who find themselves in their *riper years* (or at a *ripe old age*) could also be described as *mellow* – in other words, 'soft and fully flavoured from ripeness', as my dictionary defines it. There are also expressions like *mature* or *matured.* Here's a positive word. It means 'fully developed in body or mind', something we would presumably become in our late teens. Some of you might recall the World Fair in New York in the mid 1960s. There you could find the 'Dynamic Maturity Pavilion' – a garden and benches where 'mature' people could rest. *Seasoned* has something of the same connotations of fulfilment and ripeness – with perhaps the additional associations of a tasty dish. And, of course, we all know what tasty dishes are!

Circumlocution – now there's an excellent strategy. Often this involves a kind of componential analysis. The senses of taboo terms are unpacked and each of the meaning components is listed. The resulting periphrasis functions as a euphemism, such as *getting on in years*, *to have seen better days*, *to pass three score years and ten*, *to be past one's prime*, *getting on a bit*, *of advanced years*, *of indeterminate age* and so on. (This is this same process that turns *doors* into *entry systems* and *teachers* into *learning facilitators.*) Shortening is the antithetical strategy. Acronyms and abbreviations, such as OAPs for 'old age persons or pensioners', also offer an effective disguise for the 'o' word. From my hospital slang days I can recall examples like *COPs* ('crotchedy old patients') and *LOLs* ('little old ladies').

Another strategy is hyperbole (or overstatement). Political correctness of the 1980s and 1990s provides an exuberance of this kind of euphemism. If it's a positive spin you want try *the chronologically gifted* or *the experientially enhanced.* (These were up for gobbledygook awards some years back; so we know they are not simply satirical inventions.) A recent addition to the 'correct' terminology of the 1990s is *the third age.* Like John Ayto, I presume that youth and middle age are the two other ages. But then what exactly is middle age – 35, 40, 50, older? Much like the labels for those body parts we'd prefer not to label, age-related terms keep shifting around. The taboos surrounding old age and death create the same instability. Clearly, imprecision is what you want in a euphemism and the most successful euphemistic substitutions always involve very general expressions. What's more, vague expressions like *venerable* and *respected* can also emphasize other (more positive) aspects of the aging process – dignity of appearance and the deference one commands.

The antithetical strategy to hyperbole is understatement. For example, some of us are *not as young as we used to be.* But then who is? This is an example of litotes – specifically, an affirmative expressed in terms of the negative of its contrary – and it's effective camouflage for old age. Another example is the expression *of a certain age.* As with the others, the span of years covered by this phrase is very imprecise. The word *certain* blurs things a bit – think of women 'in a certain condition' or people with 'a certain disease' (an early euphemism for syphilis). But if it's camouflage language you're looking for, there's nothing like a good foreign expression. French has been providing us with linguistic fig leaves for centuries. *Un certain âge* – now, that's got class.

It should be apparent that the various strategies for forming euphemisms are by no means mutually exclusive, and examples often fall into more than one of these categories – expressions such as *to be at the evening of one's days, the autumn/the winter of one's life* are metaphoric, long-winded and also hyperbolic, as are *mutton dressed up as lamb* and *long in the tooth. No spring chicken* is an example of metaphor and understatement. *Past it* illustrates the typical general-for-specific strategy and also total omission (in this case, the failure to mention 'one's prime'). And, as all of these simple examples illustrate, time inevitably blows the cover of any euphemistic disguise – in which case why bother with the linguistic anti-wrinkle creams?

Knickers in a knot

Words for trousers and undergarments have fascinating histories. Take *knickers*. The word probably comes from Dutch *knikker*. This was some sort of clay marble – it must originally have been onomatopoeic, imitating the crack or snap of the marbles hitting each other. In 1809 this word *knicker* was used by Washington Irving as a basis for the mock Dutch name of the fictitious author of his book *Knickerbocker's History of New York*. It's a jokey name, something like Rip Van Winkle. Knickerbocker then came to refer to Dutchmen generally, those among the original settlers in the area. Later it generalized again to any New Yorker (which, by the way, is how we get *Knickerbocker Glory* – this extraordinary sweet was a tribute to New York).

But back to knickers. These Dutch chaps, these knickerbockers, wore knee breeches and so the name was extended to cover those sorts of trousers gathered at the knee. People were always on the lookout for new terms for garments of this sort – just so they didn't have to utter the dreaded words 'trousers' or 'breeches'. Many of these expressions then extended to include the even-more-unmentionable underclothing. After all, this was a time when even the legs, or rather *limbs*, of the table and pianoforte were modestly concealed by frilled pantalettes, at least in the United States. We get our terms *dark meat* and *white meat* because those in nineteenth-century polite society couldn't bear to utter 'legs' and 'breasts', even when speaking of a cooked fowl. Small wonder any garment below the waist had to be cloaked in euphemism.

Many of you will be familiar with some of those invisible words of the Victorian novel like *irrepressibles*, *inexpressibles*, *unmentionables*, *indescribables*, *ineffables*, *inexplicables*, *unspeakables, untalkaboutables, unutterables, unwhisperables, don'tmentionums, mustn'tmentionums, innominables, sit-down-upons, indispensables, unhintables* – even *dittoes*! Total omission is undoubtedly a most successful euphemistic strategy. In Mrs Beeton's *Book of Household Management* all items of clothing rate a mention, with the notable exception of trousers. Perhaps she meant to include them under 'body linen' – now, here's an omnibus euphemism! She might also have sought refuge in the safe haven of complicated curiosities like *nether integuments, femoral habiliments* [*femoral* = 'pertaining to the thigh'] – even *limb-shrouders*! *Continuations* were around at that time. Presumably, trousers were viewed as continuations of the rest of one's clothing.

Of course, these camouflage words are quick to take on erotic connotations. It's not long before they're considered offensive and have to be replaced. Apparently decent ladies of the late nineteenth century couldn't even refer to a chest of drawers without blushing! This sort of richness in vocabulary is always revealing of society's preoccupations. It just goes to show how much interest there was in these sorts of garments at that time. As Joseph Epstein once said, 'the best pornographer is the mind of the reader'.

Genital flip-flop

When we look at the problems our nineteenth-century forebears had with legs, we shouldn't grow too smug. After all, ours was the century of *smalls* and *foundation garments*, not to mention *athletic supporters* and *abdominal protectors* – which leads me naturally on to a discussion of loins and groins.

Let's begin with the things called *loins*. Originally the description was quite straightforward. Loins described the bit below the ribs and above the hips (the word is related to *lumbar* and *lumbago*). In the Bible it was always the loins on which people put clothes to cover their nakedness. This was also a time when everyone was rushing around girding their loins. Consequently, loins was reinterpreted as that part of the body actually containing the unmentionable bits. This meaning was further reinforced by expressions like 'the fruit of one's loins' – the source of one's offspring.

Just as vague is *groin*, although again historically it is quite straightforward. *Groin* goes back to the Old English word *grynde* meaning 'abyss' (it's therefore related to the word *ground*). It originally referred to a channel or depression and hence was extended to mean the depression where the thigh meets the body. But how did *grynde* become the word we know as *groin*? Basically, the 'd' dropped out and through a series of predictable vowel changes the word changed to *grine*. Not predictable, however, was the curious later shift *grine* to *groin*. The most likely explanation is that *grine* was contaminated by *loin* – *grine* changed to *groin* to be more like *loin*. And like the loin, the groin's location made it a kind of all-purpose euphemism for anything unmentionable in that general area. What a relief when we can shift focus to the approximate area where unmentionable body parts are situated! Technically, it's still a unisex word, but with all these sporting 'groin injuries' going around, groin, like loin, has become very male-oriented. Do female athletes have 'groin confidence', I wonder? I suspect women will have to start reclaiming body parts like *groin* and *loin*.

Now we come to the true location of the *groin*. Like so many of these anatomical 'below' words, no one is really sure where the groin actually is, and of course we're all too polite to ask. This nicely illustrates the start of a phenomenon known as 'genital flip-flop'. (I am grateful to my colleague Robert Bauer for alerting me to this handy linguistic label.) What is striking about unmentionable anatomical terms is that they keep changing their referent. The words start life being deliberately vague, and then as they lose their euphemistic sheen they start to narrow. But because of their initial vagueness, they can narrow in different ways in different varieties of English. Because these terms are never fully understood and no one dares ask, so they move around in reference. Hence the ambiguity of slang anatomical terms such as *fanny*, *prat* and even *tail*, which have all at some stage in their history meant both 'buttocks', 'female pudendum' and in the case of *tail* the 'virile member' as well!

Rest assured the linguistic confusion surrounding these offending organs is by no means confined to English. 'Genital flip-flop' is a linguistic phenomenon found in many languages of the world and is a source of great confusion and embarrassment – as any American who has tried to buy a *fanny bag* outside of the States will tell you.

'Like a worm i' th' bud'

Deodorizing language and offensive language clearly go hand in hand. We see this in the language of modern-day political correctness. PC language is subject to precisely the same perennial narrowing and deterioration that accompany any taboo expression. Take something as straightforward as terms for the poor countries of the world in the post-colonial era. According to lexicographer John Ayto, one of the earliest was *backward*, a word with a euphemistic sheen so badly tarnished by connotations of mental illness and lack of civilization that it's difficult to even imagine it as euphemism. In the late forties *underdeveloped* was substituted, and then in the fifties *less developed*, or better still, *lesser developed* (the use of the comparative ensures the description is a little fuzzier around the edges). In the 1960s appeared the more positive *developing*, followed closely by *emerging* or *emergent.* But the smack of colonialism soon rendered all these taboo, and as Ayto points out, today we tend to retreat to the safe territory suggested by geographical labels like *Third World* and more recently *The South* – or else an acronym like HIPCs 'highly indebted poor countries', as described on page eight of the *Australian Financial Review* on 22 February 1999.

During the controversy in 1992 surrounding British Mencap's refusal to change the name *mental handicap*, their director of marketing observed: 'It is only a matter of time before even the most right-on expression becomes a term of abuse. It has been the same since people talked about village idiots, and "learning difficulties" is no exception. Children are already calling each other LDs as an insult'. If society's prejudices continue to bubble away, undermining the euphemistic value, the negative connotations soon reattach themselves. *African-American*, and the more recent

Saints' names

A spectacular example of the deterioration of euphemisms can be found in saints' names. During medieval times there existed a euphemistic practice of labelling the most feared of diseases with the names of saints. Some 130 saints were invoked to serve as protectors and comforters of the sick. St Antonius' Fire referred to an epidemic which raged periodically throughout the Middle Ages, killing and deforming on a huge scale. St Vitus' Dance suggests a joyous romp; it certainly conveys nothing of the horror and suffering that attended this particularly nasty psychotic disorder. So great was the terror surrounding the plague that it masqueraded under a number of different saints' names: St Adrian's/St Christopher's/St Valentine's/St Giles'/St Roch's Disease. But if ever a euphemistic practice backfired, it was this one. The contamination of the euphemisms became so great that, much to the horror of the Church, it even provoked a dramatic return to pagan worship (and for a time the cult of saints was tabooed). The diseases became so closely associated with the names of the saints that the saints themselves came to be seen as the actual source of the sickness – not as comforters and protectors of the faithful, but rather as wrathful tyrants to be feared as perpetrators of the diseases themselves. In the minds of the sufferers of herpes zoster, or shingles, it became St Antonius who was stoking the fire of their burning hot blisters, and St Louis who covered their bodies with ulcers. This is without doubt the most striking illustration I've encountered of the pejorative path euphemisms can take.

Member of the African Diaspora, now replace *black*, which earlier replaced *Negro* and *coloured*.

Euphemism and dysphemism are never far apart, in the sense also that censorship and repression, whether full-blown legal sanctions or just social niceties, always seem to provide a nursery for new 'dirty words' to thrive. The most exuberant periods of dirty talk are also periods of great reticence and linguistic restraint in our society. We need only to look at the oxymoronic behaviour of the Victorian middle classes. When sex ceased to be talked about openly it went underground, and so did dysphemism. Geoffrey Hughes' book on the history of English swearing shows clearly how, during the Renaissance period, the first ever organized form of linguistic censorship coincided with a flourishing of linguistic subterfuge – a whole new collection of profane and blasphemous language in the form of 'dismembering oaths' like *zounds* or *sfoot*. Today we see precisely the same curious mix of exuberance and restraint. Jonathan Green's recent collection *Words Apart* shows that, next to the PC etiquette of current public discourse, there is a burgeoning lexicon of bigotry – 'dirty words', this time in the form of racial abuse. Green's collection highlights new arrivals on the linguistic scene, 'a whole new litany of dislike' as he describes it. As a grim irony, American coinages make up the largest proportion of dysphemistic language in his book. The land of immigrants and aliens, and birthplace of PCdom, tops his list of abusers. To borrow from William Shakespeare, like some kind of dysphemistic worm in the euphemistic bud, offensive language always seems to thrive on social sweetness.

Euphemism – a dirty word

It's not surprising euphemism has itself become a dirty word these days. Most of us associate it with double-speak – unwanted jargon, language that's value-laden and which we suspect is used primarily to obfuscate and disguise ordinary and inconvenient facts. Such expressions include *collateral damage* to describe the killing of civilians, and *surgical strikes* and *pinpoint accurancy*, which try to give the impression that buildings not people are being bombed. This is the sort of language that turns *war* into *violent peace*, *failure* into *incomplete success* and *death* into *terminal living* – the sort of language that George Orwell once described as being 'designed to make lies sound truthful and murder respectable, and to give an appearance of solidity to pure wind'. Certainly, it is very much an Orwellian-inspired view of euphemism that has come to dominate public discussion. And people are right to be suspicious of this kind of euphemism.

All euphemisms are in a sense dishonest – but here the motives are much more malign than others. Understandably, we become concerned at what seem to be attempts to manipulate our thoughts and opinions. Understandably, we grow impatient with what we see as the pretence that sweeter words produce a sweeter world. But it is neither fair nor accurate to paint all euphemism in this way. Many euphemisms are there to make life easier for us. They serve human interests by avoiding the things which threaten to cause distress and offence. Technology may have made many things in our lives easier, but it can't help us greatly with the reality that, whether we like it or not, we are still firmly rooted in nature – and it's here we will end up.

So, while there might be something initially attractive about a no-frills, say-it-as-it-is euphemism-free world, think about it – what would life be like if we all said exactly what was on our minds, and in the plainest and most explicit of terms? We as human beings would have to change beyond all recognition for the need for euphemism to disappear.

References

Aitchison, Jean *Language Change: Progress or Decay?* Cambridge University Press, Cambridge 1991.

— *Linguistics* (Teach Yourself Books) Hodder & Stoughton, London 1992.

— *Words in the Mind* Basil Blackwell, Oxford 1994.

Algeo, John *Problems in the Origins and Development of the English Language* (third edition) Harcourt Brace Jovanovich, San Diego 1966.

Allan, Keith and Burridge, Kate *Euphemism and Dysphemism: Language Used as Shield and Weapon* Oxford University Press, New York 1991.

Andersson, Lars-Gunnar, and Trudgill, Peter *Bad Language* Penguin Books, Harmondsworth 1990.

Ayto, John *Euphemisms* Bloomsbury Publishing, London 1993.

— *A Gourmet's Guide: Food and Drink from A to Z* Oxford University Press, Oxford 1994.

Barfield, Owen *History in English Words* Faber, London 1954 (1926).

Bauer, Laurie *Watching English Change* Longman, London 1994.

Blamires, Harry *The Queen's English: The Essential Companion to Written English* Bloomsbury, London 1994.

Bolinger, Dwight *Aspects of Language* Harcourt Brace Jovanovich, New York 1975.

— *Language the Loaded Weapon* Longman, London 1980.

Buczacki, Stefan *The Conran Beginner's Guide to Gardening* Conran Octopus, London 1988.

Burgess, Anthony *A Mouthful of Air: Language and Languages, Especially English*, Vintage, London 1993.

Burridge, Kate and Mulder, Jean *English in Australia and New Zealand* Oxford University Press, Melbourne 1998.

Bybee, Joan 'Mechanisms of Change in Grammaticization: the Role of Frequency' in Brian D. Joseph and Richard D. Janda (eds.) *The Handbook of Historical Linguistics* Blackwell, Oxford 2003.

Byron, George Gordon *The Complete Poetical Works* (ed. by Jerome J. McGann) Clarendon Press, Oxford 1980.

Cameron, Deborah *Verbal Hygiene* Routledge, London 1995.

Castiglione, Baldesar *The Book of the Courtier* (trans. by G. Bull) Penguin, Harmondsworth 1976.

Chen, Matthew and Wang, William 'Sound Change: Actuation and Implementation' in *Language* 51: 255–81, 1975.

Cowper, William *The Poetical Works of William Cowper* (ed. by H. S. Milford) Oxford University Press, Oxford 1963.

Crystal, David *The Cambridge Encyclopedia of the English Language* Cambridge University Press, Cambridge 1995.

Cutler A., McQueen, J. and Robinson, K. Elizabeth and John 'Sound Patterns of Men's and Women's Names' in *Journal of Linguistics* 16: 471–82, 1990.

Defoe, Daniel 'Of Academics' in W. F. Bolton (ed.) *The English Language: Essays by English and American Men of Letters 1490–1939*, pp. 91–101, Cambridge University Press, Cambridge 1966 (1697).

Eliot, Thomas Stearns *Complete Poems and Plays* Faber and Faber, London 1969.

Emerson, Ralph Waldo *The Collected Works* Belknap Press of Harvard University Press, Cambridge, Mass. 1971.

Epstein, Joseph 'Sex and Euphemism' in D. J. Enright (ed.) *Fair of Speech: The Uses of Euphemism*, pp. 56–71, Oxford University Press, Oxford 1985.

Greene, Amsel *Pullet Surprises* Scott, Foresman and Co., Glenview, Ill. 1969.

Grose (Captain) Francis *Dictionary of the Vulgar Tongue*, London 1811 (1783).

Harmer, Wendy 'Wounded by a Glance' in *The Age Good Weekend*, p. 16, Melbourne 29 April 1995.

Herbert, George *The Temple: Sacred Poems and Private Ejaculations* Chadwyck-Healey, Cambridge 1994.

Hock, Hans Heinrich *Principles of Historical Linguistics* Mouton de Gruyter, Berlin 1991.

Hock, Hans Heinrich and Joseph, Brian D. *Language History, Language Change, and Language Relationship* Mouton de Gruyter, Berlin 1996.

Horace, Quintus Horatius Flaccus *The Art of Poetry* (*Ars Poetica*; trans. by James Hynd) State University of New York, New York 1974.

Householder, Fred *Linguistic Speculations* Cambridge University Press, Cambridge 1971.

Hughes, Geoffrey *Words in Time* Basil Blackwell, Oxford 1988.

— *Swearing: A Social History of Foul Language, Oaths and Profanity in English* Basil Blackwell, Oxford 1991.

Jespersen, Otto *Language, its Nature, Development and Origin* Allen and Unwin Ltd, London 1922.

Langacker, Ronald 'Syntactic Reanalysis' in Charles Li (ed.) *Mechanisms of Syntactic Change*, pp. 57–139, University of Texas Press, Austin 1977.

Lewis, C. S. *Studies in Words* Cambridge University Press, Cambridge 1970.

Lipton, James *An Exaltation of Larks or The Venereal Game* Penguin Books, Harmondsworth 1977.

Lowell, Robert *Near the Ocean* Farrar, Straus & Giroux, New York 1967.

Noonan, Peggy 'Toward Candor and Courage in Speech' in Katherine Anne Ackley (ed.) *Essays from Contemporary Culture*, pp. 368–76, Harcourt Brace & Co., Fort Worth 1998.

Orwell, George 'Politics and the English Language' in *Shooting an Elephant and Other Essays* Harcourt, Brace and World, New York 1946.

Palmer, Leonard *Descriptive and Comparative Linguistics: A Critical Introduction*. Faber and Faber, London 1978.

Partridge, Eric *Adventuring Among Words* Andre Deutsch, London 1961.

Peters, Pam *The Cambridge Australian English Style Guide* Cambridge University Press, Cambridge 1995.

Pinker, Stephen *The Language Instinct: New Science of Language and Mind* Penguin Books, London 1994.

Porter, Roy Interview 'Coining it' in Simon Elmes (ed.) *The Routes of English (2)* BBC Education Productions, London 2000.

Read, Allen Walker 'The Sources of Ghost Words in English' in *Word* 20: 95–104, 1978.

Sapir, Edward *Language* Harcourt, New York 1921.

Shakespeare, William *The Complete Works* Collins Clear-Type Press, London 1938.

Taylor, Geoffrey *Some Nineteenth-Century Gardeners* The Anchor Press, Essex 1951.

Thorpe, Patricia *The American Weekend Garden* Random House, New York 1988.

Weiner, E. S. C. *The Oxford Miniguide to English Usage* Oxford University Press, Oxford 1983.

Weinreich, Max *The History of the Yiddish Language* (trans. Shlomo Noble with Joshua A. Fishman) University of Chicago Press, Chicago 1973.

Wilkes, Gerald Alfred *Exploring Australian English* ABC Books, Sydney 1993.

Winter, Jack 'How I Met My Wife' *The New Yorker* 25 July 1994.

Wright, Judith *Woman to Man* Angus & Robertson, Sydney 1949.

Wyld, Henry C. *A History of Modern Colloquial English* Blackwell, Oxford 1920/1936.

Index